Crafting a Global Field

Six Decades of the Comparative and International Education Society

CERC Studies in Comparative Education

33. Erwin H. Epstein (ed.) (2016): *Crafting a Global Field: Six Decades of the Comparative and International Education Society.* ISBN 978-988-14241-4-3. 316pp. HK$250/US$38.

32. Mark Bray, Ora Kwo & Boris Jokić (eds.) (2015): *Research Private Supplementary Tutoring: Methodological Lessons from Diverse Cultures.* ISBN 978-988-14241-3-6. 292pp. HK$250/US$38.

31. Bob Adamson, Jon Nixon, Feng Su (eds.) (2012): *The Reorientation of Higher Education: Challenging the East-West Dichotomy.* ISBN 978-988-1785-27-5. 314pp. HK$250/US$38.

30. Ruth Hayhoe, Jun Li, Jing Lin, Qiang Zha (2011): *Portraits of 21st Century Chinese Universities: In the Move to Mass Higher Education.* ISBN 978-988-1785-23-7. 486pp. HK$300/US$45.

29. Maria Manzon (2011): *Comparative Education: The Construction of a Field.* ISBN 978-988-17852-6-8. 295pp. HK$200/US$32.

28. Kerry J. Kennedy, Wing On Lee & David L. Grossman (eds.) (2010): *Citizenship Pedagogies in Asia and the Pacific.* ISBN 978-988-17852-2-0. 407pp. HK$250/US$38.

27. David Chapman, William K. Cummings & Gerard A. Postiglione (eds.) (2010): *Crossing Borders in East Asian Higher Education.* ISBN 978-962-8093-98-4. 388pp. HK$250/US$38.

26. Ora Kwo (ed.) (2010): *Teachers as Learners: Critical Discourse on Challenges and Opportunities.* ISBN 978-962-8093-55-7. 349pp. HK$250/US$38.

25. Carol K.K. Chan & Nirmala Rao (eds.) (2009): *Revisiting the Chinese Learner: Changing Contexts, Changing Education.* ISBN 978-962-8093-16-8. 360pp. HK$250/US$38.

24. Donald B. Holsinger & W. James Jacob (eds.) (2008): *Inequality in Education: Comparative and International Perspectives.* ISBN 978-962-8093-14-4. 584pp. HK$300/US$45.

23. Nancy Law, Willem J Pelgrum & Tjeerd Plomp (eds.) (2008): *Pedagogy and ICT Use in Schools around the World: Findings from the IEA SITES 2006 Study.* ISBN 978-962-8093-65-6. 296pp. HK$250/US$38.

22. David L. Grossman, Wing On Lee & Kerry J. Kennedy (eds.) (2008): *Citizenship Curriculum in Asia and the Pacific.* ISBN 978-962-8093-69-4. 268pp. HK$200/US$32.

21. Vandra Masemann, Mark Bray & Maria Manzon (eds.) (2007): *Common Interests, Uncommon Goals: Histories of the World Council of Comparative Education Societies and its Members.* ISBN 978-962- 8093-10-6. 384pp. HK$250/US$38.

20. Peter D. Hershock, Mark Mason & John N. Hawkins (eds.) (2007): *Changing Education: Leadership, Innovation and Development in a Globalizing Asia Pacific.* ISBN 978-962-8093-54-0. 348pp. HK$200/US$32.

19. Mark Bray, Bob Adamson & Mark Mason (eds.) (2014): *Comparative Education Research: Approaches and Methods. Second edition.* ISBN 978-988-17852-8-2. 453pp. HK$250/US$38.

18. Aaron Benavot & Cecilia Braslavsky (eds.) (2006): *School Knowledge in Comparative and Historical Perspective: Changing Curricula in Primary and Secondary Education.* ISBN 978-962-8093- 52-6. 315pp. HK$200/US$32.

17. Ruth Hayhoe (2006): *Portraits of Influential Chinese Educators.* ISBN 978-962-8093-40-3. 398pp. HK$250/US$38.

16. Peter Ninnes & Meeri Hellstén (eds.) (2005): *Internationalizing Higher Education: Critical Explorations of Pedagogy and Policy.* ISBN 978-962-8093-37-3. 231pp. HK$200/US$32.

15. Alan Rogers (2004): *Non-formal Education: Flexible Schooling or Participatory Education?.* ISBN 978-962-8093-30-4. 306pp. HK$200/US$32.

Earlier titles in the series are listed at the back of the book.

CERC Studies in Comparative Education 33

Crafting a Global Field

Six Decades of the Comparative and International Education Society

Edited by Erwin H. Epstein

Comparative Education Research Centre
The University of Hong Kong

Comparative Education Research Centre
Faculty of Education, The University of Hong Kong,
Pokfulam Road, Hong Kong, China

Copyright © Comparative Education Research Centre.
First published 2016
ISBN 978-988-14241-4-3 Paperback

CERC Studies in Comparative Education
ISBN 978-3-319-33185-0   ISBN 978-3-319-33186-7   (eBook)
DOI 10.1007/978-3-319-33186-7

Library of Congress Control Number: 2016945035

Cover design and layout: Gutsage
Layout: Emily Mang

Printed on acid-free paper

This Springer imprint is published by Springer Nature
The registered company is Springer International Publishing AG Switzerland

Contents

Abbreviations and Acronyms

AACTE	American Association of Colleges of Teacher Education
AERA	American Educational Research Association
AESA	American Educational Studies Association
AFR	Africa
ASA	American Sociological Association
CEIMA	Comparative Education Instructional Materials Archive
CER	*Comparative Education Review*
CERC	Comparative Education Research Centre
CES	Comparative Education Society
CIECAP	Comparative and International Education Course Archive Project
CIDE	Comparative and International Development Education
CIE	comparative and international education
CIEDR	Center for International Education, Development and Research
CIEGSA	Comparative and International Education Graduate Student Association
CIES	Comparative and International Education Society
CIESC	Comparative and International Education Society of Canada
CV	Curriculum Vitae
GEC	Gender and Education Committee
GLE	Globalization and Education
HED	Higher Education
HES	History of Education Society
HKU	The University of Hong Kong
IBE	International Bureau of Education
IEPM	International Education Policy and Management
IIE	Institute for International Education
IU	Indiana University
JDS	John Dewey Society

JOTS	Journal Office Tracking System
MDG	Millennium Development Goal
KMb	Knowledge Mobilization
NAFSA	National Association of Foreign Student Advisors
NEA	National Education Association
NGO	non-governmental organization
NIE	National Institute of Education (Singapore)
NSCTE	National Society of College Teachers of Education
OISE	Ontario Institute for Studies in Education
OSI	Open Society Institute
PES	Philosophy of Education Society
PISA	Programme for International Student Assessment
SBEC	Brazilian Comparative Education Society
SIDEC	Stanford International Development Education Center
SIG	Special Interest Group
SPE	Society of Professors of Education (formerly NSCTE)
SUNY	State University of New York
TC	Teachers College, Columbia University
TCE	Teaching Comparative Education
TEP	Teacher Education and the Teaching Profession
UCLA	University of California at Los Angeles
UCP	University of Chicago Press
UNESCO	United Nations Educational, Scientific and Cultural Organization
UREAG	Under-represented Racial, Ethnic, and Ability Groups
USAID	U.S. Agency for International Development
WCCES	World Council of Comparative Education Societies

List of Tables

List of Figures

Foreword

Mark BRAY

I have great pleasure in writing this Foreword, finding that I do so in a convergence of roles. One role, as Director of the Comparative Education Research Centre (CERC) at the University of Hong Kong (HKU), is editor of the series CERC Studies in Comparative Education in which the book appears. CERC's principal mandate is to advance scholarly work in the field of comparative education, and the series has established a reputation for valuable work in this domain. The present book indeed maintains and enhances that reputation.

A second role is President-Elect of the Comparative and International Education Society (CIES), i.e. the body on which this book focuses. Under the CIES system, the person elected Vice-President in any given year becomes President-Elect the following year and then in turn President and Past-President. The major role for the President-Elect is organization of the society's annual conference. This book has been prepared in time for the 60th anniversary conference in Vancouver, where it has been accorded a place of prominence to help participants both celebrate and learn about the Society's history.

A third role concerns my own history in a path that parallels that of the book's editor. Just as Erwin H. Epstein was once President Elect and then President of the CIES, both of us have been Presidents of the World Council of Comparative Education Societies (WCCES), an umbrella body which brings together 44 national, sub-national, regional and language-based

Erwin H. Epstein (ed.) (2016): *Crafting a Global Field: Six Decades of the Comparative and International Education Society*. Hong Kong: Comparative Education Research Centre (CERC), The University of Hong Kong, and Dordrecht: Springer. © CERC

societies of comparative education. Erwin Epstein was President from 1980 to 1983, and I was President from 2004 to 2007. An earlier volume in the series CERC Studies in Comparative Education is entitled *Common Interests, Uncommon Goals: Histories of the World Council of Comparative Education Societies and its Members* (edited by Vandra Masemann, Mark Bray and Maria Manzon, 2007). That volume contains a chapter on the CIES alongside accounts of the histories of the other WCCES member societies at the time of preparation. The present volume complements its predecessor by focusing on one Society and its evolution. The accounts include the contributions of the CIES and the WCCES to each other.

More broadly, this book assists in the academic maturation of the field of comparative and international education. It shows how forces have shaped the contours and boundaries of the field over the decades, and it will help to strengthen the identity of the field for future generations.

Both the CIES itself and the HKU Comparative Education Research Centre express great appreciation to the editor for the thorough, diligent and enlightening ways in which he has prepared this book. The CIES is the oldest and largest professional society for comparative and international education. It is based in the United States but has many members in other countries (including myself), and has a global influence. The various chapters map the paths traversed during the decades since 1956, and they also point to a future in which developments will build on a rich heritage and strong foundations.

Finally, I mention that the book can be read in conjunction with a pair of videos. Gita Steiner-Khamsi of Teachers College, Columbia University, worked with colleagues to record interviews of CIES past-presidents for the 50th anniversary of the Society, and prepared an update for the 60th anniversary. Some highlights are explained in her chapter in this book, and the video recordings themselves can be accessed on the CIES website: www.cies.us. Thus the written words can be accessed in conjunction with the spoken words and the visual images.

Introduction: Building a Home

Erwin H. EPSTEIN

Home is the sailor, home from the sea,
And the hunter home from the hill.
-Robert Louis Stevenson (from "Requiem")

For more than a half century the Comparative and International Education Society (CIES) has been my professional "home from the sea and home from the hill." To be sure, I have worked in many places – universities, states, countries – but year after year the Society has enriched my professional career in a truly special and unique way as an intellectual home.

I used to tell people that CIES was a warm, friendly association, where the members knew each other. You could count on renewing warm friendships at CIES meetings. I believe that is still mostly true, but with a membership that has grown incrementally to more than 2,500 people from about 800 people 50 years ago (see Epstein 1997), retaining warm friendships at meetings is not as easily assumed as it used to be. People pass on, of course; it is long since I could regularly count on seeing familiar faces like those of Anderson, Bereday, Brickman, Eggertsen, Farrell, Foster, Paulston, Shafer, and Wilson. Now, instead, I see an increasingly large number of *new* faces.

As we remember those who have contributed so much to this organization, we welcome the many who are just starting out in the Society and choosing it as their new home. It is a home with a remarkable history and structure, an understanding of which is this book's aim. It is a home with

Erwin H. Epstein (ed.) (2016): *Crafting a Global Field: Six Decades of the Comparative and International Education Society*. Hong Kong: Comparative Education Research Centre (CERC), The University of Hong Kong, and Dordrecht: Springer. © CERC

many rooms to accommodate its 2,500 member inhabitants. To serve as a useful guide to the Society's 60-year journey, I have assembled a stellar team of scholars, some of whom are rising stars and others of whom are time-honored, to produce *Crafting a Global Field*.

Consider this "Introduction" as the home's basement upon which all the floors, rooms, stairways, and passageways rest. Above the basement lie six floors representing the Society's development and growth. Each floor is a section containing chapters; consider them the floor's rooms.

The first floor (section), "Institutionalization", begins with a "room" by Elizabeth Sherman Swing who writes about setting the Society's foundation. The second room, by Alexander W. Wiseman and Cheryl Matherly, shows how the Society has advanced the profession, followed by Allison Blosser's description of how the Society has promoted the development of institutional programs, and, then a final room by Sahtiya Hosoda and Maria Ishaq Khan describing the Society's support of new scholars. The second floor, "Internationalization", has a room (by Louis Berends and Maria Trakas) that elaborates how and why international education became embodied in the name of the Society, and another (by Vandra L. Masemann) that describes the relationship between the Society and the World Council of Comparative Education Societies. The rooms on the third floor, "Intellectual Currents", consider how the Society has shaped the intellectual landscape of the field (by José Cossa), how the *Comparative Education Review* became the field's leading journal (by Bjørn H. Nordtveit), how the Society has mobilized knowledge (by Iveta Silova, Robyn Read, and Karen Mundy), and how Special Interest Groups have formed to advance specialty areas (by Oren Pizmony-Levy). This floor also contains a chapter on gender and education (by Nelly P. Stromquist, Halla B. Holmarsdottir, and Caroline Manion).

The top floors feature leaders and resources. The fourth floor's rooms describe how leadership in the Society has been shaped (by Ratna Ghosh and Mariusz Galczynski) and the foundational contributions of Isaac L. Kandel, William W. Brickman, and C. Arnold Anderson (by Erwin H. Epstein), and those of Gerald Read and George Z.F. Bereday (by Linda F. Robertson and Kenneth Cushner). On this floor too, Gita Steiner-Khamsi describes efforts to document the work of the Society's officers, Maria Manzon portrays other prominent Society members, and Hilary Landorf and Bahia Simons-Lane explain the means the Society uses to honor individuals with distinguished records of scholarship and service. The fifth floor's rooms contain some of the Society's prime resources: its Archive (by Erwin H. Epstein), Newsletter (by Martha C. Merrill), the Comparative and International Education Course Archive Project (by Kathleen M. Stone), and the Comparative Education Instructional Materials Archive (by Patricia K. Kubow). Atop all these floors is an attic featuring my "Conclusion" to this resplendent structure.

Figure 0.1 illustrates how the staircases and passageways link the floors (sections) and rooms (chapters). The box on the left is the name of the Society, as it was transformed from the Comparative Education Society through the insertion of "International", as depicted in the linkage shown in the middle boxes. The boxes on the right are the floors representing the book's sections, within which lie the rooms, or chapters. The linkages between the middle boxes and the boxes on the right explain how the Society acquired its current name. The arrows linking the boxes on the right are the staircases that connect floors, or sections. One of these arrows links "Institutionalization" and "Distinguished Shapers and Doers", a linkage that explains the construction of the original Comparative Education Society. Another arrow shows the link between "Distinguished Shapers and Doers" and "Internationalization".

Figure 0.1: Shifting the Name to the Comparative and International Education Society

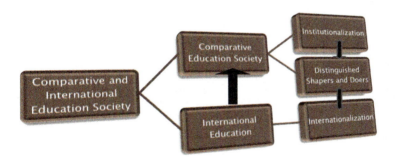

The rubrics at the right of Figure 0.2 display the chapters, or rooms (contained in the sections, or floors, shown in Figure 0.1) that were involved in the Society's change of name. The rooms (chapters) within each floor (section) are themselves linked by "passageways" that inform its section. For example, chapters by Ratna Ghosh and Mariusz Galczynski, Epstein, Cushner and Robertson, Steiner-Khamsi, Manzon, and Landorf and Simons-Lane, are linked to form the "Distinguished Shapers and Doers" section. In turn, the chapters by Swing, Wiseman and Matherly, and Blosser, comprising the section on "Institutionalization", are "staircased" to "Distinguished Shapers and Doers" to explain how the Society achieved its original name: Comparative Education Society. The chapters by Berends and Trakas, and by Masemann, comprising the "Internationalization" section, address the role of international education in the Society's transformation to its current name and state, as well as its relationship to the field beyond its North American context.

Figure 0.2: Passageways Between Rooms/Chapters

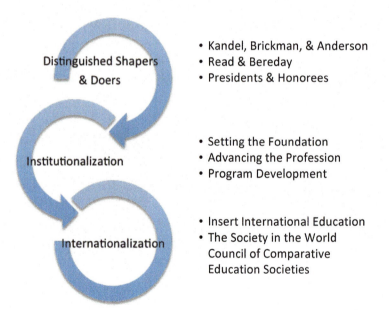

Distinguished Shapers & Doers
- Kandel, Brickman, & Anderson
- Read & Bereday
- Presidents & Honorees

Institutionalization
- Setting the Foundation
- Advancing the Profession
- Program Development

Internationalization
- Insert International Education
- The Society in the World Council of Comparative Education Societies

By similarly cross-referencing sections/floors and chapters/rooms of this book, the reader can craft illustrations of many other topics in the development of the Comparative and International Education Society. For example, epistemological developments affecting the Society can be discerned by "staircasing" all of the sections, and thereby linking chapters, or rooms, across and between sections, or floors. Hence, the reader can "discover" different epistemological topics by viewing relationships among several chapters, especially Setting the Foundation, Advancing the Profession, Shaping the Intellectual Landscape, and The Mobilization of Knowledge.

The use of forums to advance the Society's objectives likewise can be viewed in all sections, but especially in the sections on Intellectual Currents and Prime Resources, and within them, chapters on Shaping the Intellectual Landscape, The Comparative Education Review, The Mobilization of Knowledge, and Developing the Newsletter. To understand how the Society has influenced instruction, the reader should access the sections on Institutionalization, Intellectual Currents, and Prime Resources. Particularly useful within these sections will be the chapters on Program Development, The Social Organization of Special Interest Groups, The Comparative and International Education Course Archive Project, and The Comparative Education Instructional Materials Archive. All sections contain chapters on institutional memory, but Setting the Foundation, Advancing the Profession, Shaping the Intellectual Landscape, Developing the Archive, Choosing Leaders, and the two chapters on Early Leaders are especially applicable to that topic. The reader is invited to discern many other staircases and passageways among these sections and chapters that might shed light on particular interests.

So, you see, CIES is a large home with many floors and rooms. Yet a home has more than these, along with its stairways and passageways. No volume of this size could possibly cover everything in this house, and it perforce leaves out some of the Society's spaces. In particular, the book does not contain chapters on the Society's constitution and bylaws, its annual and regional meetings, its website, and its endowments. The areas not extensively covered in this volume must await future treatment.

This book is a tribute to the many leaders and members of the CIES, who, over 60 years, built a home worthy of emulation by comparativists and internationalists around the world. The production and distribution of this volume, in concert with the 2016 60th anniversary CIES Conference in Vancouver, represent a celebration of the dedication and craftsmanship of those who have labored so hard over the years to build a global field.

Reference

Epstein, Erwin H. 1997. "Editorial". *Comparative Education Review* 41(3): 241-243.

Institutionalization

I
Setting the Foundation

Elizabeth Sherman SWING

Prehistory, 1954-56

The New York University Conferences

The Comparative and International Education Society (CIES) evolved from annual conferences on comparative education organized by William W. Brickman at New York University in 1954. Brickman's conferences reflected the spirit of the times (Editor's note: See the chapter by Erwin H. Epstein on Early Leaders in this book). The post-World War II period was an era of proliferating international educational institutions, including UNESCO; the Centre for Comparative Education at the University of Ottawa (Canada); and the Research Institute of Comparative Education and Culture, University of Kyushu (Japan). It was also an era when a distinguished group of European senior scholars, including Joseph A. Lauwerys, Nicholas Hans, Isaac Kandel and Friedrich Schneider, set a standard for what might be achieved in comparative education scholarship. Brickman's concern was the low status of comparative education in the United States, "the apparently widespread feeling that the comparative study of foreign systems of education is decorative rather than functional and hence of little value to the teacher" (Brickman 1954). Although only 35 people participated in the initial New York University conference, Brickman labeled his edition of their papers: "Proceedings for the *First* Annual Conference on Comparative Education" (1954, emphasis added). In doing so, he signaled that this group would henceforth occupy comparative education turf in the United States.

Erwin H. Epstein (ed.) (2016): *Crafting a Global Field: Six Decades of the Comparative and International Education Society*. Hong Kong: Comparative Education Research Centre (CERC), The University of Hong Kong, and Dordrecht: Springer. © CERC

The first objective was to rescue the term "comparative education" from association with "junketlike tours abroad and the resultant courses" run by amateurs (Brickman 1977, 398) – to gain for the field "recognition in the academic and professional world as a group of scholarly-minded, serious specialists with high standards of teaching, research, and publication" (Brickman 1966, 8). Brickman's remedy was a rigorous program of post-doctoral study, research, foreign language training and school visits. The eminent scholar, Robert Ulich of Harvard University, who was keynote speaker at the first conference, also stressed foreign language and travel (Ulich 1954, 14). Like Brickman, Ulich located the field within a humanist tradition in which the frame of reference was Eurocentric and the dominant tools were history and languages.

The humanist frame of reference notwithstanding, the focus of the New York University conferences was also prescriptive, pragmatic, and pedagogic. The theme of the first conference, 'The Role of Comparative Education in the Education of Teachers' (1954), was followed by 'The Teaching of Comparative Education' (Brickman 1955), 'Comparative Education in Theory and Practice' (Brickman 1956a), and 'Comparative Education and Foreign Educational Service' (Brickman 1957a). The Comparative Education Society (CES), which evolved from these conferences, began its existence as a branch of the National Society of College Teachers of Education.

Formation of the Comparative Education Society

In 1954, shortly after the first New York University conference, William W. Brickman, Gerald H. Read of Kent State University, and Bess Goodykoontz of the United States Office of Education met in Washington, DC "to explore the possibility of designing a program that would provide a significant and first-hand experience in Europe for professional educators who had a responsibility for teaching course … that dealt with education in other lands" (Brickman 1966, 7) [Editor's note: See the chapter by Linda F. Robertson and Kenneth Cushner in this book]. Although discussion of a formal organization had antedated this meeting, the impetus for action was the discovery that group rates for study tours required a pre-existing group. To meet this requirement, at the close of the Third New York University Conference on April 27, 1956, Brickman and Read proposed that participants form a society (Brickman 1956b). Read's report in the minutes of the event is succinct:

Those present voted in favor of the formation of a Comparative Education Society. The Society came into being the next day (Read, Minutes, April 27, 1956).

The CES would hold annual meetings in Chicago in conjunction with the American Association of Colleges of Teacher Education, the National Society of College Teachers of Education, and the Association of Student Teaching. In addition, it would organize a Comparative Education Section of the National Society of College Teachers of Education. Summer meetings would take place during annual study tours.

Membership in the CES was to be "open to professors and students of comparative education and other Foundations of Education, to those persons who have responsibilities in the area of comparative education in organizations other than colleges and university, to those persons in professional education and other disciplines who are interested in comparative education" (Read, Minutes, April 27, 1956). Its goals were ambitious: to promote and improve the teaching of comparative education in colleges and universities; to encourage scholarly research in the field; to interest professors of all disciplines in the comparative and international dimensions of their specialties; to promote inter-visitation of educators and on-the-spot studies of school systems throughout the world; to cooperate with specialists in other disciplines in interpreting educational developments in a wider cultural context; to facilitate the publication of studies and up-to-date in-formation on comparative education; to encourage cooperation among specialists in comparative education in studies, exchange of documents and first-hand description of education; to cooperate wherever possible with such organizations as UNESCO, the International Institute of Education, and the Organization of American States," CES would "publish newsletters, monographs, yearbooks and other publications, either independently or in cooperation with other organisations." It would also sponsor programs of visitation to other lands and would even call upon its members to serve as hosts to foreign educators in the United States (Read, Minutes, April 27, 1956).

William W. Brickman was elected President; Robert Sutton, Ohio State University, Vice-President; and Gerald H. Read, Kent State University, Secretary-Treasurer. A Board of Directors was established, "with members selected from each of the various regions of the United States" (Read, Minutes, April 27, 1956). The first Board consisted of Claude Eggertsen, University of Michigan; George Z.F. Bereday, Teachers College, Columbia University; David Scanlon, Newark State Teachers

College; Bess Goodykoontz, US Office of Education; Flaud Wooton, University of California; Harold R.W. Benjamin, Peabody College for Teachers; William Johnson, University of Pittsburgh; and Robert Ulrich, Harvard University. Thereafter, an invitation was sent to 500 educators to become charter members of the society for a fee of US$2.00 per year. The society had 155 members after this solicitation (Read, Minutes, April 27, 1956).

Brickman later pointed out that the group who formed the Comparative Education Society consisted of junior scholars. "One might have expected an initiative from such internationally recognized scholars as Professor Joseph A. Lauwerys of England, Professor Walther Merck, Dr. Franz Hilker, and Professor Reich Hulla of West Germany; and Professors Robert King Hall, Thomas Woody, and Flaud C. Wooton of the USA, but none was forthcoming" (Brickman 1977, 398). In Brickman's view, therefore, the founding of the society "could be regarded as an act of rashness perpetrated by a relatively younger generation rather than as the outcome of deliberation by the outstanding experts of the field." Nevertheless, Brickman persuaded senior scholars such as Flaud Wooton and Robert Ulrich to join the first Board of Directors.

About the founding of the Comparative Education Society, George Z.F. Bereday, the first editor of the *Comparative Education Review*, had a similar but somewhat different perspective. In a letter to Walter F. Cronin, Office of Intelligence Research, Department of State, about his plans for the *Review*, Bereday noted that:

> Originally the Society germinated in a small group of people. Few of those have established a claim to competence in some aspects of comparative education; for most, their interest in the fields was far greater than their competence. After some deliberation at the college [Teachers College, Columbia University], I have decided to join and support the Society rather than creating factions and splinter groups in the field.... At present the demand for comparative education has far outrun the supply and many teach the subject who from the point of view of training they received have no business teaching it.

Bereday went on to provide an overview of the academic interests of several founding fathers:

> At present two of the men at the helm of the Society major in research in the Soviet area. William Johnson, the vice-president,

represents George Count's political-educational school. I myself represent the sociological, Harvard Russian Research Center orientation.... William Brickman, the president, has also some interest in the area. I think this is an overemphasis.... Fortunately my first major is not Soviet but Western Europe, England in particular; David Scanlon, one of our directors is working on Africa and Fundamental Education. This points in the direction of the kind of general coverage in which I am interested for the *Review* and for the Society (Letter, Bereday to Cronin, July 29, 1957).

Defining Institutional Directions, 1956-60

Study Tours

The newly-minted CES faced an immediate challenge: to implement the program of seminars and study tours planned by Brickman, Read and Goodykoontz. During the summer of 1956, a group of educators and academics led by Brickman and Read visited schools and universities in Denmark, Germany, Switzerland, France, the Netherlands and England. In the course of this tour, the Society held its first international meeting in Geneva, Switzerland, where on 1 September 1956 tour participants heard papers on the study of education in Switzerland and in the USA and on schools in Germany. George Z.F. Bereday was concerned about "unsettledness" in the society because of foreign tours (Letter to Walter F. Cronin, July 29, 1957), an issue over which Isaac Kandel later resigned from the Board of Directors. Nevertheless, the society sponsored an imaginative series of excursions to Venezuela, Brazil, Argentina, Chile, Peru, Ecuador, Japan, Korea, Ethiopia, Kenya, Tanganyika, South Africa, the Republic of Congo, Nigeria, Ghana, and Liberia. During the society's first six years, Brickman and Read led groups to five continents and 24 countries. Of particular significance was the five-week trip to the Soviet Union in 1958 at a time when the US State Department had not yet obtained an exchange agreement with the Soviet Union (Bereday et al. 1960).

The First Constitution

The CES held its first annual meeting in Chicago on February 14, 1957, with 39 members present (Read, Minutes). At that time, a series of practical decisions was made. The fiscal year was to start on January 1,

1958, and those who were members at that date would become charter members. A committee chaired by Kathryn G. Heath, US Office of Education, was appointed to frame a Constitution. At the second annual meeting in Chicago, February 20, 1958, with 111 members present, drafts of a Constitution were discussed. At the third annual meeting in Chicago, February 12, 1959, the decision was made to poll the membership by mail for ratification of the Constitution. This process was officially completed on June 1, 1959.

The first Constitution (1959) defined the shape and scope of the society. It called for annual elections and an annual professional and business meeting; a President and a Vice-President, each elected for a one-year term but eligible for a second term; a nine-member Board of Directors elected three at a time, each for a three-year term; and two Executive Committee Officers appointed by the Board, the Secretary-Treasurer and the Editor of the *Comparative Education Review*. The Constitution was amended in 1975 to provide for one-year successive terms by the Vice-President, President-Elect, and President respectively, and thus a two-year preparation for the Presidency. Several other revisions have been made in more recent years. The Society, however, has remained recognizably the organization created in the Constitution of 1959.

Provision in the first Constitution for election by the membership of the President, Vice-President, and the Board of Directors, rather than their appointment by a group in power, reflected the political traditions in which the Founders of the society were acculturated. The fact, moreover, of term limits for officers, board members, and appointed officers ensured that no clique would dominate the society for long. This outcome appears to be intentional. In March 1964, George Z.F. Bereday wrote a letter to Robert E. Belding of the University of Iowa in which he noted: "The founders and directors of the CES are most anxious not to dominate its affairs, hence their desire to stay in the background as much as possible." This posture, however, plus the rapid turnover of officers prescribed by the Constitution, has led to an unanticipated outcome in the years that followed: a loss on the Board of members with historical memory.

The Constitution called for Regional Meetings (Article IV, Section 2) to be arranged by the Executive Council. What has developed instead is an active network of geographical groups whose meetings are encouraged but not coordinated by the parent organization. The New York University conferences continued until 1959. Thereafter, Northeast

Regional Meetings of the CES took place respectively at Columbia University Teachers College, Jersey City State College, the US Office of Education, Syracuse University, the Pan American Union, and the University of Bridgeport. By 1965, there were regional conferences in Pittsburgh, Pennsylvania; Madison, Wisconsin; Berkeley, California; and Montreal, Quebec (Canada).

Comparative Education Review

Article V, Section 1, of the first Constitution directed the society to publish a professional journal "which shall be distributed to members without further cost other than membership dues." On April 25, 1957, a few months after the first annual meeting, William W. Brickman, David Scanlon, George Z.F. Bereday, and William Johnson "met to discuss the probability of publishing a *Comparative Education Review [CER]*" (Read, Minutes). [Editor's note: See the chapter by Bjorn Nordtveit in this book.] The journal first appeared in June 1957 with George Z.F. Bereday as Editor and Gerald H. Read as Business Editor. It has been published continuously ever since. Columbia University Teachers College financed the first issue; New York University, Harold Benjamin of Peabody Teachers College, and William W. Brickman, the next two issues. Thereafter, the journal relied on members' subscriptions and dues (Read, Minutes, 1957-1965; Bereday 1958). The first issue contained a brief introductory statement by Brickman, in which he prophesied that the *Review* would "become an organ of importance in the United State and abroad" (1957b, 1).

Reception of the new journal was mixed. Bereday received letters of congratulations from Benjamin, Ulich, Cronin, and Eggertsen, although the latter expressed some concern that the *Comparative Education Review* might overlap with his *History of Education Journal*. A negative assessment was penned by Joseph A. Lauwerys, of the University of London Institute of Education, who wrote to Bereday on June 13, 1957: "I am by no means clear in my mind whether it is a good thing to have such a Review. There is already in existence the *Hamburg Journal*, our own *Year Book*, the *Journal of Education Studies*...." Bereday replied that Brickman would have put out something if he [Bereday] hadn't (Letter to Lauwerys, June 19, 1957), showing that even Founding Fathers had professional rivalries.

After seeing the first issue of the *CER*, Lauwerys expressed even greater concern. "I cannot see what good a publication of this kind can do–indeed it is likely to do harm.... Forgive my bluntness. There are involved here academic and professional standards" (Letter to Bereday, n.d., June or July 1957). After learning more about the journal, Lauwerys recanted. "Don't get worried. All is well. I suppose as you think and say, I wrote in the heat of the moment" (Letter to Bereday, July 15, 1957). He went on to say that he would have responded differently had he known of Bereday's plans to review, in a subsequent issue of the *CER*, the *Year Book of Education*, of which he and Bereday were joint editors. He had been concerned that the British contribution to comparative education might be slighted.

Foreign Relations

Given Lauwerys' response to the launching of the new journal, the diplomatic skills displayed by Bereday in rounding up senior scholars, particularly international scholars, to give legitimacy to the fledgling *Comparative Education Review* were all the more remarkable. [Editor's note: See the chapter by Jose Cossa in this book.] Both Joseph Lauwerys and Nicholas Hans eventually joined the *Review*'s Editorial Board, but only after a careful balancing act. In response to Bereday, Hans had written to Bereday (March 15, 1959): "I am quite willing and ready to take part in your publication on the condition that Lauwerys is also on the Board. As I am working now in his department, I would not like to represent the Institute of [Education in] London without him." Meanwhile, Bereday approached Isaac Kandel, to whom he wrote (March 3, 1959):

> Your point about the younger generation not measuring up to the older in Comparative Education is well taken, humiliating as this fact is to me personally. But, in any case, we in our culture don't make nearly enough use of elder statesmen, and if our discipline is to thrive in the future, we need to have your support and blessing.... So please, please agree to being on our Board and I shall profit as I have always tried to do so in the past, from your experience and guidance.

By then, Bereday had persuaded James Bryant Conant, former President of Harvard, Franz Hilker, and Robert Ulich to join his Board, and in the next few years he enrolled Friedrich Schneider of Germany, Pedro Rosselló of Switzerland, and Torsten Husén of Sweden.

The Board of Directors of the *Review*'s parent organization, the Comparative Education Society, also reached out to established scholars from beyond the United States. During the 1960s, its Board included Edmund J. King, Vernon Mallinson, and Joseph Lauwerys, United Kingdom; Pedro Rosselló, Switzerland; Joseph Katz and Reginald Edwards, Canada; Irma Salas, Chile; and Philip J. Idenburg, the Netherlands. In addition, during this era two Canadians served as President – Joseph Katz in 1961 and Reginald Edwards in 1969. By 1962, 47 of the Comparative Education Society's 564 members, were "foreign" (Read, Minutes). In 1965 Gerald H. Read (Minutes) reported an "all-time high of 1,082 active members spread all over the world." In 1966 there were members from 44 countries (*CES Newsletter,* No. 5, June 1966).

Organization Building, 1960-75
Leadership, Finances, and Constitutional Revision
In the years following the founding of the CES, a core group assumed positions of leadership. William W. Brickman served as President from 1957 to 1959, and Gerald H. Read as Secretary-Treasurer from 1957 to 1965. Table 1.1 below gives details on the organizational leadership during this period.

Table 1.1: Presidents and Secretaries-Treasurer of the CES/CIES*

Term of Office	President	Term of Office	Secretary-Treasurer
1956-58	William W. Brickman	1957-65	Gerald H. Read
1959-60	William H.E. Johnson	1965-67	Franklin Parker
1960-61	Joseph Katz	1967-72	Barbara Yates
1961-62	C. Arnold Anderson	1972-75	Val Rust
1962-63	Claude Eggertsen		
1963-64	R. Freeman Butts		
1964-65	Donald K. Adams		
1965-66	David G. Scanlon		
1966-67	William W. Brickman		
1967-68	Stewart E. Fraser		
1968-69	Reginald Edwards		
1969-70	Philip Foster		
1970-71	Andreas M. Kazamias		
1971-72	Cole S. Brembeck		
1972-73	Harold J. Noah		
1973-74	Robert F. Lawson		
1974-75	Rolland G. Paulston		

*Editor's Note: This book's Appendix B contains a list of the presidents to date.

George Z.F. Bereday was founding editor of the *CER*. Bereday served as *Comparative Education Review* editor from 1957-1966, except for 1962-63, when he was replaced temporarily during a sabbatical leave by Hu Chang-tu of Columbia University. Harold Noah of Columbia University served as editor from 1967 to 1971. He was followed by Andreas M. Kazamias, University of Wisconsin-Madison, who served from 1971 to 1978.

This was an era of incremental financial growth. In 1957 Gerald H. Read reported a balance of US$554.11 in the society's accounts; in 1963, a balance of US$8,409.68. In 1968 there were total assets of US$21,624.02 (*CIES Newsletter,* No. 10, March 1968). By then, the Society was preparing for annual professional audits. There were nevertheless recurring concerns over solvency and over the need to increase membership, over the fact that officers frequently 'bootlegged' secretarial assistance from their home institutions, a theme that would echo in the years that followed. In the 1960s, however, non-financial issues dominated: constitutional revision, the question of a name change, and the decision to hold separate instead of joint meetings with groups with which the society was affiliated.

Constitutional revision was a consensus undertaking. As Gerald H. Read pointed out at the Board of Directors Meeting on February 15, 1967, the draft revision of the Constitution, which appeared in the December 1966 *Newsletter*, "formalized procedures which have been in operation for the last few years." The revised Constitution gave student members of the society the same rights and privileges as active members. It designated as officers of the society: the President, Vice-President, immediate Past President, the nine Directors, the Secretary, the Treasurer, the Editor, and the Business Manager. It also specified that the Vice-President succeed to the office of President after one year. Changes were discussed at the Annual Meeting in Chicago, February 17, 1967, and submitted thereafter to the membership by mail ballot for ratification. The *CIES Newsletter* for January 1968 reported that the revised Constitution was now official.

The Name-Change Issue

Of greater concern than the Constitution was the issue of a name change. [Editor's note: See the chapters by Louis Berends and Maria Trakas and by Alexander Wiseman and Cheryl Matherly in this book.] According to the January 1966 *Newsletter*, the instigator of the change was Joseph Katz, University of British Columbia (Canada), who suggested that Comparative *and International* Education Society might better indicate the global character of the organization. At the next annual Business Meeting on February 16, 1967, R. Freeman Butts put the issue before the membership. Twenty-four were in favor of a change, 14 against, and two abstaining. The following year the Committee on a Change of Name, chaired by Reginald Edwards, submitted, after exhaustive exploration, a very thorough report (*CIES Newsletter*, No. 10, March 1968). Among names discussed in the Edwards Report were Society for *Comparative* and International Education, International and Comparative Education Society, International Education Society, and, of course, Comparative and International Education Society. It cannot be a total coincidence that Joseph Katz, who initiated the name change, became the first president of the Comparative *and International* Education Society of Canada, which held its first meeting in 1967.

The Edwards Report reflected a heated debate. Opinions ranged from support of no change to strong support for a change that would emphasize the idea of international education. Reasons for and against were both theoretical and practical. It was argued that responsibilities such as cultural exchanges, student exchanges, Peace Corps, UNESCO, United States Agency for International Development, the International Education Act, world colleges, and university-to-university programs had transformed the academic discipline of comparative education as it was practiced during the era of Michael Sadler and I.L. Kandel. Professionals in administration, guidance and curriculum, it was asserted, were more likely to want affiliation with an international organization than with an exclusively academic organization. A change in name would bring together people different from the academics attracted by comparative education, would better describe the membership of the society, and would provide a basis for special interests. There was also the practical concern that government and non-governmental agencies dispensing funding might overlook the Comparative Education Society if it did not have the word *international* in its title.

Members of the Society were far from unanimous on this issue. Included in the 1968 Edwards Report is the following fervent statement (quoted in the CES Minutes, February 14, 1968):

> There are two major reasons why I would not wish to see a change of name at this juncture. The first concerns the different natures of the two topics – Comparative Education and International Education – and the second, a negative one, concerns the

'opportunist' thinking which seems to attach to some aspects of international education. It has taken rather more than 10 years to get this far in Comparative Education, and only now are we beginning to lay serious claim to being able make any worth- while comparisons, and to adopt methods which are presumed to underlie our studies. We have lacked good data, good methods, good training, and above all, as in so many aspects of education, we have lacked good theories. Now that these deficiencies are less obvious in Comparative Education, it might be preferable to capitalize on the skills we have acquired. In this respect International Education remains a more diffuse, more amorphous concept, and I cannot see many testable theories emerging in this area.

In an undated essay in the CIES Collection and in a 1968 letter to the Editor of *Comparative Education Review* (Vol.12, No.3, 376-378), Erwin H. Epstein, who was later to become editor of the journal, questioned the motives for the change. From his perspective, broadening the base of support for the field might realign factions "and even alter the nature of the field itself." For Epstein the word *international* connoted a "less analytic type of activity ... concerned more with practice and *implement- ing* [in contrast to the study of] policy" than was comparative education, which was more academic. These arguments still reverberate.

These concerns notwithstanding, on February 14, 1968, the Board of Directors unanimously approved a name change. The issue was put before the Business Meeting two days later, following which mail ballots were sent to the membership. The September 1968 *CES Newsletter* reported 200 ballots returned: 149 in favor of a change and 51 opposed. "Thus, Article I, Section I, of the Constitution is now amended to read: The name of this organization shall be the Comparative and International Education Society." The December 1968 *CIES Newsletter*, now using the new name, reported: "By vote of the membership the name of the Society has been changed to Comparative and International Education Society. From this issue onward, the title [of the Newsletter] will be *Comparative and International Education Society Newsletter*."

The Separate Meeting Issue
Until 1970 the Comparative Education Society met annually in Chicago during February, coordinating its meetings with those of the American Association of Colleges of Teacher Education, the National Society of

College Teachers of Education, and the Association of Student Teaching – organizations with which it affiliated at the time of its inception. In an era, however, when George Z.F. Bereday, Brian Holmes, Harold Noah and Max A. Eckstein were exploring new methodologies in comparative education, identification with teacher education was beginning to weaken. In 1964 the Board talked of coordinating their meetings with the American Educational Research Association (AERA) while retaining identification with teacher education. By 1965, there was talk of autonomous meetings or of meetings in which the intellectual focus was oriented more toward philosophy and the social sciences than toward teacher education.

In 1966, the year William W. Brickman gave an address on "Ten Years of the Comparative Education Society," the annual February meeting was still taking place in Chicago in conjunction with the National Society of College Teachers of Education (NSCTE). There were, however, difficulties identifying a sufficient selection of useable papers; also difficulties when the American Association of Colleges of Teacher Education (AACTE) announced its own central theme (Minutes, Executive Committee, October 11-12, 1966). In February 1968, the fact that the Society needed to seek permission from the NSCTE in order to plan three of its own sessions came under Board scrutiny. In October of that year, the Executive Committee examined ongoing problems of coordination, and it also discussed the "larger question of where and with whom the Society should meet annually." By March 1969, the Society was ready to experiment with a meeting independent of the AACTE/NSCTE in Chicago but to continue cooperation with the other societies on a reduced scale.

The September 1969 *CIES Newsletter* announced plans for a separate annual meeting in Atlanta in 1970:

> For the year 1969-70 our Society decided to separate the holding of a meeting in Chicago from the holding of the annual meeting. Thus, still in conjunction with NSCTE, and along with the History of Education Society, the John Dewey Society, the Philosophy of Education Society, and the American Education Studies Association, we shall also arrange a meeting at Chicago, in February 1970, in addition to the Annual Meeting to be held in Atlanta in March 1970.

It is not difficult to figure out which of the meetings was more important. The Chicago meeting would feature only graduate students, whereas senior scholars would meet in Atlanta. Meanwhile, the Executive Committee decided that the Vice-President would decide each year on the location of the annual Meeting (Executive Committee Minutes, October 10-11, 1969).

The CIES continued to interact with education societies from its past, but in a muted way. In 1970 R. Freeman Butts chaired meetings of the Foundational Coordinating Committee, which consisted of: the American Educational Studies Association (AESA), the CIES, the History of Education Society (HES), the John Dewey Society (JDS), the Philosophy of Education Society (PES), and the Society of Professors of Education (SPE, formerly NSCTE). Three of these societies were willing to have AACTE do administration and secretarial tasks through a joint secretariat in Washington. The other three, including the CIES, were not (*CIES Newsletter*, No.17, March 1970). In March 1970, the Board discussed plans for the CIES sessions at the AACTE Chicago meeting but decided instead to hold its own Annual Meeting in San Diego in 1971. At this point, Philip Foster proposed that the site of the Annual Meeting move around the country and be located in a different region each year.

Three CIES conferences took place in 1973: San Antonio, site of the annual meeting; Chicago, where a group from the CIES met with education associations from the past; and the University of Iowa, which held a Regional Conference (*CIES Newsletter*, No.27, 1973). However, not every CIES member was happy with these geographical experiments. Philip G. Altbach called on the Society "to reconsider our decision of a few years ago to hold our conventions separately from the AACTE meetings in Chicago" (*CIES Newsletter*, No.27, 1973). Altbach's concern was that recent recipients of the PhD degree needed access "to a wide range of employment opportunities" for which the AACTE format would be superior. "The situation of comparative education and that of the academic profession generally has changed greatly in the past few years and ... it would be at least a good idea to think about returning to the 'fold' of the broader community of teacher educators." Altbach also noted the central location of Chicago as an airline travel hub for faculty members in an era when travel funds appeared to be drying up.

Altbach's was not the only voice on this issue. Ursula Springer also spoke of the need to continue contact with "foundations" societies, especially the American Educational Studies Association (AESA). In her report for the Committee on Professional Concerns (*CIES Newsletter*, No.28, May 1973), Springer noted the low visibility of the CIES in the education profession and the danger of losing support in the colleges. She also pointed out "that it would be in our professional interest to develop a set of 'competencies' that we can accept and publicize in our *Newsletter*, so that the CIES members may utilize them if their situation and interest calls for it." At the Business Meeting in 1973, a sub-committee was formed to draft this set of "competencies", an effort that reflected a preoccupation in the world of teacher education at that time. Concern about competencies was short-lived, but it was symptomatic of the degree to which the CIES had strayed from an earlier professional focus.

No CIES-sponsored sessions were held at the AACTE Conference in Chicago in February 1974. The Board, however, expressed "support for participation at the Conference in order to provide Mid-Western members with participatory opportunities" (Minutes, March 1974). In a letter to the Board (May 21, 1974), Robert Lawson, the incoming CIES President, announced San Francisco as the site of the CIES conference in 1975. There would be an extra day for sessions, but "our thought that we might arrange the meeting in cooperation with one or more other Societies could not be worked into the conference pattern." A Chicago session, coordinated with AACTE, was to be run by Malcolm Campbell. In a letter to W.D. Halls, Oxford University, United Kingdom (May 23, 1975), Lawson clarified the situation: "The CIES meetings held annually in Chicago are continued as a contribution to the annual meeting of the American Association of Colleges of Teacher Education. The annual CIES conference is held separately, this past year in San Francisco, March 26-29, 1975." Lawson noted that a group unrepresentative of the CIES was to be found in Chicago, thus making it clear that the San Francisco meeting represented the real CIES, an organization with its own identity.

Growth and Consolidation, 1975-90
Relationship with Other Societies
After 1975, the CIES, although now meeting independently from other organizations, continued to seek collaborative relationships with other professional groups. In 1980 it appointed Leo Leonard (University of Portland) and Edward Berman (University of Louisville) to represent the

CIES at the annual meeting of the Council of Learned Societies in Education.

Throughout the 1980s, the CIES maintained relationships with organizations such as AERA, UNESCO, and the United States Office of Education (Executive Committee Minutes, Atlanta, March 16, 1988), all professional organizations with an international scholarly thrust (*CIES Newsletter*, No.94, May 1990). In 1990 the Society had affiliations with the Council of Learned Societies in Education; with NCATE (National Council for Accreditation of Teacher Education), to which it contributed an annual fee of US$200; as well as with the Alliance for Education in Global and International Studies, to which it contributed US$150 dues.

Besides the Council of Learned Societies in Education, which consisted of member societies in various areas of the social foundations of education, another "umbrella" organization of which the CIES has been a member (in fact a founding member) is the World Council of Comparative Education Societies (WCCES) [Editor's note: See the chapter by Vandra Masemann in this book]. In 1974, there was concern that *ratifying* the WCCES Constitution would mean endorsing a "super-society" (*CIES Newsletter*, No.34, December 1974). However, Robert Lawson and others successfully argued for ratification.

Moreover, in the 1980s, the CIES committed itself explicitly to support the WCCES. A statement issued by the Board at the Society's 1985 annual meeting, and again endorsed by the Board at the 1986 meeting, spelled out this commitment: the CIES encouraged members to attend WCCES congresses, to appoint CIES representation to WCCES committees when requested to do so, to publish news of the WCCES in the *CIES Newsletter*, to contribute dues assessed by the WCCES, and to expect that CIES members would assume the cost of participation in committees or congresses of the World Council. Within this framework, many CIES members regularly attended WCCES congresses and served on WCCES committees. In 1997 the CIES Board decided that the official CIES representative to the WCCES should be a Past President, who would serve for two years, thus skipping a Past President every other year (Minutes of the Board of Directors, March 23, 1997). However, a 2014 revision of the CIES Bylaws provided that the Immediate Past President serve as the Society's formal representative to associated organizations, including the WCCES. The term of representative is thus one year, although the Immediate Past President can delegate that responsibility.

Establishing Historical Memory: Creation of the Archives

A measure of the growing maturity of the CIES was the establishment in 1980 of the Society's own archives [Editor's note: See the chapter by Erwin H. Epstein on Developing the Archive in this book]. Formal discussion of the need to preserve the past dated from a proposal by Beatrice Szekely in 1978 that was distributed to the Board the following year by Philip G. Altbach. At the time, the Board endorsed a motion by Gail P. Kelly that archives be established as a long-term project. To get started, the Board voted a grant of US$600 to Beatrice Szekely for the current year and another US$600 for the following year.

Although Beatrice Szekely was subsequently unable to undertake supervision of this project, the idea slowly gained momentum. One possibility explored by President George Male would have used the "Papers in Comparative and International Education" collection at Teachers College, Columbia University, for the CIES papers. Such an arrangement, however, would have excluded Brickman, Anderson, Eggertsen, and others not connected with Columbia. It also required an initial financial outlay. Male then appointed an Archive Committee, consisting of Franklin Parker, Claude Eggertsen and William W. Brickman. Thereafter, at the urging of Philip G. Altbach (Letter to Kim Sebaly, May 19, 1980), Kim Sebaly submitted a proposal for a CIES Collection in the Special Collections department of the Kent State University Archives. This proposal was promptly accepted.

The CIES Collection in the Kent State University department of Special Collections and Archives has become an important resource in the field of comparative education. It now occupies approximately 92 cubic feet, of which 57 cubic feet are processed and included in its online inventory. The CER Editors' files are currently undergoing review and are being re-processed. The Collection holds records from before the founding of the CIES, *CER* records, issues of the *CER* and the *CIES Newsletter*, correspondence by CIES officers, minutes of Board meetings, and video interviews of past CIES Presidents. Kent State University also hosted the WCCES archival collection from 1996 to 2014. Kent State University archivists, Nancy Birk, and her successor, Cara Gilgenbach, have guided the day-to-day supervision of the CIES Collection. Of particular importance is the work of Kim Sebaly, a Kent State University faculty member and long-time CIES member who generously donated his time and expertise to the Collection.

Societal Recognition Marker: Honorary Fellows

A first attempt to honor "Elder Statesmen" was introduced at the CIES Annual Business Meeting in 1970, at which time the Board recommended an honorary membership category limited to 10 members. This proposal, which was defeated by a vote of 13 in favor, 20 opposed, was premature (Minutes, Annual Business Meeting, March 23, 1970). The idea re-emerged in 1981 in a memo to the Board from Erwin H. Epstein suggesting that CIES find a way to honor "some of our *illuminati* who have retired or are about to retire" (Epstein, Memo to Board, 7 July 1981).

In 1983, the Awards Committee proposed that the CIES appoint selected senior members as "Fellows of the CIES" (*CIES Newsletter,* Nos. 67-68, April/June 1983). Thereafter, criteria for the Honorary Fellow designation were prepared by Philip J. Foster, Chair of the Awards Committee; Thomas J. La Belle; and Vandra Masemann, later aided by Noel McGinn. Of particular concern was the question of posthumous awards. (George Z.F. Bereday had just died.) The membership, however, voted to reject "Posthumous Honorary Fellow" status (Business Meeting Minutes, April 20, 1985). Nevertheless, in 1990 an article in the *CIES Newsletter* (No.95, September 1990) refers to George Z.F. Bereday as an Honorary Fellow, thus confounding historical memory. The criteria agreed upon in 1985 limited the number of Honorary Fellows to five *"living"* members" per year until 15 are identified (later limited to one a year, with provision for holding over nominations if more than one name is submitted). The age of 60 was set as the minimum age for an Honorary Fellow but changed in 1990 to evidence of a "long and distinguished career." All nominations, plus recommendations from at least five active members of the society, were to be forwarded by the Awards Committee to the Board of Directors, which would make the final decision. More recently, the total number of living Honorary Fellows has been increased.

The first two Honorary Fellows, Claude Eggertsen and C. Arnold Anderson, were appointed in 1987; the second two, Harold Noah and Philip Foster, in 1990. These were followed by Mary Jean Bowman, Andreas Kazamias, Gerald H. Read, and R. Murray Thomas – all appointed in 1991. Thereafter came Max A. Eckstein (1994), Noel McGinn (1997), Don Adams (1998), Rolland Paulston (1999), Elizabeth Sherman Swing (2000), Norma Tarrow (2001), Mathew Zachariah (2002) and Robert Arnove (2003). Joseph Farrell and William Rideout received the honor in 2007, and Vandra Masemann received it in 2008. In more recent years the Honorary Fellows have been Martin Carnoy (2009), John

Hawkins (2010), Ruth Hayhoe (2011), Erwin Epstein (2012), Val Rust (2013), David Evans (2014), Robert Lawson (2015), and Jack Schwille (2016).

Systemic Change: The Constitution of 1998
The Constitution and By-Laws of 1998 brought systemic change to the CIES. In the past, amending the constitution had been a cumbersome process that involved soliciting approval of two thirds of CIES members by mail over a three-month time period. In a Memo to the Board of Directors on March 3, 1991, Val Rust argued for a less complicated system:

> As you know, we have never had a set of By-Laws. Rather, as issues have arisen we have been content to change the CIES Constitution [and] this has resulted in a fairly complicated document that has procedural detail in it not appropriate for a constitution.

The Constitution of 1998, of which Rust was a major author, was divided into two parts: a semi-permanent, but lean Constitution, followed by the Society's first set of By-Laws. Amending the Constitution still requires two-thirds approval by mail ballot. Passing or rescinding a By-Law, however, requires no more than a two-thirds affirmative vote by a quorum of the Board, a procedure that can take place during a regular Board meeting (Article XII, Sections 1 and 2). It can also take place electronically (By-Laws, Article V, Section c). In 2000, using streamlined procedures in the new Constitution, the Board amended the By-Laws to convert three newer committees from Ad Hoc to Standing Committee status: the Investment Committee, the Gender and Education Committee, and the Under-Represented Ethnic and Ability Groups (UREAG).

In addition to By-Laws, the Constitution of 1998 created a new officer – Historian, an office with a three-year renewable term and Executive Committee status. The CIES Historian is charged with supervising archive maintenance, with ensuring the deposit of necessary documents therein, with advising the society on "matters of historical fact," with facilitating research projects, with coordinating communications with other collections related to the society, with serving as Parliamentarian, and with reporting annually to the Board of Directors. In 1999, the Board of Directors appointed as its first Historian, Elizabeth

Sherman Swing, whose PhD dissertation advisor was William W. Brickman, the first President of the society.

Systemic Change: Expansion of the Committee Structure
A significant development was a trend toward a decentralization of CIES activities through expansion of the committee structure and through Special Interest Groups. At the time the Constitution of 1998 was ratified, the CIES had three Standing (permanent) Committees: the Nominations Committee, the Awards Committee, and the New Scholars Committee. The Nominations Committee (Constitution, Article VI, Section 2) which was composed of members "who are not holding office in the Society," was responsible for selecting a slate of candidates for the annual election: two each for the office of Vice-President and for three members of the Board of Directors [Editor's note: See the chapter by Ratna Ghosh in this book]. The Awards Committee, which came into being in 1981 in order to select the winner of an award for the best article each year in the *CER* (since 1990 called the Bereday Award), selects the Gail P. Kelly Dissertation Award winner and the Joyce Cain Award winner, and submits Honorary Fellow nominations to the Board for final vetting [Editor's note: See the chapter by Hilary Landorf and L. Bahia Simons-Lane in this book]. The New Scholars Committee, which traces its origin to a student caucus at the annual meeting in 1988 (*CIES Newsletter*, No.86, January 1988), converted from Ad Hoc to Standing Committee status in 1991 [Editor's note: See the chapter by Maria Khan and Sahtiya Hosoda Hammell in this book]. At that time it changed its name from Young Scholars Committee to New Scholars Committee, "to reflect age diversity among students and scholars who are entering the field of comparative and international education." This well-established group has its own website, runs highly successful dissertation workshops, and has assumed responsibility for video-taping interviews of former CIES Presidents. Other committees had different origins. The Investment Committee, for example, was a response to a 2000 endowment of US$100,000 from George F. Kneller, a UCLA professor of the philosophy of education. Terms of the endowment included a directive that the bequest be made "in securities that will appreciate along with the factor of inflation," that it be controlled and managed "as an autonomous entity" rather than mingled with other funds, and that income from the bequest be used for an annual lecture "to be presented before the general assembly or

members (and others) by a distinguished scholar or personage," and be called the George F. Kneller Lecture (Secretariat Report, March 7, 2000).

The Gender and Education Committee represented a response to other concerns [Editor's note: See the chapter by Nelly Stromquist, Carly Manion, and Halla Holmarsdottir in this book]. That gender had become a dominant issue in the CIES in part reflected the women's movement in the larger society. It also reflected the pioneering work of Gail P. Kelly, a prolific scholar who was Associate Editor of the *CER* (1979-88) and President of the CIES (1986). Gender equality was not a pressing concern in the early years of the CIES. Minutes of a 1961 discussion by the Board of the characteristics looked for in a Vice-President describe the ideal candidate as "a young *man* who shows potentiality in the field of comparative education" (italics added). It was not until 1976 that the society elected its first female President, Susanne Shafer. Up to 2006, Barbara Yates, Gail P. Kelly, Beverly Lindsay, Vandra Masemann, Nelly Stromquist, Ruth Hayhoe, Heidi Ross, Karen Biraimah, and Kassie Freeman served in this office. Between 2006 and 2015, a much higher proportion of women served as President – Gita Steiner-Khamsi, Maria Teresa Tatto, Ratna Ghosh, Karen Mundy and N'Dri Assié-Lumumba. In total, of the 58 CIES Presidents, 43 have been men and 15 have been women.

The structural response of the CIES to gender issues dates from 1989 when President Vandra Masemann created a Gender and Education Committee with Nelly Stromquist as Chair. Subsequent chairs were Karen Biraimah, Heidi Ross, Margaret Sutton, Mary Ann Maslak and Shirley Miske. In 1990 this Committee set out to explore what was still unfamiliar territory: participation of women on boards of professional organizations and as contributors to journals, gender issues in doctoral dissertations in comparative education, and the position of women as university professors and in international agencies. Its request, for example, that the editors of the *CER* provide them with a breakdown by gender of the number of articles submitted, accepted or rejected was the first such inquiry in the history of the *CER* (Minutes, Board of Directors, March 24, 1990). In addition to its role in setting up the Gail P. Kelly Award in 1994 for the best dissertation with social justice and equity issues in an international or comparative context, the Gender and Education Committee hosted well-attended pre-conference workshops. Tangible evidence of the increasing importance of the committee structure, and of this committee in particular, is the fact that three of the

Gender Committee chairs – Nelly Stromquist, Karen Biraimah, and Heidi Ross – became CIES Presidents.

The Under-Represented Ethnic and Ability Groups Committee (UREAG) also came into being because of perceived grievances. The UREAG Committee traces its genesis to 1990 when Kassie Freeman, Paul Emongu and Victor Kobayashi petitioned to convene a committee to investigate how to ensure "greater ethnic equity in all dimensions of our professional activities: the Board unanimously approved this proposal (Minutes, March 24, 1990). Subsequently, concern over access to CIES meetings for those with physical disabilities came under the purview of this committee. The UREAG Committee leaders have not hesitated to ask that their voices be heard (Gezi 1995) or that slots be available in the conference schedule for presentations and "Global Village Dialogue". Kassie Freeman has written eloquently of the "reluctance, almost resistance, to acknowledge that there are different cultures within the 'USA that warrant greater understanding and inclusion'" (Freeman 1995).

UREAG maintains its own website and has supported members with travel grants to attend CIES meetings. In 2000 it established an Award for Distinguished Research on African Descendants, named after Joyce Lynn Cain, in honor of a faculty member at Michigan State University, "a colleague and a devoted scholar of comparative education" (*CIES Newsletter*, No.124, May 2000). Kassie Freeman, the first chair of UREAG, became a CIES President. She also ran a highly successful conference in New Orleans (2003) hosted by Dillard University, a historically black institution.

Political and Ideological Concerns
During the 1990s and beyond, the CIES grappled with an increasing number of political and ideological issues. Particularly troubling was the issue of apartheid in South Africa. Should CIES welcome at its annual meeting representatives of a regime that denied justice to a majority of its people (*CIES Newsletter*, No.93, January 1990)? A Norwegian scholar, Yngve Nordkvelle, wanted to keep all South Africans, including those opposed to apartheid, out of conferences as a way of putting pressure on a corrupt political system (Letter from Nordkvelle, February 6, 1989). Joseph Di Bona of the CIES saw a different challenge: "Nothing can be so unsettling, and therefore so morally enlightening, as face-to-face interaction with real champions of policies we detest. We need to teach our students the link between racism at home and fascist policies of South

Africa" (Letter to Masemann, June 5, 1989). The society eventually decided not to adopt a boycott. What it did do was to approve a statement that subsequently appeared on much of its correspondence until apartheid ended: "The Comparative and International Education Society is opposed to apartheid in South Africa and condemns that country's laws and policies which deny basic human rights."

There were other contentious issues. After the 1989 Beijing Tiananmen Square incident, the CIES opposed selection of Beijing as the site of the next WCCES Congress. In 1997, it recorded opposition to gender discrimination in education in Afghanistan. In 2003 it wrote to US President George Bush concerning difficulties encountered by foreign students and scholars in getting visas for entry to the United States.

A different set of issues erupted over the so-called World Bank Bibliography. This database across academic disciplines called for an annotated bibliography on education reform and management resources to be prepared by members of the CIES with World Bank funding (*CIES Newsletter,* No.124, May 2000). After the first installment was published, some CIES members questioned whether this project represented a partnership between the CIES and the World Bank – an uncomfortable prospect for a vocal group in the organization. Once the project ended, the issue receded; but it remains an example of a fundamental difference in worldview between liberal academics and pragmatic researchers which was reminiscent of the comparative education/international education cleavage of the 1960s.

The Last Ten Years

Total individual memberships have risen incrementally to over 2,500, of which 43 percent are students. In the last decade, many of the activities initiated earlier have grown in size and complexity.

The length of the annual meetings has increased over the years from the average three days in the 1970s. Now the newcomer will see a great choice of professional workshops held in the day or days before the official conference opening. The impact of computer technology is also evident as proposals for papers must be done online and the entire registration and payment process is done electronically. The fact that a paper conference program must be ordered and purchased is evidence of a fundamental change in this regard.

Special Interest Groups have proliferated and sponsor many

interesting panels at the annual conference. [Editor's note: See the chapter by Oren Pizmony-Levy in this book] Indeed there has been speculation that their development might lead to the fragmentation of the Society. The very large number of attendees in recent years means that people can attend and may never see a specific colleague. The increased use of electronic means of communication obviates this problem.

There has also been increased activity of the New Scholars Committee and proliferation of sessions aiding new scholars, such as the very popular mentoring programs for doctoral students. The number of travel grants for New Scholars has been increased. Highly successful workshops related to writing and publishing have been held.

The CIES has established new committees, including some dealing with relatively new topics such as investments. To the average member, the discussion at annual meetings focuses much more on financial reserves and planning than formerly as a result of increased attendance at annual meetings. Already existing committees, such as the Gender Committee and the UREAG Committee, are very active. The Awards Committee also has an increased amount of work relating to its various sub-committees, as the numbers of awards increase.

The *Comparative Education Review* has become a top flight journal world-wide and measures up well in terms of numbers of citations and computer downloads of articles. William Brickman's vision of elevating the status of comparative education has certainly been realized in the reputation of the journal. Overall, the fact that the conference attracts many members from North America as well as from over 100 other countries each year is a testament to its success.

Afterword

For those to whom it speaks, the CIES has become more than just a professional association. Loyalty runs deep and long. The members' list for June 1966 includes a roster of familiar names of those who remained active five decades later. Even among the younger generation, the CIES conferences have a special ambience. Asked what the CIES has meant to her, a graduate student member of the Board of Directors offered this heartfelt testimony (Maria Fatima Rodrigues, *CIES Newsletter*, No.121, May 1999):

The annual CIES conference creates a social space where human beings from many different parts of the world connect on topics of mutual interest and learn from one another (even from those [with whom] they may strongly disagree). The greatest value of being a member of this society has come from my interactions with people who have different frames of reference and different realities.

It is possible to argue that the CIES is still a work in progress, but it is one whose "different frames of reference and different realities" give it strength.

References

Altbach, Philip G., Robert F. Arnove, & Gail P. Kelly, eds. 1982. *Comparative Education*. New York: Macmillan.

Altbach, Philip G., & Gail P. Kelly, eds. 1986. *New Approaches to Comparative Education*. Chicago: University of Chicago Press.

Bereday, George Z.F. 1958. Editorial. *Comparative Education Review* 1(3): 1-4.

Bereday, George Z.F., William W. Brickman, & Gerald H. Read, 1960. *The Changing Soviet School*. Cambridge: Riverside Press.

Brickman, William W. 1954. "Report on New York University's First Annual Conference on Comparative Education", in *The Role of Comparative Education in the Education of Teachers*, ed. William W. Brickman. Proceedings of the First Annual Conference on Comparative Education. New York: School of Education, New York University, April 30: 8-9.

Brickman, William W., ed. 1955. *The Teaching of Comparative Education*. Proceedings of the Second Annual Conference on Comparative Education. New York: School of Education, New York University April 29.

Brickman, William W., ed. 1956a. *Comparative Education. A Symposium*. Proceedings of the Third Annual Conference on Comparative Education on 'Comparative Education in Theory and Practice.' Reprinted from *Journal of Educational Sociology* 30(3): 113-160.

Brickman, William W. 1956b. 'Report on New York University's Third Annual Conference on Comparative Education'. In Brickman, William W. (ed.), *Comparative Education: A Symposium*. Reprint from *Journal of Educational Sociology* 30(3): 113.

Brickman, William W., ed. 1957a. *Comparative Education and Foreign Educational Service*. Proceedings of the Fourth Annual Conference on Comparative Education. New York: School of Education, New York University (April 26).

Brickman, William W. 1957b. "A New Journal in Comparative Education." *Comparative Education Review* 1(1): 1.

Brickman, William W. 1966. "Ten Years of the Comparative Education Society." *Comparative Education Review 10*(1): 4-15.

Brickman, William W. 1977. "Comparative and International Education Society: An Historical Analysis." *Comparative Education Review 21*(2/3): 396-404.

Comparative Education Society/Comparative and International Education Society. *Newsletters*. CIES Collection, Special Collections and Archives. Kent State University, Kent OH, USA.

Constitution of the Comparative Education Society 1959. *Comparative Education Review 3*(2): 37-40.

Constitution of the Comparative and International Education Society of 1998 and its By-Laws.

Epstein, Erwin H. n.d. "A Rose under Any Other Name." (Undated typescript)

Epstein, Erwin H. 1983. "Currents Left and Right: Ideology in Comparative Education" (Presidential Address). *Comparative Education Review 27*(1): 3-29.

Freeman, Kassie. 1995. "Marginalisation on the Eve of Globalisation." *CIES Newsletter* 108 (January).

Gezi, Kal. 1995. "Increasing Underrepresented Groups in Education." *CIES Newsletter,* 108 (January).

Hackett, Peter 1988. "Aesthetics as a Dimension for Comparative Study" (Presidential Address). *Comparative Education Review 32*(4): 389-399.

Kelly, Gail P. 1987. "Comparative Education and the Problem of Change: An Agenda for the 1980s" (Presidential Address). *Comparative Education Review 31*(4): 477-489.

Masemann, Vandra. 1990. "Ways of Knowing: Implications for Comparative Education" (Presidential Address). *Comparative Education Review 34*(4): 465-473.

Rust, Val D. 1991. "Postmodernism and its Comparative Education Implications." *Comparative Education Review 35*(4): 610-626.

Ulich, Robert 1954. "Keynote Speech", in Brickman, W.W. (ed.). *The Role of Comparative Education in the Education of Teachers.* Proceedings of the First Annual Conference on Comparative Education. New York: School of Education, New York University (April 30), p.14.

2
Professionalizing the Field

Alexander W. WISEMAN and Cheryl MATHERLY

The debate concerning the professional status of comparative and international education has a relatively short yet tumultuous history, beginning roughly in the mid-twentieth century. Two professional organizations, in particular, have been at the center of this debate, and are now among the oldest comparative and international education (CIE) associations. The Comparative and International Education Society (CIES) was established in 1956, and NAFSA (The Association of International Educators) was established in 1948.[1] Yet, comparative researchers and international educators are still struggling to distinguish themselves as belonging to a unique profession. In fact, the debate as to the status of comparative and international education as a profession began about the time these associations were founded (Heath 1958), and has ebbed and flowed ever since.

The existence of a commonly agreed upon set of characteristics of a profession is key to the process of professionalization. A well-established literature grounded in the works of Larson (1977) and Abbott (1988) defines the fundamental characteristics of a profession related to: (1) expert knowledge, (2) training and credentials, (3) self-policing and ethical codes, (4) occupational domain, and (5) the workplace. In order to achieve professionalization, members of an occupation collectively struggle "to define the conditions and methods of their work, to control 'the production of producers,' and to establish a cognitive base and legitimation for their occupational autonomy" (DiMaggio & Powell 1991, 70).

The theoretical foundation laid by sociological neo-institutionalism suggests that university programs and professional associations in any

Erwin H. Epstein (ed.) (2016): *Crafting a Global Field: Six Decades of the Comparative and International Education Society*. Hong Kong: Comparative Education Research Centre (CERC), The University of Hong Kong, and Dordrecht: Springer. © CERC

field become institutionalized as professional entities and structures through a process of legitimation (DiMaggio & Powell 1991; Jepperson 1991, 2002; Meyer & Rowan 1977). This process occurs as these associations and programs follow established and accepted scripts for legitimate activity and content. Within the established structures and norms there will be some "loose coupling" of day-to-day activity (Pierson & Skocpol 2002), meaning that university programs and professional association members' institutional affiliation may vary. But, any variants will mostly fall within the larger, legitimate, taken-for-granted structural and organizational boundaries of university programs and professional associations affiliated with comparative and international education.

The primary characteristic of professionalization, then, is the development of a legitimate knowledge base through the development of specialized university degree or training programs. In his seminal work on professionalization, Wilensky (1964, 142, 144) highlights this characteristic by asserting that once people "start doing full time the thing that needs doing," the next step is to develop a training school–usually in a university. Universities and training institutions develop legitimate norms for formal education and a knowledge base. The next step in professionalization is to develop a professional association. And, so a profession is newly born. Professional associations then develop legitimate norms for professional networks and behavior. DiMaggio and Powell (1991, 71) build on the sociology of professions literature (specifically Abbott 1988; Larson 1977) by explaining how these two aspects of professionalization are important sources of organizational change.

The organizations and institutions of a field embody the efforts of that field to perpetuate itself epistemologically (Cook, Hite & Epstein 2004, 148). The purpose of the present study is to identify, describe, and analyze trends in the professionalization of the field of comparative and international education, as indicated by the founding, expansion, and evolution of various university programs and professional associations serving the field. No historical development is inevitable, and it is important for those working in the field to understand why and how some routes were taken when others were avoided or even abandoned. This understanding is important to individuals working in the field of comparative and international education as agents of reform, development, policymaking, or classroom teaching, as well as to those who rely on the services that others in the field provide to students, schools, education systems, national governments, and international organizations. A firm understanding of the field's professional knowledge base and association trends will enable both academics and practitioners to better plot a course for the future of comparative and international education.

To discern the degree to which the field of comparative and international education has professionalized, we look at these two important characteristics of professionalization: expert knowledge base and professional association. Specifically, we look at the development of "knowledge" in comparative and international education both in terms of how it has been studied and in terms of where the legitimate expert knowledge base resides. Next, we consider the development and demographics of one of the first and largest professional associations in the field, the Comparative and International Education Society (CIES). To frame this investigation in more empirical terms, we analyze historical documentation as well as the characteristics of the Comparative and International Education Society membership to examine the degree to which comparative and international education has become professionalized. The first step is to define the language and terms used to describe both the field and its professionalization.

Definitions of the Field

An analysis of the professionalization of comparative and international education relies upon developing an understanding of both the institutionalization of the field of comparative and international education and the institutions that represent the profession (i.e., associations and graduate programs) and the synergistic convergence of two related fields (international and comparative) into one. One of the cornerstones of the debate over the professionalization of comparative and international education concerns the definition of comparative versus international education. The definitions provided by Epstein (1994, 918) in the *International Encyclopedia of Education* provide the basis for our perspective. It should be noted, however, that Epstein himself was one of the original critics of combining the two fields of comparative and international education (Epstein 1968). In his encyclopedia definition of the two fields, Epstein alludes to this by pointing out,

"Comparative education" and "international education" are often confused. The former refers to a field of study that applies historical, philosophical, and social science theories and methods to international problems in education.... Comparative education is primarily an academic and interdisciplinary pursuit.... International education ... fosters an international orientation in knowledge and attitudes and, among other initiatives, brings together students, teachers, and scholars from different nations to learn about and from each other.... Many practitioners of international education are experts on international exchange and interaction.... However, there is some disagreement on the specific range of activities encompassed by international education. Halls (1989) categorized it as a subfield of comparative education, consisting of 'international pedagogy'. This would include such items as education for international understanding, internationalization of teaching norms, and the study of international education institutions. Others characterize it as an applied field attached to comparative education.

Whether international education is a pedagogical subfield of comparative education or the application of comparative education concepts to global educational problems is still a matter for debate. In fact, the difficulties in describing and differentiating the "twin" fields of comparative and international education are still the subject of much discussion (Arnove 2001; Phillips & Schweisfurth 2014; Wilson 1994). One of the reasons to suggest that merging comparative education (representing the more theoretical side of the field) and international education (representing the more practical side) is that "a profession is based upon a systematic body of knowledge which is both theoretical and practical" (T.R. Horowitz 1985, 297; Hughes 1963). Therefore, it is possible that by merging the comparative and the international a whole (rather than a semi-) profession was created. The yin and yang of theory and practice in education in general and in the comparative and international education field in particular is therefore an important element to consider both in defining the field and in analyzing the degree to which the field has professionalized.

Analysis of the Professionalization of Comparative and International Education

The question of professionalization in the field of comparative and international education, then, fundamentally depends on (1) the establishment of a legitimate knowledge base through university (i.e., graduate) training and (2) the development of specific professional networks and behavior guidelines through the establishment of a professional association dedicated to the unique concerns of the field. Our analyses examine institutionalization of professional norms, values, and expectations related to comparative and international education through the establishment and reach of professional institutions (which include both university programs and associations).

Our analysis of the professionalization of comparative and international education is driven by two fundamental research questions:

1. Do university programs and professional associations in comparative and international education contribute to the development of or secure control over expert knowledge, training and credentials?

We specifically focus on the degree to which graduate university programs and professional associations in comparative and international education have contributed to or secured control over expert knowledge, training, and credentials – with expert knowledge being the key – because "... a field's process of inducting its own membership must include ... a cohesive transmission of a particular and identifiable body of knowledge" (DiMaggio & Powell 1983; 1991) [Editor's note: See the chapter by Allison Blosser in this book]. Theoretical and methodological knowledge bases are often the special domain of disciplines that lead to specific professionalization. Hawkins and Rust (2001, 508) make the point:

> Methodology usually has a central role in the training of those coming into the field, and it also represents part of the glue that defines a field and provides a sense of being part of a professional community. If the research strategies become too fragmented and disparate, the field could begin to gyrate with such force that it may spin out of control, losing any sense of the identity and cohesiveness necessary for a field to grow and thrive.

Hawkins and Rust suggest that expert knowledge, training, and credentials cannot be established under the domain of comparative and international education if they are not comprised of one unifying disciplinary methodology. This could indeed be a problem for the professionalization of the field if is found that the fragmentation of comparative and international education by discipline (e.g., economics, sociology, political science, etc.) has resulted in a hodgepodge of methodologies operating disparately under the name of comparative and international education. A related question concerns the impact that merging comparative with international education has had on the field.

2. Has the merging of "comparative" and "international" education contributed to the professionalization of the field?

We believe that it is highly significant that the previously distinct fields of "comparative education" and "international education" have converged in the Comparative and International Education Society, in particular. They are still in many ways two sides of the same coin: research vs. teaching, basic vs. applied, theory vs. practice (Cook et al. 2004). But, in the words of a former CIES President David N. Wilson (1994, 450), "the merger of the two perspectives has resulted in the education of a new breed of academic-practitioner, who has brought this 'scientific' perspective to bear on his or her melioristic international education activities." We rely on Wilson's description of "a new breed of academic-practitioner" as a benchmark for investigating and evaluating the degree to which the field of comparative and international education has been professionalized.

To analyze the phenomenon of professionalization of the field of comparative and international education, we use historical institutionalism as one methodological approach. This approach is used frequently in political science, historical, and sociological analyses to (1) develop explanatory arguments by specifying sequences and tracing transformations and processes of varying scale and temporality, and (2) analyze macro contexts and hypothesize about the combined effects of institutions and processes rather than examining just one institution or process at a time (e.g., Beland & Vergniolle de Chantal 2004; Steinmo, Thelen & Longstreth 1992).

To investigate historical trends in the professionalization of comparative and international education, we consulted published histories of the professional associations associated with the field of comparative and international education. The analysis of these histories included coding for key terms related to the core constructs of expert knowledge, training, and credentialing in comparative and international education associations and university programs. We noted the temporal sequence of the terms we identify, context in which these terms occurred, and developmental trends that arose. Of particular interest to us is the way that professional associations and university programs either intersect with or complement each other related to key professionalization constructs.

The evidence shown below comes from several different sources. The authors and their graduate assistants collected some of it. But, we also rely upon the work done by CIECAP at Loyola University Chicago; especially regarding the specific author and course content information for the introductory course in comparative and international education [Editor's note: See the chapter by Kathleen Stone in this book]. Lastly, we benefited from the anonymous CIES membership information made available by the University of Chicago Press.

Historical Evolution of the Knowledge Base and Professional Network in Comparative and International Education

This section traces two threads in the professionalization of comparative and international education regarding the development of a legitimate knowledge base. One is an examination of the evolution of the study of comparative and international education from area studies, to disciplinary studies, to development studies. Another is the shift in comparative and international education research toward more positivist, social science approaches. We trace these threads making two assumptions. First, that being Americans we predominantly understand the field of comparative and international education from a U.S. perspective. We do so while recognizing that there is a rich and important history of comparative education outside North America, which deserves more attention in future work on this topic (Epstein 2008a, 2008b). Second, despite the fact that the roots of comparative and international education can be traced to the late 19th century, this study is limited to post World War II because of the rapid growth in comparative and international education activities during this period.

To induct members into the field of comparative and international education, there must be "a cohesive transmission of a particular and identifiable body of knowledge" (Loxley 1994). But, for the field of comparative and international education, is this a true and accurate statement? Is there a cohesive transmission of knowledge related to comparative and international education? And, is there anything particularly identifiable about comparative and international education knowledge? This is the crux of the professionalization of comparative and international education as a field, and the focus of the following analysis.

We use Hawkins and Rust's (2001) framework to trace the evolution of comparative and international education since World War II. They define *area studies* as a perspective that chooses a specific place and culture as the unit of analysis, and typically requires scholars to have language skills, area expertise, extensive field experience, and a social science or humanities background. *Disciplinary studies* place primacy on the scholars' discipline and aim to explain a phenomenon in terms of context-independent elements. Researchers do not use national setting as the unit of analysis, but rather as the setting where problems, theory, and methods can be examined. Hawkins and Rust contend that these researchers typically do not have extensive language and cultural preparation, and field experience in a particular setting is rare. They describe *development studies* as a complex mixture of area studies and discipline studies. Development scholars use a transdisciplinary approach to the social sciences, and also use a holistic approach common to area studies, to understand social and economic change. Hawkins and Rust do not suggest that area, disciplinary, and development studies are mutually exclusive – indeed all three were used immediately following World War II – but that the study of comparative and international education suggests that each held sway as a dominant approach to the scholarship.

These perspectives can be loosely tracked chronologically. The origin of comparative education research is in area studies, beginning with research that described educational systems in other countries. Typical of these works were Moehlman and Roucek's *Comparative Education* (1952), which used nation-states as the unit of analysis for systems of education, and M.M. Chambers' *Universities of the World outside U.S.A.* (1950), compiled for the American Council on Education. There were a number of influences on this scholarship, including returning WWII soldiers who had exposure to foreign systems of education; new ideological concerns (such as the Cold War) that sought to cast education systems in terms of national interest; an increase in the number of U.S. students studying abroad and foreign students studying in the U.S.; and funding for foreign assistance through institutional development projects by organizations such as USAID and UNESCO (Altbach 1991; Brickman 1966). This suggests that from the outset, the activities and scholarship of comparative education were fragmented and directed towards many competing agendas: educational exchange, political relations, and international development.

In this environment, a primary motive for the formation of the Comparative Education Society (later renamed the Comparative and International Education Society) was to claim control of the term "comparative education." The founding scholars claimed the term was being used too loosely and irresponsibly. They believed that forming this association would raise the standard of scholarship and create initial standards for who could claim to be part of the profession. Brickman (1966, 8), the founding President of the Comparative Education Society, said its purpose was to "gain recognition in the academic and professional world as a group of scholarly-minded, serious specialists with high standards of teaching, research and publication." The founders were concerned that there was no recognized way to access the field and "anyone who so desired could leap into the vacuum." The Comparative Education Society was founded in 1956 with ambitious goals (Brickman 1966, 7):

> To promote and improve the teaching of comparative education in colleges and universities; 2) to encourage scholarly research in comparative and international studies in education; 3) to interest professors of all disciplines in the comparative and international dimensions of their specialties; 4) to promote intervisitation of educators and on-the-spot studies of school systems throughout the world; 5) to cooperate with specialists in other disciplines in interpreting educational developments in a wider cultural context; 6) to facilitate the publication of studies and up-to-date information on comparative education; 7) to encourage cooperation among specialists in comparative education throughout the world in joint studies, exchange of documents, and first-hand descriptions of education; 8) to cooperate whenever possible with such organizations as UNESCO, International Institute of Education [sic], Organization of American States, etc.

In an obvious effort to rescue comparative education from "junketlike tours abroad and the resultant courses" run by amateurs (Brickman 1977, 398), the early CES meetings were to be held in conjunction with the

American Association of Colleges of Teacher Education, the National Society of College Teachers of Education, and the Association of Student Teaching — all forums in which scholars could influence the teaching of the subject (see the chapter by Swing in this volume). Among the Society's first activities was a European study tour that involved faculty from comparative education as well as history and philosophy of education, philosophy, psychology, and theology in visits to schools, teachers colleges and universities in Denmark, England, France, Germany, Holland, and Switzerland. The organization subsequently sponsored similar trips to Africa, Latin America, and the Soviet Union in 1958, at a time when the U.S. State Department had not yet established an exchange agreement with the Soviet Union (Swing's chapter in this book).

By the late 1950s, there were several programs in comparative education in the USA at Harvard, Peabody College (Vanderbilt), Teachers College (Columbia), and the University of Michigan (Altbach 1991). The program in comparative education at Teachers College, Columbia University provides a useful snapshot of early graduate studies. The tradition of comparative and international studies at Teachers College dates back to World War I. By the mid-1950s it was squarely in the academic tradition of area studies, concentrating on both defining and refining the methods for studying comparative education and with the application of liberal disciplines to the study of education. In 1958, there were three faculty in the department of Comparative and International Foundations of Education, each specializing in a geographic area: East Asia and India; Sub-Sahara Africa and the Middle East; and Europe, the Soviet Union, and Latin America. Altogether they taught 20 courses that were grouped as general (Fundamentals of Comparative and of International Education; Seminars on Methods and Problems in Comparative and International Education); problems (courses dealing with mass culture, nationalism, cross-cultural concepts, problems of undeveloped areas); and area studies (course on Europe, Asia, and Africa). Of the 20 doctoral students completing their dissertations, five were in European studies; two in Soviet studies; three in African studies; and one each in Canada, Australia, and the Middle East. Significantly, only one of the dissertations was considered "comparative". The remainder completed research that analyzed the educational system within a single country, albeit a foreign one (Bereday 1960).

The motive of many of the early scholars studying schools in foreign countries was to improve their own classroom practices and school systems. The area studies tradition, which stemmed from the early scholars' roots in the traditions of history and philosophy, gave way to the introduction of social science methods, which seemed better suited to the increasing interest in education as a policy tool. While economists in particular led the move towards the consideration of the education system of a nation as its means for investing in human potential and developing national resources, researchers were aware that the survival of a nation also depended on its success in dealing with political and social problems. Nations were for the first time considering how education could address a myriad of social needs: achieving a sense of national unity among disparate subpopulations, ameliorating gross disparities in status and opportunity among social classes, and improving people's skills and quality of life.

The shift in comparative and international education away from area to disciplinary studies coincides with the rise of the positivistic, social science approach to the field of education in general represented by Noah and Eckstein's (1969) analysis of the "science of comparative education." Noah and Eckstein's work marked the shift to a disciplinary studies approach, because it clearly advocated for the use of empirical social science methods in education by calling for the application of positivist methods in comparative education studies. The social sciences were perhaps an inevitable evolution from the predominantly historical and philosophical approaches of earlier comparative educators. Researchers were now concerned with causal relations: What factors in school systems or in the social, political, or other social structures explain differences in student achievement, administrative structures, school financing, and instructional methodology? What are the similarities and differences in educational practices among nations, and what are their outcomes (Eckstein 1975). The real-world application of these ideas can be seen in such programs as the Peace Corps and USAID, which positioned education as an engine of national development and social change (Hawkins & Rust 2001).

Development studies, or "education aimed at the modernization of technological activities in order to provide better for their material and cultural needs, and at the adaptation of their political machinery and other society institutions in such a way as to make possible the most effective use of this modernization in the satisfying of those needs," was a logical next step in the application of social science practices on comparative and international education.

After 1960, several major U.S. schools of education established centers or departments concerned with the field of international development education that were clearly influenced by the social sciences. Among the most influential were at Stanford (Stanford International Development Education Center); Teachers College, Columbia (International Studies); Chicago (Center for Comparative Education); Harvard (Center for Studies in Education and Development); Pittsburgh (International and Development Education Program); and Syracuse (Center for Development Education) (Spaulding, Singleton & Watson 1968). By 1967, a review of the curriculum and faculty at these institutions suggests how far these programs had evolved from that in Comparative Education at Teachers College 10 years earlier. The Stanford program recruited faculty from economics, anthropology, and political science to work in multidisciplinary teams with professional educators. The University of Chicago and Syracuse University stressed economics and sociology as their core disciplines. Columbia emphasized approaches that considered how to strengthen educational systems and organizations from an applied social science perspective. Harvard integrated economic and educational planning. Pittsburgh emphasized educational methods, techniques, and strategies for development. Underscoring the now primacy of the social sciences, anthropologists were central in the programs at Stanford, Columbia, and Pittsburgh, while sociologists held sway at Chicago and Syracuse, and they were increasingly concerned with the predictive characteristics of quantitative data (Spaulding et al. 1968).

It is this shift towards disciplinary studies that provides context for the debates over changing the name of the Comparative Education Society to indicate a more global nature of the organization. Although the board of directors of the association unanimously voted to change their name to the Comparative and *International* Education Society on February 14, 1968, the heated debates by the membership reflect the larger question of what the terms include (Swing's chapter in this book). Many working in the field hotly contested this shift. For example, in his CIES presidential address, Reginald Edwards (1970, 254) conceived, "the meeting ground of social science and comparative education to be a three dimensional space, with unequal distribution of comparative educators and social scientists throughout the space." In other words, the exact boundaries of the field of comparative and international education were in a constant state of flux between comparative education, international education, and social science disciplines. This suggests an ambiguity regarding both the legitimacy of the knowledge base and the professional association of those working in the field of comparative and international education.

Justification for and against changing the association's name was both theoretical and practical. Some wanted a name that was inclusive of the growing responsibilities included in international education, such as student exchanges, Peace Corps, UNESCO, USAID, and university-to-university programs. There was also a practical interest in ensuring that the association would be competitive for government and non-governmental funding for international education activities (Swing's chapter in this book). Some opponents argued that this was precisely the reason to not make the change – that broadening the base of the field might alter the nature of the field itself. Others considered the move "opportunistic." One member, quoted in the February 14, 1968 CES minutes, suggested that the shift undercut the efforts on the part of the association to lay claim to a consistent body of knowledge – a key factor contributing to the professionalization of the field. This member said,

> We have lacked good data, good methods, good training, and above all, as in so many aspects of education, we have lacked good theories. Now that these deficiencies are less obvious in Comparative Education, it might be preferable to capitalize on the skills we have acquired. In this respect International Education remains a more diffuse, more amorphous concept (Swing's chapter in this book).

By the late 1970s, however, the interest in comparative education declined precipitously in the context of a general decline in higher education, a U.S. economic recession, decline in foreign aid budgets, a general anti-internationalism brought on in part by U.S. defeat in the Vietnam War, and a reconsideration of the role of education in national development as many third world economics failed to take off. This was also a period marked by growing fragmentation in the epistemology of comparative education.

Altbach (1991) identified several factors that contributed to the decline of established approaches of the 1960s: the failure of traditional ideas to explain educational developments worldwide, notably that only a few developing countries were actually developing despite considerable educational expenditure, and social movements, such as the women's movement, that pointed to new and important elements that needed extensive further analysis. Kazamias (2001) used the cover of a 1977 issue of *Comparative Education Review* on which Humpty Dumpty sits on a cracked-wall map of the USA looking at the words "structural functionalism", "cost-benefit", "production", "pedagogy", "development", and "mankind" as an illustration of the debates in the field during the 1970s. This was the beginning of the rise of critical theory, post-structuralism, post-modernism, various feminist theories, as well as a growing array of methodological data collection options, ranging from surveys, literature reviews, historical studies, content analyses, inter-views, questionnaires, and participant observation.

The paradigmatic struggles in the field of comparative education essentially mirrored what was happening in other fields of social science, further indicating the extent to which comparative education had become multidisciplinary. The social sciences, with which comparative and international education was now firmly aligned, experienced a flowering of perspectives: critical race theory, Marxism, feminism, queer theory. But concomitant with the excitement of these new approaches also came a withering of established authority. New people entered the field without deference to the existing expertise, since all perspectives were valid, and increasingly there was no fixed star by which to measure expertise anyway. Authority gave way to competing theories. In aban-doning its humanistic origins, comparative education was now subject to the fits, fancies, and hysterias of other social sciences.

The 1980s saw a modest renewal of U.S. interest in comparative education, in large part because the World Bank became a major source of research in comparative education. By the end of the 1980s, the World Bank was probably the largest producer of comparative research on education (Altbach 1991). World Bank staff published in journals on comparative education, and several of its publications, such as *Education in Sub-Saharan Africa*, became influential.

This historical analysis has shown how the comparative and inter-national education knowledge base shifted in the U.S. from area studies to disciplinary studies to development studies over the course of the 20th century, but especially post-World War II. The establishment of compa-rative and international education university programs has paralleled this shift in the content and focus of the courses and research coming out the field. Also, the post-World War II era is marked by the merging of comparative education and international education as evidenced by the renaming of the Comparative Education Society as the Comparative and International Education Society.

The Degree of Professionalization of Comparative and International Education

In reviewing these historical trends in the development of both expert knowledge and professional association, the following promises and problems are keys to understanding the professionalization of the field of comparative and international education through the struggle to establish a legitimate knowledge base and professional network:

1. There is a developing professional knowledge base for the field of comparative and international education that reflects the progression of studies and research approaches to the field summarized above.

2. The shift towards social science disciplines encouraged a methodological and theoretical fragmentation of the field because those working in the field sometimes more closely aligned with their primary disciplines (e.g., economics, sociology, political science) more than the field of comparative and international education itself.

These issues help us understand how comparative and international education has developed as a professional field in its contemporary form and speak directly to the dual trends in the development of expert knowledge in the field of comparative and international education. On the one hand, the development of a professional "canon" for the field represents the professionalization of the field through the establishment of a legitimate base of expert knowledge (Stinchcombe 1982); in other words, the comparative and international education canon consists of "what is taught" in university programs that specialize in the field (Dowd 1991, 317). On the other hand, the fragmentation of the field into various methodologies and theoretical perspectives based in different social science disciplines suggests that the base of expert knowledge is not unified, meaning there is no cohesive base of expert knowledge (I.L. Horowitz 1993). Thus, we suggest that the professionalization of comparative and international education is characterized by both promise and problem.

As the fledgling Comparative Education Society finalized its original Constitution and Bylaws, one of the more shrewd reflections on the development of comparative and international education appeared in an early article in the *Comparative Education Review*. Heath (1958) summarized 10 key characteristics of a professional discipline and posed pointed questions about each, challenging readers to define and justify comparative education in those terms. She asserted that disciplines have a specialized body of knowledge, educational foundation, specialized training, in-service learning process, clear career path, unique function, clear path of entry, code of procedure, service to humanity, and a formal association. These 10 characteristics map nicely onto the professionalization concepts of an expert knowledge base and association network discussed in the sociology of professions and professionalization literature (Abbott 1988; Gispen 1988; Guillen 1992; Hall 1968; Hoyle 1982; Larson 1977; Meriam 1937; Montagna 1968; Ritzer 1975; Rothblatt 1995; Waters 1989; Wilensky 1964). Heath's article also emphasized that since the field was first "professionalized" through the establishment of the Comparative Education Society, there have been questions about the process.

The historical development of a knowledge base in comparative and international education outlined in the previous section suggests that the field of comparative and international education has not yet emerged as a fully-vested profession, although it is certainly more professionalized than a semi-profession as defined by Etzioni (1969). This is in part due to the persistent variability in knowledge base and formal training that characterizes individuals working in the field. For example, those working in the field of comparative and international education include university professors, development consultants, bank representatives, classroom teachers, research assistants, study abroad directors, foreign student advisors, and social program managers around the world. Professionals in the field are spread across both private and public communities, and academic and commercial organizations. Cook, Hite, and Epstein (2004, 145) call this a "flexible professional identity," but realistically it means that there is no single or 'best' method for training and credentialing these individuals.

While there are about 30 graduate programs in comparative and international education in the U.S., many more universities offer an introductory course in comparative education than there are degree or academic programs specializing in the field. Post, Farrell, and Ross (1995) discussed this phenomenon in the mid-1990s. They also went on to discuss how university faculty teaching and researching in the field of comparative and international education did so in "comparative isolation" (Ross, Post & Farrell 1995, 4), which suggests a need for a "more general diffusion of knowledge" related to the field across disciplines and technical training opportunities. In other words, many scholars in universities are teaching or doing research in comparative and international education, but doing so as individuals rather than as part of a more cohesive department or program structure. Likewise, Crossley and Watson (2003, 31) assert, "Because comparative and international research in education is influenced by many different intellectual, disciplinary and professional foundations it cannot lay claim to any one single theoretical or methodological perspective." This diversity within the field highlights the potential for "comparative isolation" among individuals working in comparative and international education.

One of the ways to estimate the extent of "comparative isolation" in the field is by simply counting the number of institutions that have just one member of the Comparative and International Education Society affiliated with them. Table 2.1 shows the number of CIES members affiliated with such institutions. In 2015, which is 59 years after the founding of the Comparative and International Education Society, 542 individuals were the only recorded CIES members at their institution.[2] This means that of the 720 CIES members with recorded institutional affiliations, 75 percent were the only recorded CIES members at their institutions. Twenty two percent of CIES members with recorded affiliations were affiliated with institutions having five or fewer CIES members. Only 25 institutions had more than five CIES members affiliated with them. These numbers suggest that professionals in the field of comparative and international education are still working in comparative isolation, although most of the CIES members who give their institutional affiliation are at universities.[3] So, while individuals who identify themselves as professionals in comparative and international education are largely isolated from other individuals in the same field, they are also part of a larger community by virtue of the broader institutional association they all share. Since "comparative education" has traditionally been seen as the more scholarly side of the field, a large affiliation of CIES members with universities might suggest that the field was still more comparative than international. Wilson (2003, 18), however, asserts that with the merging of the comparative and the international there came "a new breed of individual, the academic-practitioner, who has been equipped with a viable academic understanding of comparative education and who has used that orientation to further the meliorative function common to both international and comparative education in his or her subsequent international activities." The question then is whether those individuals working as academic-practitioners in the field of comparative and international education demonstrate that there is a specific body of expert knowledge, training, and credentials unique to their professional field.

Table 2.1 Number of CIES Members Affiliated with Unique Institutions (2015)

Indicator of "Comparative Isolation"	f
Institutions with only 1 recorded CIES member	542
Institutions with only 2 recorded CIES members	90
Institutions with only 3 recorded CIES members	29
Institutions with only 4 recorded CIES members	20
Institutions with only 5 recorded CIES members	14
Institutions with >5 recorded CIES members	25

One way to estimate whether there are academic-practitioners working in the field versus either academics or practitioners is to consider the institutional affiliations of CIES members. Using the online membership tool and supplementing it with anonymous data from the *Comparative Education Review* subscription list, we have an estimate of the institutional affiliation of most of the members whose address is in the U.S. We identified three main categories of members' institutional affiliations, which are:

- **University or tertiary education**
  CIES members included in this category are affiliated with a university or other tertiary educational institution (such as a community or technical college) as their primary institutional affiliation. Examples include the larger, better-known universities with comparative and international education programs like Stanford University and Teachers College, Columbia University, as well as smaller private universities like Lehigh

University, and other higher education institutions with a more practical focus such as the Milwaukee Area Technical College and Minneapolis Community and Technical College.

- **Development, research, and policy**
  CIES members included in this category are affiliated with a development, research, or policy organization as their primary institutional affiliation. Development organizations are those that are primarily financial, such as the World Bank, as well as those that address social justice and community development, such as Give a Child a Life or Plan International. Research organizations are those that may be involved in development or policy as well, but are largely focused on the collection, analysis and interpretation of comparative and international education data. Examples of research organizations include the American Institutes for Research and the Council of American Overseas Research Centers. Finally, policy organizations are those that count among their primary functions the analysis and development of educational policy. Examples of policy organizations are the Institute for Higher Education Policy and the National Education Association.

- **Education (Other)**
  CIES members in this category are affiliated with educational organizations that are not at the tertiary level and could be either classroom or administration-related. For example, educational organizations in this category could include the Baltimore Board of Education or the private Lake Forest Academy.

Table 2.2 presents the number of CIES members worldwide in 2015 who had recorded institutional affiliations and the categories into which these institutions fall. Overwhelmingly, CIES members were affiliated with universities and other tertiary educational institutions. Sixty two percent of the Society's members were graduate students, faculty, or high-ranking administrators in university contexts. Those who were more application-oriented worked either in organizations dedicated to development, research, and policy-making (37 percent) or other areas of education systems (one percent). In determining the degree to which comparative and international education has a legitimate, professional knowledge base, it is significant that so many of the members of CIES are institutionally affiliated with a university. Universities are repositories of official and legitimate knowledge. By affiliating themselves with both universities and the main professional organization related to comparative and international education, these members strengthen the assertion that there is a knowledge base in the field.

Table 2.2 Institutional Affiliation of CIES Members (domestic/U.S. and international, 2015)

Institutional Affiliation	N	% of Valid N	% of Total N
University or Tertiary Education	813	62	27
Development, Research & Policy	492	37	16
Education (Other)	11	1	0
Valid N	1316	100	
Missing	1743		57
Total N	3059		100

The extensive affiliation of CIES members with universities also suggests that there is not as much of an academic-practitioner model as Wilson asserted but instead more of a majority academic professional model and a minority practitioner-oriented professional base. Granted, many CIES members are graduate students in university programs training to work in the field of comparative and international education, but that does not change the fact that either these graduate students disassociate with CIES when they graduate from university or they stay affiliated with universities after graduating. For example, some may leave CIES once they graduate and join other professional associations that are more specific to their actual occupational responsibilities. However, since formal training is a key component to the establishment and professionalization of a knowledge base, the overwhelming number of members affiliated with universities remains significant.

The large group of university-affiliated members of the CIES may also suggest a higher degree of loyalty to the profession of comparative and international education among those who professionally reside in departments or degree programs specifically dedicated to comparative and international education. Wallace's (1995) study of organizational and professional commitment in professional organizations showed that professional commitment is less related to the structural characteristics of organizations and more related to the potential distribution of opportunities and rewards. Simply put, the professionals in comparative and international education will have a greater potential for opportunity and reward in university programs specifically dedicated to the field. For example, professionals working for the World Bank–even though they may consider themselves to be working in the field of comparative and international education–will be less committed to the field of CIE than they will be to the field of economics or another social science discipline, because the potential for reward is greater from a disciplinary perspective than from a CIE perspective.

It is important to note, however, that a significant shift of members' institutional affiliation is underway. In 2008, the data show that about 80 percent of CIES members were affiliated with university or tertiary education, whereas in 2015 that had dropped to 62 percent. Likewise, whereas affiliation with development, research, or policy institutions was around 20 percent in 2008, in 2015 that percentage has grown to 37 percent. So, while the academic-practitioner model envisioned by Wilson (2003) may not have been fully-realized, there might be a change afoot among the membership of CIES, with more of a balance between academics and practitioners in the field than previously reported.

The struggle to professionalize, therefore, is measured for the field of comparative and international education primarily through the ability of members of the field to define and legitimate an expert knowledge base as well as to regulate their own training and credentials. The results are, quite frankly, mixed. On the one hand, professionalization has occurred through the growing homogeneity across university degree programs and courses in the field coupled with the strong institutional association between universities (as repositories of legitimate knowledge) and the predominant professional association in the field. On the other hand, the diversity in the content of the knowledge base, dominant methodologies, exact degree program, university or other institution suggests that professionalization has not fully arrived for comparative and international education through the unification or standardization of knowledge. Instead, there is likely another phenomenon at work.

Abbot (1988, 20) argued that the "central phenomenon of professional life" is the "link between a professional and his work," which he calls "jurisdiction." Dingwall and King (1995, 21) paraphrased jurisdiction as "the rights of an occupation to a piece of territory defined by the division of labor," but they suggest that this is misguided and the central phenomenon of professional life is actually "contract." Contract encompasses the "terms that govern interchanges among occupational groups and between them and their various publics." In estimating the degree to which comparative and international education has professionalized, this idea of negotiating interchanges among discipline-related methodologies and theoretical perspectives to understand and embrace comparative and international education is more appropriate. Rather than Wilson's academic-practitioner, the historical and contemporary evidence suggests that there is significant variation in the ways that knowledge and training in comparative and international education occurs. But, the common threads of university-based training and institutional affiliation among those identifying themselves as professional members in the field suggest that a professionalized field in comparative and international education does indeed exist.

Table 2.3 shows a list of 30 American universities with graduate programs specifically dedicated to comparative and international education. It is significant that these universities range from large public universities to selective private universities to smaller regional universities. The fact that there are multiple types of universities offering degrees in comparative and international education suggests that the field has become legitimate enough as a program of study to survive even in university communities that may only have a small number of faculty dedicated to the program. It is also important to note that while the exact name of the program varies from university to university, all of the programs are variations on the same theme: comparative and international education. Some include the terms "culture" or "social" or "policy", but all address these issues from comparative and international perspectives. There are, of course, more universities than those listed here that train people to work in the field of comparative and international education–often through educational policy or administration programs. For example, Michigan State University has a long history of preparing professionals for the field, but it does not offer a degree specifically in comparative and international education. Table 2.3 also does not include all of the programs that send graduates to work in the field, but train these graduates in specific disciplinary foci like economics or sociology.

Table 2.3 U.S. University Graduate Programs emphasizing Comparative and International Education (2015)

University	Name of Program	Degres Offered
American University	International Training and Education	M.A.
Bowling Green State University	Cross-Cultural and International Education	M.A.
DePaul University	Social and Cultural Foundations in Education	MA, M.Ed.
Drexel University	Global and International Education	M.S.
Florida International University	International and Intercultural Development Education	M.S.
Framingham State University	International Education Program	M.Ed., M.A.
Harvard University	International Education Policy	M.Ed.
Indiana University	International and Comparative Education	M.S.Ed., Doctoral Minor
Iowa State University	Historical, Philosophical, and Comparative Studies in Education	M.S., M.Ed., Ph.D.
Kent State University	Cultural Foundation of Education	M.A., M.Ed., Ph.D.
Lehigh University	Comparative and International Education	M.Ed., M.A., Ph.D.
Loyola University, Chicago	Cultural and Educational Policy Studies	M.A., M.Ed., Ph.D.
University of Maryland	International Education Policy	M.A., Ph.D.
New York University	International Education Policy	M.A., Ph.D., Advanced Certificate
Pennsylvania State University	Comparative and International Education	M.A., Ph.D. (Dual Degree)
SIT Graduate Institute	International Education	M.A.
Stanford University	International Comparative Education	M.A., Ph.D.
State University of New York, Albany	The Comparative and International Education Policy Program	M.A., Ph.D.
State University of New York, Buffalo	Comparative and Global Studies	M.Ed.
Teachers College, Columbia University	International and Comparative Education	M.A., Ed.M., Ph.D.
University of California, Los Angeles	Social Science and Comparative Education	M.A., Ph.D.
University of Central Florida	Global and Comparative Education	Certificate
University of Hawaii	Educational Foundations	M.Ed., Ph.D.
University of Maryland	International Education Policy	M.A., Ph.D.
University of Massachusetts, Amherst	International Education	M.A., Ed.D.
University of Minnesota	Comparative and International Development Education	M.A., Ph.D.
University of Pittsburgh	Social and Comparative Analysis in Education	M.Ed., M.A., Ed.D., Ph.D.
University of San Francisco	International and Multicultural Education, Human Rights Education	M.A., Ed.D.
University of Utah	Education, Culture and Society	M.Ed., M.A., M.S., Ph.D.
University of Wisconsin, Madison	Education Policy Studies-Comparative and International Education	Ph.D.

As the brief history presented in this paper illustrates, the pathways into comparative and international education have historically been many–political science, economics, sociology, international relations, business and banking–and can be tracked against trends in national politics, international affairs, international teaching and higher education administration, all fields which have also been subject to profession-alizing trends in recent decades. While these different pathways each indicate a different body of expert knowledge with its own training and credentials, there are nonetheless a finite number of subject areas that overlap in significant ways. For instance, both the comparative education researcher and the international educator understand the importance of culture and are trained to account for or accommodate the contextualized impact of culture on their specific work in the field. One may be more theoretical and one more pragmatic, but both share an understanding and training related to the same construct, namely, culture. Recognizing and understanding the convergence and institutionalization of expert

knowledge, training, and credentials are important to the professionalization of the field of comparative and international education.

One of the ways to investigate the degree to which an expert
knowledge base in comparative and international education exists is to
look at the topics and readings covered in university courses relevant to
the field. As Phillips & Schweisfurth (2014, 39) suggest: "There is a body
of established literature produced by leading figures in comparative
studies from the late nineteenth century onwards." This established body
of literature is what would comprise a knowledge base in the field, if one
exists. And, if a knowledge base exists to some degree, then we would
expect that similar topics and a core "canon" of readings would be the
focus of these relevant courses. Table 2.4 uses data gathered through an
extensive outreach to all of the university programs listed in Table 2.3.
Comparative and international education and related programs were
contacted and instructors were asked to share their most recent syllabus
for their introductory comparative education or closely-related course.
These data allow us to calculate the percentage of introductory comparative education courses in 30 different universities that cover various
topics. If a legitimate knowledge base is forming in comparative and
international education, we expect that the number of topics that are
covered extensively would be relatively consistent.

Table 2.4 shows that instructors teaching introductory comparative
education in 32 different courses indicated that they taught a total of 162
different topics. Of those 162 different topics only 32 were explicitly
taught in more than 10 percent of the courses. Eleven topics were taught
in 13 percent of the courses: teaching or teachers, society, reform, poverty,
post-colonial, language, feminist theory, economics, dependency theory,
critical theory, and conflict or conflict resolution. Six topics were taught
in 16 percent of the courses: research, neo-liberalism, higher education,
curriculum, comparative education, and assessment. Three topics were
taught between 19-22 percent of the time: policy borrowing, neo-
institutionalism, and culture. Four topics were taught in 25 percent of the
courses: modernization, international education, human capital, and
centralized and decentralized governance. And, finally, eight topics were
taught more than 25 percent of the time: history of the field (31 percent),
gender (31 percent), equity (31 percent), policy (34 percent), methodology
(38 percent), development (38 percent), theory (41 percent), and globalization (44 percent). This means that 130 other unique topics are taught in

less than 10 percent of the 32 introductory comparative education or related courses sampled here.

Table 2.4 Introductory Course in or related to Comparative Education – Topics Covered Across 32 Courses and Instructors (% of total)

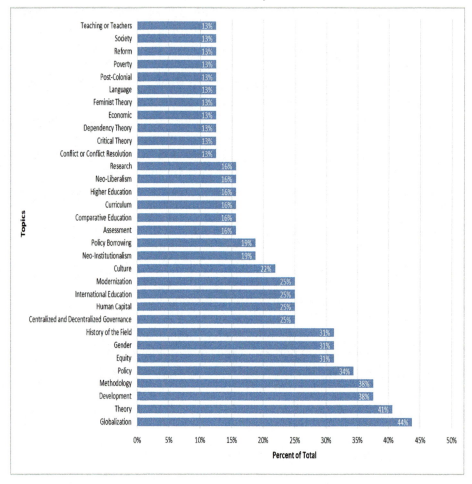

This distribution of topics in the introductory comparative education and related courses suggests two things. First is that while the topics of history, gender, equity, policy, methodology, development, theory, and globalization are not overwhelming indicators of a core expert knowledge base, they do indicate that there is some consistency in the major topics that comprise the expert knowledge base in comparative and international education. And, second, this knowledge base is grounded in explaining educational phenomena in comparative and international using theoretical frameworks (i.e., theory), deals largely with developing nations or societies (i.e., development), recognizes the importance of history in understanding both why and how comparative education has developed, asserts that gender differences are one of the core concerns of the field's knowledge base (i.e., gender, equity), focuses on decision-making related to education worldwide (i.e., policy), and is concerned with global trends and phenomena related to education (i.e., globalization).

Table 2.5 shows the degree to which there is a developing "canon" of literature in comparative and international education as evidenced by the frequency and extent to which particular authors' works are assigned as readings, unique publications, and across universities in introductory comparative education and related courses. This table represents the single or first authors whose work was assigned at least four times in unique syllabi across different courses and universities. Table 2.5 specifically shows the number of different readings assigned by each author in the introductory comparative education or related course in 32 different courses. The top six assigned authors are Carnoy (18), Epstein (15), Stromquist (15), Bray (9), Mundy (9), and Steiner-Khamsi (9). This suggests that a core group of readings is assigned across universities and introductory comparative education courses, which comprise a core of knowledge in the field.

It is also possible to consider the core knowledge base of comparative and international education by identifying the most frequently assigned readings across universities and courses, which include the following books more than many other texts:

- Arnove, R. & Torres, C.A. (Eds.). (1999/2013). *Comparative Education: The Dialectic of the Global and the Local.* Lanham, MD: Rowman & Littlefield.
- Phillips, D. & Schweisfurth, M. (2007/2014). *Comparative and international education: An introduction to theory, method, and practice.* New York: Bloomsbury Academic.
- Baker, D. & LeTendre, G.K. (2005). *National differences, global similarities: World culture and the future of schooling.* Stanford, CA: Stanford University Press.

Table 2.5 Most Frequently Assigned Readings by Single/First Authors in the Introductory Comparative Education or Related Course (32 courses/instructors reporting, 2004-2015)

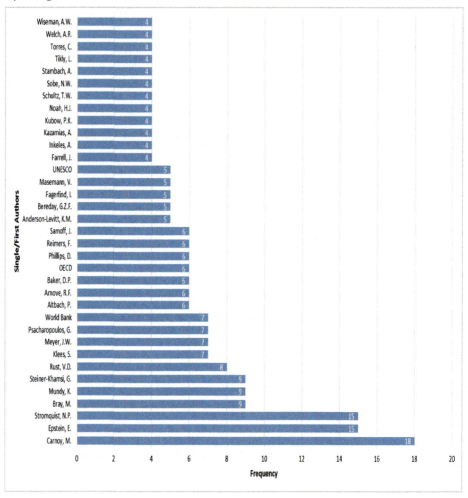

Of course there are other core readings that comprise the comparative and international education expert knowledge base that are not complete books. And, there are some authors whose work is part of the core of knowledge but is distributed across several different (but less frequently assigned) readings. Martin Carnoy's work is a good example. He is one of the most frequently assigned authors in the introductory comparative education course, but there is not one specific text by Carnoy that is included more often than the others. Nelly Stromquist is another good example. While she, too, is one of the most frequently assigned authors in the introductory comparative education course, her most frequently assigned work is a chapter on women's education from the Arnove & Torres (1999/2013) edited book cited above.

So, while literally hundreds of unique texts and authors are assigned as part of the core of knowledge taught in introductory comparative education courses, a handful of authors and texts are included more frequently than others. It is significant that all of the most frequently assigned texts are edited volumes. And, most of the chapter authors in these volumes are people that most individuals trained and working in the field of comparative and international education would readily recognize. Again, this evidence suggests that a professional knowledge base does exist – albeit as a varied base – and serves as a foundation rather than as an exclusive domain. The same is true of the actual work members of the profession perform, as suggested by the institutional affiliation of CIES members. There is no monopoly on the work of comparative and international education, but there is a professional network among those working in the field through the kinds of institutions with which they affiliate as well as through the professional association. This affiliation, however, is not the end result of professionalization but rather one part of a larger process.

Where is the Professionalization of Comparative and International Education Headed?

This study addresses just some of the many elements of professionalization, specifically, expert knowledge base and training and credentials. The importance of self-policing and ethical codes, exclusivity of occupational domain, and control over the workplace are other important elements of professionalization, which are not covered here. For example, in contrast to the Comparative Education Society, the early associations in the field of international educational exchange (such as NAFSA) were founded in order to self-police the quality of their programs, as opposed to exerting control over expert knowledge.

This point highlights an area of the field that this study does not fully explore, namely, the "other half" of comparative and international education: international education. International education, when defined independently from comparative education, is a field concerned with cross-national relations as well as cooperation and exchanges of educational information and personnel. The three major areas of interest initially associated with international education are (1) international relations and cooperation in education; (2) cross-national movements of educational materials, students, teachers, consultants, and aid; and (3) education for international and cross-cultural understanding. The Fulbright Program, for instance, primarily positioned international education as programs for the exchange of people (Spaulding et al. 1968).

One international education organization, the Institute for International Education (IIE), was founded in 1919 as a postwar organization committed to promoting world peace through formal educational exchange (Hoffa 2007). With regards to establishing and maintaining standards, IIE established the Junior Year Abroad oversight committee in 1927, which after WWII took on the task of setting standards for study abroad and restraining rampant and seemingly uncontrolled growth of abroad programs. The histories of other early international educational exchange organizations reveal similar origins: the Council on International Educational Exchange traces its roots to activities to monitor transatlantic travel for U.S. students for student, work, volunteer and travel abroad, and NAFSA began as an organization interested in training personnel to effectively advise foreign students studying in the U.S. (Hoffa 2007; Mikhailova 2002).

Therefore, a next step in the analysis of the professionalization of comparative and international education is to examine the "twin" profession of international education and the ways that it has both converged and diverged with comparative education. In particular, international education should be examined regarding the various indicators of professionalization of the field (e.g., self-policing and ethical codes, exclusivity of occupational domain, and workplace control).

Promises and Problems in the Professionalization of Comparative and International Education

We began by posing two general research questions. First, we asked whether university programs and professional associations in comparative and international education contribute to the development of or secure control over expert knowledge, training and credentials. Second, we asked whether the merging of "comparative" and "international" education contributed to the professionalization of the field. The evidence presented above suggests that the best answers to these questions are yes and yes, but not always for the obvious reasons.

Indeed the institutionalization of an expert knowledge base for the field of comparative and international education through the establishment of university programs in the field, the isomorphic development of a preliminary professional "canon" in comparative and international education, and the establishment of a professional association specifically dedicated to the field is important. But, also important is the fact that there is significant variation in the topics covered in university programs, the type of universities offering programs in comparative and international education, and the range of readings assigned as part of the introductory comparative education course. These all suggest that one of the surprising strengths of the field is the development of disciplinary studies as a characteristic of research and knowledge in the field.

One of the ways that the field actually moved itself forward toward professionalization in spite of (rather than because of) its dual character as both comparative and international was by changing the name of the Society from CES to CIES. When professionals in a field rename themselves they are, in fact, establishing that field as their domain through the ritual of naming (Caplow 1954; Lounsbury 2002). The renaming of the Society, therefore, was not only a move toward professionalization of the field because of merging the two areas under one umbrella but also because it demonstrated the authority of those working in the field and associating with each other through a particular professional network to control their own professional nomenclature.

This is important because the professionalization of the field is as much about the establishment of a *rationalized cultural system* as it is the overt domination of knowledge and networking. Scott and Meyer (Scott 1991, 172; Scott & Meyer 1991) both point out that fields in the process of professionalization will increasingly "prefer weaker and more decentralized administrative structures that locate maximum discretion in the hands of practitioners." This means that as the field of comparative and international education professionalizes there will naturally be fragmentation at the individual level. This is exactly what has happened with the shift toward disciplinary studies and the merging of similar but nonidentical fields into one under the moniker of the Comparative and International Education Society.

On a more overt level, comparative and international education has experienced a robust professionalization over the past 50 years as evidenced by "the robustness of graduate training programs [and] the vitality of professional and trade associations" (DiMaggio & Powell 1991, 77). There is no "universality of credential requirements" for the field, nor may there ever be, but there are a growing number of universities offering degrees specifically in the field under the name of comparative and international education rather than educational policy, economics, or international development. That is a significant move toward continued professionalization. Yes, there is a "more general diffusion of knowledge" (Ross et al. 1995), but that has become a strength of the field rather than a weakness. The diversity of the profession's methodological and disciplinary base is one of its greatest strengths. Those of us working in the field should strive to capitalize on the diverse approaches growing out of our profession.

Acknowledgment

Much of this chapter is based on Wiseman & Matherly (2009). The authors gratefully acknowledge permission to reproduce material from that article.

Notes

[1] The National Association of Foreign Student Advisors (NAFSA), a practitioner-oriented international education association, was founded in 1948 to promote the professional development of American college and university officials responsible for assisting and advising the 25,000 foreign students who had come to study in the United States after World War II. Like the founders of CES, the academic institutions, government agencies, and private organizations that combined to form NAFSA were concerned about training specialists working in the field.

[2] Baker (1994) previously used the term "in comparative isolation" in his discussion of the relatively low impact that comparative research has on American sociology of education.

[3] 1,727 CIES members worldwide had no recorded institutional affiliation.

References

Abbott, A. 1988. *The System of Professions: An Essay on the Division of Expert Labor.* Chicago: University of Chicago Press.

Altbach, Philip G. 1991. Trends in Comparative Education. *Comparative Education Review,* 35(3): 491-507.

Altbach, Philip G. & Gail Kelly, eds. 1986. *New Approaches to Comparative Educa-tion*. Chicago: University of Chicago Press.

Arnove, Robert 2001. Comparative and International Education Society (CIES) Facing the Twenty-First Century: Challenges and Contributions. *Comparative Education Review, 45*(4): 477-503.

Arnove, Robert, Philip G. Altbach & Gail Kelly, eds. 1992. *Emergent Issues in Education: Comparative Perspectives*. Albany: State University of New York Press.

Arnove, Robert & Carlos A. Torres, eds. 1999. *Comparative Education: The Dialectice of the Global and the Local*. Lanham, MD: Rowman & Littlefield.

Baker, David P. 1994. "In Comparative Isolation: Why Comparative Research Has So Little Influence on American Sociology of Education." In A. Pallas, ed. *Research in Sociology of Education and Socialization*. Greenwich, CT: JAI Press, Vol. 10, pp. 53-70.

Beland, D. & F. Vergniolle de Chantal 2004. "Fighting 'Big Government': Frames, Federalism, and Social Policy Reform in the United States." *Canadian Journal of Sociology 29*(2): 241-264.

Bereday, George Z.F. 1960. "Comparative Education at Columbia University." *Comparative Education Review 4*(1): 15-17.

Brickman, W.W. 1966. "Ten Years of the Comparative Educaiton Society." *Comparative Education Review 10*(1): 4-15.

Brickman, W.W. 1977. "Comparative and International Education Society: An Historical Analysis." *Comparative Education Review 21*(2/3): 396-404.

Caplow, T. 1954. *The Sociology of Work*. Minneapolis: University of Minnesota Press.

Chambers, M.M. 1950. *Universities of the World Outside U.S.A.* Washington, DC: American Council on Education.

Cook, B.J., S.J. Hite & E.H. Epstein. 2004. "Discerning Trends, Contours, and Boundaries in Comparative Education: A Survey of Comparativists and Their Literature." *Comparative Education Review 48*(2): 123-149.

Crossley, Michael & Keith Watson. 2003. *Comparative and International Research in Education: Globalisation, Context and Difference*. New York: RoutledgeFalmer.

DiMaggio, P. & W.W. Powell. 1983. "The Iron Cage Revisited: Institutional Isomorphism and Collective Rationality in Organizational Fields." *American Sociological Review 48*(April): 147-160.

DiMaggio, P. & W.W. Powell. 1991. "The Iron Cage Revisited: Institutional Isomorphism and Collective Rationality." In W.W. Powell & P. DiMaggio, eds. *The New Institutionalism in Organizational Analysis*. Chicago: University of Chicago Press, pp. 63-82.

Dingwall, R. & M.D. King. 1995. "Herbert Spencer and the Professions: Occu-pational Ecology Reconsidered." *Sociological Theory 13*(1): 14-24.

Dowd, J.J. 1991. "Revising the Canon: Graduate Training in the Two Sociologies." *Teaching Sociology 19*(3): 308-321.

Eckstein, Max 1975. "Comparative Education: The State of the Field." *Review of Research in Education 3*: 77-84.

Edwards, Reginald. 1970. "The Dimensions of Comparison, and of Comparative Education." *Comparative Education Review 14*(3): 239-254.

Epstein, Erwin H. 1968. "Letter to the Editor." *Comparative Education Review 12*(3): 376-378.

Epstein, Erwin H. 1994. "Comparative and International Education: Overview and Historical Development." In T. Husen & T.N. Postlethwaite, eds. *International Encyclopedia of Education*. London: Elsevier.

Epstein, Erwin H. 2008. "Crucial Benchmarks in the Professionalization of Comparative Education." In C. Wolhuter et al., eds., *Comparative Education at Universities World Wide* [2nd edition]. St. Kliment Ohridski University Press (Bulgaria).

Epstein, Erwin H. 2008. "Setting the Normative Boundaries: Crucial Epistemological Benchmarks in Comparative Education." *Comparative Education 44*(4): 373-386.

Etzioni, A. 1969. *The Semi Professions and Their Organization*. New York: Free Press.

Gispen, C.W.R. 1988. "German Engineers and American Social Theory: Historical Perspectives on Professionalization." *Comparative Studies in Society and History 30*(3): 550-574.

Guillen, M.F. 1992. "German Professions: Historical Perspectives and Sociological Concerns." *Contemporary Sociology 21*(3): 378-380.

Hall, R.H. 1968. "Professionalization and Bureaucratization." *American Sociological Review 33*(1): 92-104.

Halls, W.D., ed. 1989. *Comparative Education: Contemporary Issues and Trends*. London: Jessica Kingsley and Paris: UNESCO.

Hawkins, John N. & Val D. Rust. 2001. "Shifting Perspectives on Comparative Research: A View Form the USA." *Comparative Education 37*(4): 501-506.

Heath, K.G. 1958. "Is Comparative Education a Discipline?" *Comparative Education Review 2*(2): 31-32.

Hoffa, W. 2007. *A History of Study Abroad: Beginnings to 1965*. Frontiers, PA: Frontiers.

Horowitz, I.L. 1993. *The Decomposition of Sociology*. New York: Oxford.

Horowitz, T.R. 1985. "Professionalism and Semi-Professionalism among Immigrant Teachers from the U.S.S.R. and North America." *Comparative Education 21*(3): 297-307.

Hoyle, Eric 1982. "The Professionalization of Teachers: A Paradox." *British Journal of Educational Studies 30*(2): 161-171.

Hughes, E. 1963. "The Professions." *Daedalus 92*: 19-27.

Jepperson, R.L. 1991. "Institutions, Institutional Effects, and Institutionalism." In W.W. Powell & P. DiMaggio, eds. *The New Institutionalism in Organizational Analysis*. Chicago: University of Chicago Press, pp. 143-163.

Jepperson, R.L. 2002. "The Development and Application of Sociological Neo-institutionalism." In J. Berger & M. Zelditch, Jr., eds. *New Directions in Contemporary Sociological Theory*. Lanham, MD: Rowman & Littlefield, pp. 229-266.

Kazamias, Andreas M. 2001. "Re-Inventing the Historical in Comparative Education: Reflections on a Protean Episteme by a Contemporary Player." *Comparative Education* 36(3): 279-296.

Larson, M.S. 1977. *The Rise of Professionalism: A Sociological Analysis*. Berkeley, CA: University of California Press.

Lounsbury, M. 2002. "Institutional Transformation and Status Mobility: The Professionalization of the Field of Finance." *The Academy of Management Journal* 45(1): 255-266.

Loxley, William 1994. "Comparative and International Education: Organizations and Institutions." In T. Husen & T.N. Postlethwaite, eds. *International Encyclopedia of Education*. Oxford: Pergamon.

Meriam, L. 1937. "The Trend toward Professionalization." *Annals of the American Academy of Political and Social Science* 189: 58-64.

Meyer, J.W. & B. Rowan. 1977. "Institutionalized Organizations: Formal Structure as Myth and Ceremony." *American Journal of Sociology* 83(2): 340-363.

Mikhailova, L. 2002. *A History of the Council on International Educational Exchange, 1947-1994*. New York: CIEE.

Moehlman, A.H. & J.S. Roucek, eds. 1952. *Comparative Education*. New York: Dryden Press.

Montagna, P.D. 1968. "Professionalization and Bureaucratization in Large Professional Organizations." *The American Journal of Sociology* 74(2): 138-145.

Noah, Harold J. & Max A. Eckstein 1969. *Toward a Science of Comparative Education*. New York: Macmillan.

Phillips, David & Michele Schweisfurth. 2014. *Comparative and International Education: An Introduction to Theory, Method and Practice*. New York: Continuum International.

Pierson, P. & T. Skocpol. 2002. "Historical Institutionalism in Contemporary Political Science." In I. Katznelson & H. Milner, eds. *The State of the Discipline*. New York: Norton.

Post, David, Joseph Farrell & Heidi Ross. 1995. "Prologue to the Investigation of Comparative and International Education Graduate Programs in North America: Part I." *CIES Newsletter*, January (108), 4, 14, 18.

Ritzer, G. 1975. "Professionalization, Bureaucratization and Rationalization: The Views of Max Weber." *Social Forces* 53(4): 627-634.

Ross, Heidi, David Post & Joseph Farrell. 1995. "Prologue to the Investigation of Comparative and International Education Graduate Programs, Part II." *CIES Newsletter*, September (110), 1, 4-5.

Rothblatt, S. 1995. "How 'Professional' Are the Professions?" A Review Article. *Comparative Studies in Society and History* 37(1): 194-204.

Scott, W.R. 1991. "Unpacking Institutional Arguments." In W.W. Powell & P. DiMaggio, eds. *The New Institutionalism in Organizational Analysis*. Chicago: University of Chicago Press, pp. 164-182.

Scott, W.R.J. & J.W. Meyer. 1991. "The Organization of Societal Sectors: Propositions and Early Evidence." In W.W. Powell & P. DiMaggio, eds. *The New Institutionalism in Organizational Analysis*. Chicago: University of Chicago Press, pp. 108-142.

Spaulding, S., J. Singleton & P. Watson. 1968. "The Context of International Development Education." *Review of Educational Research 38*(3): 201-212.

Steinmo, S., K. Thelen & F. Longstreth, eds. 1992. *Structuring Politics: Historical Institutionalism in Comparative Analysis*. Cambridge: Cambridge University Press.

Stinchcombe, A.L. 1982. "Should Sociologists Forget Their Mothers and Fathers?" *American Sociologist 17*: 2-11.

Swing, Elizabeth Sherman 2007. "The Comparative and Internaitonal Education Society (CIES)." In Vandra Masemann, Mark Bray & Maria Manzon, eds. *Common Interests, Uncommon Goals: Histories of the World Council of Comparative Education Societies and Its Members*. CERC Studies in Comparative Education 21. Hong Kong: Comparative Education Research Centre, The University of Hong Kong, and Dordrecht: Springer, pp. 94-115.

Wallace, J.E. 1995. "Organizational and Professional Commitment in Professional and Nonprofessional Organizations." *Administrative Science Quarterly 40*(2): 228-255.

Waters, M. 1989. "Collegiality, Bureaucratization, and Professionalization: A Weberian Analysis." *The American Journal of Sociology 94*(5): 945-972.

Wilensky, H.L. 1964. "The Professionalization of Everyone?" *The American Journal of Sociology 70*(2): 137-158.

Wilson, David N. 1994. "Comparative and International Education: Fraternal or Siamese Twins? A Preliminary Genealogy of Our Twin Fields." *Comparative Education Review 38*(4): 449-486.

Wilson, David N. 2003. "The Future of Comparative and International Education in a Globalised World." *International Review of Education 49*(1/2): 15-33.

Wiseman, Alexander W. & Matherly, Cheryl 2009. "The Professionalization of Comparative and International Education: Promises and Problems." *Research in Comparative and International Education* 4 (4): 334-355.

3
Program Development

Allison H. BLOSSER

In 1958, George Z.F. Bereday, one of the forefathers of comparative and international education (CIE), claimed that within the field, "there ought to be a greater consensus on what to teach," because without such consensus, "comparative education will suffer from the embarrassment of being unable to explain what this field is supposed to encompass" (4). Since Bereday's observation, there have been periods of renewed interest in the teaching of comparative education. One of those periods is now.

Over the past 15 years, the field of comparative and international education has witnessed several initiatives devoted to exploring how the field is taught. Key among those was the Comparative and International Course Archive Project (CIECAP), a project launched in 2003 by the Center for Comparative Education at Loyola University Chicago that was devoted to the collection, analysis, and dissemination of graduate-level introductory CIE course syllabi across universities (see the chapter by Kathleen M. Stone in this volume). Three years later the Center for International Comparative Education at Bowling Green State University created the Comparative Education Instructional Materials Archive (CEIMA) to build on CIECAP's efforts (see the chapter by Patricia Kubow in this volume). CEIMA, an ongoing initiative now managed by the Teaching Comparative Education Special Interest Group (SIG) of the Comparative and International Education Society (CIES), is devoted to collecting and analyzing a variety of course materials (e.g., course assignments, activities, syllabi, etc.) from comparative education courses across universities and programs. The Teaching Comparative Education SIG was proposed at the 2011 CIES annual conference, and it was formally

Erwin H. Epstein (ed.) (2016): *Crafting a Global Field: Six Decades of the Comparative and International Education Society*. Hong Kong: Comparative Education Research Centre (CERC), The University of Hong Kong, and Dordrecht: Springer. © CERC

approved as a SIG the following year. The SIG has grown exponentially – in 2015 it had almost 90 members and continues to increase its membership – which indicates both the interest in and need for research and dialogue around the teaching of comparative education. Further, forthcoming from this SIG are both a journal issue[1] and book[2] devoted to teaching comparative education.

This chapter discusses the nature of CIE graduate programs as a way of drawing attention to pressing issues in the field. As Post, Farrell, and Ross (1995) determined, understanding the nature of CIE's graduate programs is central for discerning the state and contours of CIE. Former CIES President David Wilson (1994, 449) adds that "graduate students constitute the continuity – and future – of the field." The chapter first reviews recent literature on CIE graduate programs. Then, using information collected from 10 university websites about the career trajectories of CIE program graduates, the chapter discusses pressing issues for CIE graduate program faculty, directors, and students, as well as practitioners in the field.

The Variability of CIE Graduate Programs

Several noteworthy studies of CIE graduate programs have been conducted over the past 20 years. The mid-1990s in particular witnessed the publication of several such studies. Wilson's 1994 CIES Presidential Address chronicled the genealogy of several prominent North American CIE graduate programs in addition to discussing the "product" (discussed in greater detail below) of such programs (449). In 1995, Post, Farrell, and Ross published a two-part article on North American CIE graduate programs in the CIES Newsletter. In Part 1, they reviewed various models of CIE graduate programs like research centers, specialized programs, and programs integrating the comparative perspective, and concluded that the diversity of CIE graduate programs contribute to the field's vitality. In Part II, they analyzed CIE course syllabi from 34 U.S. universities to determine that CIE is "indeed, a field without a canon" (Ross et al. 1995, 1). Though Part II of their essay focused less on the organization of CIE graduate programs, the authors did determine that CIE courses within those programs tended to share similar goals, namely to 1) "help students to understand and respond to research and policy interests originating outside the university," 2) encourage students "to evaluate how comparative education's historical development and methodological and theoretical debates have shaped a multi-disciplinary field capable of challenging current relationships between academic work and practice beyond the university," and 3) teach students "to critically acknowledge the potential tension between idealism – being both politically and globally relevant – and pragmatism – securing employment" (Ross et al. 1995, 1-2). They also found that CIE courses offered little opportunity for students to explore the relationship between CIE and other areas of educational research, like multicultural education. Ultimately, they made a case for wider sharing of information about the teaching of CIE and its respective graduate programs.

Also in 1995, Altbach and Tan published a global inventory of 79 CIE programs, institutes, and centers. From their analysis of programs, they determined that the geographic hub of the field rested primarily in North America and Britain even as the field was gaining momentum in East Asia. They also observed that an increasing number of comparative educators were securing jobs in governmental and other international agencies. They concluded that, "comparative and international education is a field without a research agenda, without widely accepted paradigms for research, without agreed upon methodologies, and without a clear hierarchy" (xviii), which to them suggested that the field was both creative and lacking coherence.

More recently, Wolhuter and Popov (2007) edited a volume titled *Comparative Education at Universities World Wide*. In its third edition (published in 2013), the volume contained 44 chapters, 42 of which outlined the nature of the field and its presence in universities in various regions and countries. Similarly, in 2008 CIECAP expanded its efforts and began collecting data on CIE graduate programs across the world. To collect data, CIECAP administrators at Loyola developed a Graduate Program Data Form (available in English, French, and Chinese) seeking information about the types of degree programs offered, program requirements (e.g., foreign languages, methods courses, internships, etc.), program size, course offerings, program specializations, career trajectories of program graduates, and how the department/program defines major terms in the field. While not all of this information is available via CIECAP's current website host,[3] the website does include a spreadsheet with the websites and degree options for CIE programs at 58 institutions around the world.[4]

Timothy Drake (2011) published another recent and informative analysis of U.S. CIE graduate programs. Drake analyzed the websites of

35 CIE graduate programs in the U.S. as well as survey results from 22 CIE program directors or faculty members. In addition to reporting statistics on programmatic size, Drake found that programs demonstrate the field's contemporary relevance through emphasizing globalization and development. He (2011, 205) also found that 80% of programs mention education policy on their website(s) as one of the primary areas of education that they teach, though he concluded that "there does not appear to be general consensus as to what a CIE (comparative and international education) program should teach." Finally, in examining how students will learn CIE in their respective programs, Drake (2011, 201) found that students primarily learn CIE through "regional emphases, humanities and social science disciplines, cross-cutting fields and theoretical lenses, and professional specializations." Ultimately, Drake's analysis echoed the conclusions of others by demonstrating that there is no generally agreed upon formula for what and how U.S. CIE graduate programs teach.

Finally, several scholars note the variability in models of CIE graduate programs. Some universities have distinct programs, degrees, or concentrations in CIE within colleges of education, while others integrate the comparative perspective throughout related degree programs (Post et al. 1995; Tikly & Crossley 2001; Wiseman & Matherly this volume; Drake 2011; Kubow & Blosser 2014). Tikly and Crossley (2001) share their concerns about both the specialization and integration models and propose that universities move toward a model of transformation, where-in CIE faculty envision their universities and departments as learning organizations. Such a reconceptualization, they argue, would urge CIE faculty to conduct self-audits of their international knowledge and curricula, to reach out to faculty in other disciplines, and to enhance communication and knowledge-sharing with their CIE colleagues. But ultimately, most scholars agree that even though the structural variability of the field's programs creates issues for the field, it is a reflection of the field's adaptability, an adaptability upon which CIE professionals should capitalize (Post et al. 1995; Wiseman & Matherly this volume; Drake 2011).

Career Trajectories of CIE Program Graduates
Perhaps now more than ever, CIE programs must assert their importance and necessity in the field of education. Foremost among the reasons they

should do so is that there is a declining emphasis on the social foundations of education across U.S. colleges of education (Wolhuter et al. 2008; Kubow & Fossum 2013; Kubow & Blosser 2014). In addition, CIE graduate programs find themselves competing with other areas of emphasis in education like "school leadership, curriculum, teacher training, education finance, policy studies and special education" (Drake 2011, 192). Further, recent declines in the numbers of students enrolled in teacher preparation programs may also bear on CIE programs as schools and colleges of education are looking for alternative means to stay afloat (Sawchuk 2014). While CIE programs could potentially attract students and thereby revenue, programs and courses that are not deemed essential for teacher credentialing (as are most CIE programs and courses in the U.S.) are often the first on the chopping block (Wilson 1994). Simply put, CIE graduate programs need to attract students and demonstrate their contemporary significance.

One way CIE graduate programs appear to be attracting students is through advertising the wide array of career trajectories for graduates of their programs. Several scholars (e.g., Altbach & Tan 1995; Post et al. 1995; Wilson 1995; Wiseman & Matherly 2009; Kubow & Blosser 2014) observe that those working in the field of CIE are employed in many types of organizations, not only universities. Wiseman and Matherly (2009, 342) claim that because of such variability, "there is no single or 'best' method for training and credentializing these individuals." Kubow and Blosser (2014) argue that the varied career trajectories of graduates of CIE programs, coupled with trends in the educational establishment toward more data-driven policies and practices, are changing the nature of CIE programs and courses toward the practical.

I reviewed CIE graduate program websites at 10 universities to better understand the types of careers CIE programs are preparing their students to enter.[5] If a university had both masters and doctoral programs and/or multiple CIE programs with different emphases, I reviewed all of the program descriptions for mention of career trajectories. Further, I made sure to include in my sample both public and private universities from various regions across the U.S.

Table 3.1 demonstrates that government agencies, NGOs, universities, and other research organizations/firms are deemed prime places of potential employment for CIE program graduates. Other career trajectories commonly mentioned were private-sector consulting, school system positions, and positions within international development organi zations.[6] Further, all 10 universities mentioned educational policy analysis as a type of work for which program graduates are prepared and that work could be conducted in any of the aforementioned organizations. Drake's (2011) analysis of CIE graduate programs corroborates these findings as he found that education policy and education research were the top two areas of programmatic emphasis mentioned on CIE graduate program websites, representing, respectively, 80 percent and 57 percent of CIE graduate programs.

Table 3.1: Most frequently advertised career trajectories on CIE graduate program websites

Career Trajectory	Number of university websites (out of 10) that mentioned career trajectories
Government Agencies	10
NGOs or Non-profit Organizations	10
Universities (teaching and research)	10
Other Research Organizations	9
Private Consulting Firms/Agencies	8
School Systems	6
International Development Organizations	6

University teaching and research is only one of many widely advertised career trajectories for CIE program graduates, despite the fact the universities are still the predominant institutional affiliation of U.S.-based CIES members (Wiseman and Matherly this volume). This may be due to the fact that my analysis included the advertised career paths of master's program graduates, and master's program graduates are not likely (at least in the U.S.) to have the academic credentials to get hired as faculty members. An alternative explanation is that CIE program graduates are increasingly seeking or accepting positions in organizations outside of the academy. And yet a third explanation is that there is an growing awareness among CIE faculty that many program graduates who take jobs in academia also find themselves doing part-time or short-term work for international agencies in addition to their jobs as professors (Wilson 1994).

Wiseman and Matherly in their chapter in this volume suggest that CIES may not be an accurate reflection of the body of professionals working within the field of CIE, because those working in non-university settings may be members of professional organizations other than CIES. Further, CIE professionals working in academia may be more inclined to join CIES than other CIE practitioners, because they are more committed to the professionalization of field. An area for further research would be to collect aggregated data on the employment trajectories and professional association membership of CIE program alumni.[7]

If the advertised career trajectories of CIE program graduates at least to some degree reflect the positions CIE graduates assume, then Wilson (1994) was likely correct in his determination that the field of CIE is largely comprised of "academic-practitioners" — that is, individuals who bring their "'scientific perspective[s]' to bear on [their] melioristic international education activities" (485),[8] even if the institutional affiliations of CIES members do not reflect it (see the chapter by Wiseman and Matherly in this volume).[9] As Wilson (1994) pointed out, the lines between academic and practitioner in CIE are blurred, because academics are producing research that tangibly aids educational policy-making, and CIE practitioners outside of academia are producing research that advances the epistemological underpinnings of the field.

The advertised career trajectories of program graduates also suggest that CIE programs are, at least in theory, striving to prepare academic-practitioners and should thereby reflect the merging of comparative education with international education. But are they? If so, how? And at what cost? Further, what are the benefits and drawbacks of separate programs, courses, or tracks for the international education student (the practitioner) and the comparative education student (the researcher)?[10] Along those lines, the Comparative and International Education Society should consider the implications of increasing its recruiting efforts among individuals working within the field of CIE, but outside of academia. This might mean following up with graduate student members after they have graduated and secured positions in the field. To answer these questions, CIE academics and practitioners alike need to invest in the teaching of comparative education through utilizing and capitalizing on the resources available to them, like the CIES Teaching Comparative Education SIG and CEIMA. They also need to have forthright conversations about how the changing nature of the field of education is bearing on CIE graduate programs and their graduates.

In the end, while the repository of knowledge on CIE graduate programs is growing, there is still more to learn. And underutilized sources of knowledge include current CIE graduate students and recent program graduates. They can attest to not only what they learned, how they learned it, and their commitment to the field, but also the knowledge and skills they needed to learn for their careers but didn't. And as a start, the Teaching Comparative Education SIG and the New Scholars Committee should join forces in addressing these pressing issues for CIE graduate programs and the field.

Notes

[1] The special edition of *FIRE* (*Forum for International Research in Education*) will be co-edited by CIES Teaching Comparative Education Co-chairs Patricia Kubow and Allison Blosser.

[2] Kubow, Patricia K. and Allison H. Blosser, eds. *Teaching Comparative Education: Trends and Issues Informing Practice*. Oxford: Symposium Books, 2016.

[3] Though CIECAP is no longer an active archival project (CEIMA is the ongoing, active archival project), the data and syllabi collected as part of CIECAP are still available on the CIES Teaching Comparative Education SIG website. See "Comparative and International Education Course Archive Project" in the References.

[4] It is this author's opinion that CEIMA, the active archive project for CIE, should renew CIECAP's efforts to collect data on CIE graduate programs worldwide.

[5] The universities I selected all had doctoral programs or doctoral level concentrations in comparative and international education. Universities included in the analysis were: Florida State University, Indiana University, Lehigh University, Loyola University Chicago, University of Minnesota, New York University, Stanford, Teachers College-Columbia, University of California-Los Angeles, and Vanderbilt University.

[6] Some of the other career trajectories mentioned by CIE programs but not included in the table (because they were mentioned by fewer than half of the websites) were study abroad facilitation (n=3), instructional design (n=3), and multicultural/intercultural education (n=3).

[7] Aggregated by level of program (i.e., master's program graduates versus doctoral program graduates).

[8] Wilson attributed the creation of the "academic-practitioner" to the merging of "Comparative Education," a more academically centered, research-driven discipline, with "International Education," a more practitioner-based discipline.

[9] Wiseman and Matherly found that 84% of the U.S.-based CIES members listed universities as their institutional affiliation.

[10] Some universities, like Teachers College at Columbia, have separate graduate programs that reflect this distinction.

Websites Accessed

"Career Opportunities in International Education." *NYU Steinhardt: Department of Humanities and Social Sciences in the Professions*. Accessed April 10, 2015. http://steinhardt.nyu.edu/humsocsci/international/CareersinInternational-Education.

"Center for Comparative Education Graduate Programs." *Loyola University Chicago*. Accessed April 10, 2015. http://www.luc.edu/cce/graduateprograms/.

"Comparative and International Development Education (CIDE) Program Track." *University of Minnesota College of Education and Human Development*. Last Modified January 20, 2015. http://www.cehd.umn.edu/OLPD/grad-programs/CIDE/ default.html.

"Comparative and International Education Course Archive Project." *CIES Teaching Comparative Education SIG*. Accessed April 7, 2015. http://www. ciestcesig.org/ciecap/.

"Comparative Education Instructional Materials Archive." *CIES Teaching Comparative Education SIG*. Accessed April 7, 2015. http://www.ciestcesig.org/ ceimahome/.

"Description of the Two Programs." *Teachers College, Columbia University*. Accessed April 10, 2015. http://www.tc.columbia.edu/its/ICE/index.asp?Id=About&Info=Description+of+the+Two+Programs.

"Frequently Asked Questions: What Kinds of Questions Do Graduates From These Programs Pursue?" *Teachers College, Columbia University*. Accessed April 10, 2015. http://www.tc.columbia.edu/its/ICE/index.asp?Id=FAQs&Info=Frequently+Asked+Questions.

"History, Philosophy & Comparative Education: Careers." *Indiana University Bloomington School of Education*. Accessed April 10, 2015. http://education. indiana.edu/graduate/programs/history-philosophy-comparative/.

"International Education: Recent Doctoral Student Job Placements." *NYU Steinhardt: Department of Humanities and Social Sciences in the Professions*. Accessed April 10, 2015. http://steinhardt.nyu.edu/humsocsci/international/ doctoralprogram/RecentPhDJobPlacements/.

"LPO Doctoral Level Concentrations." *Vanderbilt University: Peabody College*. Accessed April 10, 2015. http://peabody.vanderbilt.edu/departments/lpo/ graduate_and_ professional_programs/phd/index.php.

"M.A. Comparative and International Education: Overview." *Lehigh University College of Education*. Accessed April 10, 2015. http://coe.lehigh.edu/academics/ degrees/ciema.

"M.A. in Organizational Leadership, Policy, and Development: Comparative and International Development Education (CIDE) Program Track." *University of Minnesota College of Education and Human Development*. Last Modified January 20, 2015. http://www.cehd.umn.edu/OLPD/grad-programs/CIDE/ma.html.

"M.Ed. in International Education Policy and Management (IEPM)." *Vanderbilt University: Peabody College*. Accessed April 10, 2015. http://peabody.vanderbilt.

edu/departments/lpo/graduate_and_professional_programs/international_education_policy_and_management/.

"OLPD PhD: Comparative and International Development Education (CIDE) Track: Leadership for Intercultural and International Education Program." *University of Minnesota College of Education and Human Development*. Last Modified January 14, 2015. http://www.cehd.umn.edu/OLPD/grad-programs/CIDE/LIIE/default.html.

"PhD Comparative and International Education: Overview." *Lehigh University College of Education*. Accessed April 10, 2015. http://coe.lehigh.edu/academics/degrees/phdcie.

"PhD in Organizational, Leadership, Policy, and Development: Comparative and International Development Education (CIDE) Program Track." *University of Minnesota College of Education and Human Development*. Last Modified January 15, 2015. http://www.cehd.umn.edu/OLPD/grad-programs/CIDE/phd.html.

"SHIPS-International Comparative Education." *Stanford Graduate School of Education*. Accessed April 10, 2015. https://ed.stanford.edu/academics/doctoral/ships/ice.

"Social Sciences and Comparative Education Program Goals." *UCLA Graduate School of Education and Information Studies*. Accessed April 10, 2015. http://gseis.ucla.edu/education/academic-programs/social-sciences-comparative-education/program-goals/.

"Social Sciences and Comparative Education." *UCLA Graduate School of Education and Information Studies*. Accessed April 10, 2015. http://gseis.ucla.edu/education/academic-programs/social-sciences-comparative-education/.

"Sociocultural & International Development Education Studies." *Florida State University College of Education*. Accessed April 10, 2015. http://coe.fsu.edu/Current-Students/Departments/Educational-Leadership-and-Policy-Studies-ELPS/Current-Students/Degree-Programs/Educational-Leadership-and-Policy/ELP-Major-Areas/Sociocultural-International-Development-Education-Studies-SIDES.

References

Altbach, Philip G., & Eng Thye Jason Tan. 1995. *Programs and Centers in Comparative and International Education: A Global Inventory*. Buffalo, NY: SUNY Graduate School of Education Publications.

Bereday, George Z.F. 1958. "Some Methods of Teaching Comparative Education." *Comparative Education Review 1* (1): 4-9.

Drake, Timothy. 2011. "U.S. Comparative and International Graduate Programs: An Overview of Programmatic Size, Relevance Philosophy, and Methodology." *Peabody Journal of Education 86*(2): 189-210.

Kubow, Patricia K., & Paul R. Fossum. 2013. "Comparative Education in the USA. In *Comparative Education at Universities Worldwide, 3rd Expanded Edition*, eds.

Charl Wolhuter, Nikolay Popov, Bruno Leutwyler, & Klara Skubic Ermenc. Sofia: Bulgarian Comparative Education Society and Ljubljana University Press, pp. 183-192.

Kubow, Patricia K., & Allison H. Blosser. 2014. "Trends and Issues in the Teaching of Comparative Education." In *Annual Review of Comparative and International Education 2014*, eds. A. W. Wiseman and E. Anderson Bingley. United Kingdom: Emerald Group Publishing Limited, pp. 15-22.

Post, David, Joseph Farrell, & Heidi Ross. 1995. "Prologue to the Investigation of Comparative and International Education Graduate Programs in North America: Part I." *Comparative and International Education Society Newsletter* 108: 4, 14-15.

Ross, Heidi, David Post, & Joseph Farrell. 1995. "Prologue to the Investigation of Comparative and International Education Graduate Programs in North America: Part II." *Comparative and International Education Society Newsletter* 110: 3-5.

Sawchuk, Stephen. October 21, 2014. "Steep Drops Seen in Teacher-Prep Enrollment Numbers." *Education Week.* http://www.edweek.org/ew/articles/2014/10/22/09enroll.h34.html

Tikly, Leon, & Michael Crossley. 2001. "Teaching Comparative and International Education: A Framework for Analysis." *Comparative Education Review* 45(4): 561-580.

"Welcome to International and Comparative Education." *Teachers College, Columbia University.* Accessed April 10, 2015. http://www.tc.columbia.edu/its/ICE/.

Wilson, David N. 1994. "Comparative and International Education: Fraternal or Siamese Twins? A Preliminary Genealogy of Our Twin Fields." *Comparative Education Review* 38(4): 449-486.

Wiseman, Alexander W., & Cheryl Matherly. 2009. "The Professionalization of Comparative and International Education: Promises and Problems." *Research in Comparative and International Education* 4(4): 334-355.

Wolhuter, Charl, & Nikolay Popov, eds. 2007. *Comparative Education as Discipline at Universities World Wide.* Sofia: Bureau of Educational Services.

Wolhuter, Charl, Nikolay Popov, Bruno Leutwyler, & Klara Skubic Ermenc, eds. 2013. *Comparative Education at Universities Worldwide, 3rd Expanded Edition.* Sofia: Bulgarian Comparative Education Society and Ljubljana University Press.

Wolhuter, Charl, Nikolay Popov, Maria Manzon, & Bruno Leutwyler. 2008. "Mosaic of Comparative Education at Universities: Conceptual Nuances, Global Trends, and Critical Reflections." In *Comparative Education at Universities Worldwide, 2nd Expanded Edition*, eds. Wolhuter, Charl, Nikolay Popov, Maria Manzon, and Bruno Leutwyler. Sofia: Bureau for Educational Services, pp. 319-242.

4
Supporting New Scholars

Sahtiya Hosoda HAMMELL and Maria Ishaq KHAN

This chapter traces the origins and history of the New Scholars Committee (NSC), showing how the committee has become a significant contributor to the growth of the Comparative and International Education Society (CIES). The NSC's overarching goal is to support and engage graduate students and professionals and to develop future leaders within the field of Comparative and International Education (CIE).

Origins[1]

The NSC traces its origins to a student caucus during the 1988 CIES annual conference, after which an ad hoc Young Scholars Committee (YSC) was established. In 1991, the status, mandate, and name of the YSC were changed, and supported through a vote by CIES members at the annual conference. It became a standing committee and was renamed the New Scholars Committee. The name change reflected "age diversity among students and scholars who are entering the field" (NSC Annual Report, cited by Swing 2007, p.111).

Purpose

Since becoming a standing committee, the NSC has had three tasks: to assist the Awards Committee's development of a CIES dissertation award, to increase new scholars' participation in CIES annual conferences, and to identify new scholars to serve on relevant CIES standing

Erwin H. Epstein (ed.) (2016): *Crafting a Global Field: Six Decades of the Comparative and International Education Society*. Hong Kong: Comparative Education Research Centre (CERC), The University of Hong Kong, and Dordrecht: Springer. © CERC

and ad hoc committees (Swing 2007). This expanded mandate included drafting terms to outline the role of the NSC for the CIES bylaws, collaborating with the President and the President-elect to secure funds to support travel for some new scholars, and representing new scholars' interests on the CIES Board of Directors by administering a survey of members and developing recommendations for the NSC's structure (including a chair, vice chair, regional representatives, and three sub-committees) (Klyburg et al. 2011). It was not required that the student member serving on the Board of Directors be involved with the NSC. Mariusz Galczynski, elected Board of Directors member from 2012 to 2015, was the first student representative to have been an NSC chair or member.

Early on, the NSC focused on supporting new scholars within academia. Its focus later expanded to include practitioners within CIE, reflecting the changing nature of CIES membership. A review of NSC annual reports from the early 2000s shows that the NSC chairs and co-chairs have consistently viewed the Committee's audience as "new" or "emerging" scholars within the Society. In 2009, the NSC chair made references to new practitioners as well. By 2015, the CIES Bylaws had redefined the NSC's purpose as: to "promote scholarship during the early phases of members' career development" (Article IV, Section 5, Item c).

Objectives

From the early 1990s, the main objectives of the NSC have been to promote CIES among new members and attendees at the annual conferences and to support scholarly inquiry. Until 2008, the NSC's aims included: 1) improving and increasing new scholars' participation in the CIES, 2) disseminating information regarding the Society's activities, 3) promoting employment opportunities, and 4) encouraging new scholars' contributions and providing them with networking opportunities, primarily through the dissertation mentoring workshop. In 2009, the NSC broadened its reach to foster and support scholarly inquiry within CIE, and enhance the quality and engagement of new scholars through more innovative means, such as building a digital presence and supporting more non-academic aspects of the field. As a result of the broader conception of its role, the NSC has substantially diversified programming options over time.

Programming

Until 2006, the NSC focused on organizing and conducting the dissertation workshop and administering its associated travel grants. In 2003 the NSC began using its website to process workshop applications, and in 2006 the NSC started disseminating feedback to workshop participants through the website.

Two new NSC activities were introduced at the 2010 CIES conference: the New Scholars Essentials Seminar, a conference session for masters and new doctoral students, and the New Scholars Career Preparation Seminar, a session for recent and soon-to-be graduates (NSC Annual Report 2009). By 2013, the NSC had diversified its activities further to organize the following workshops and special sessions during the annual CIES conferences:

1) Orientation for new attendees of the CIES annual conference,
2) Dissertation Mentoring Workshop (DMW) for advanced doctoral students,
3) Publication Mentoring Workshop (PMW) for advanced graduate students and early career academics and professionals without a strong publishing background in CIE, and
4) Essential Series Workshops, covering a range of topics for students, recent graduates, and CIE professionals and academics, and open to all attendees to the annual conference.

Conference Orientation

The first Orientation took place at the 2013 annual conference. The primary aim was to welcome first-time participants and to suggest ways that they could make the most of their conference experience. At each Orientation, attendees learn about the Society and the conference as well as NSC membership. Representatives from the CIES Board of Directors, standing committees, SIGs, scholars, students and NGOs provide tips on how the new attendees can get involved and contribute to the CIES conference and community. Participants are encouraged to network with the panelists and with each other. The Orientation session takes place on the first day of the conference in the first time slot.

Dissertation Mentoring Workshop

The Dissertation Mentoring Workshop (DMW) provides an opportunity for doctoral students (PhD and EdD) to discuss their dissertation research in small groups of experienced scholars and peers with similar topical or methodological interests. Each potential participant must submit a short proposal prior to the conference, following the guidelines on the CIES conference website. Each proposal is reviewed, and participants are selected based on the merits of their proposals. Faculty or professional mentors volunteer prior to the conference to participate in the workshop. Once participants have been selected, they are matched with other students and faculty/professional mentors based on shared topics and/or methodological areas, forming groups with 4-6 student participants and 1-2 faculty/professional mentors. Participants must submit longer submissions for detailed written feedback from each of their group members five weeks prior to the conference. At the conference these groups meet for a three-hour workshop to discuss each student's work, followed by a lunch hosted by the NSC to enable all workshop participants to meet each other. The DMW has been so successful that the NSC received numerous requests for a similar workshop to support new scholars in publishing articles and book chapters, resulting in the establishment of the Publication Mentoring Workshop.

Publication Mentoring Workshop

The Publication Mentoring Workshop (PMW) was introduced at the 2013 annual conference in New Orleans. This workshop provides an opportunity for final-stage and recent PhD and EdD graduates, as well as early career professionals, to discuss papers that they have developed – or would like to refine – for publication with peers and experienced scholars. Each workshop participant receives feedback, particularly on theoretical framework, methodology, and findings. The workshop also strengthens links among peers across CIE programs. The application process for this workshop is identical to that of the DMW. Participants must submit their draft articles to their group members five weeks prior to the conference for written feedback, which is then discussed during the three-hour workshop. The PMW also concludes with a lunch hosted by the NSC.

The number of participants in the Dissertation Mentoring Workshops has increased significantly since the first one in 2007, while the Publication Mentoring Workshops has had sustained demand since it was established in 2013. Figure 4.1 shows the numbers of participants between 2007 and 2015. The numbers reflect workshop participants and not the numbers of applications or accepted participants, as each year some accepted participants are unable to attend the conference.

Figure 4.1: NSC Workshop Participation 2007-2015

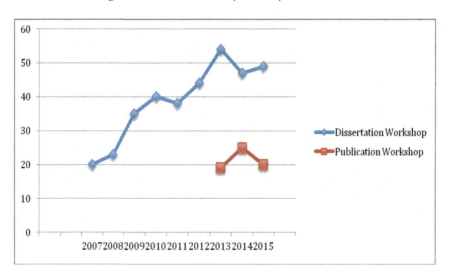

Essentials Series

The NSC organizes and facilitates the Essentials Series, a set of sessions developed to address a number of different topics with the needs of new scholars in mind. These sessions are open to all CIES conference attendees. Topics have included pursuing academic careers, non-academic career planning, writing and publishing tips, balancing family and academic life, trends in CIE, and funding, presenting and conducting fieldwork. Attendees are asked to evaluate each session and to suggest topics for the following year. The NSC Essential Series Subcommittee uses this feedback to determine the topics for the following year and then approaches experts on the topic areas from the CIES membership to conduct the sessions.

Membership

The NSC has evolved to be representative of students, recent graduates, and new CIE professionals and faculty. The size of the NSC and the NSC Board's membership is not mandated in the CIES Constitution and Bylaws, nor is the length of an appointment to the NSC Board explicitly stated in the CIES Constitution and Bylaws. However, Article IV, Section 5 of the CIES Constitution states that members of all standing committees "shall be appointed by the President in consultation with the Executive Committee." Few Presidents exercise this power, with the last memorable exception being in 2010, when the President appointed a NSC chair after 2009 members had already elected a chair in the de facto NSC election held during the committee's business meeting at the annual CIES conference. The NSC chair can serve up to two years, followed by service on the review sub-committee.

In the early years the NSC Board had six to eight members, comprising four to six faculty members and one or two student members. The Board expanded substantially in 2007, when three subcommittees were formed for outreach, workshop, and website/technology. The Board demographics have shifted towards graduate students and recent graduates who are professionals in CIE rather than faculty members. The growth and shifting demographics of the NSC Board are a response to changes in the membership of the whole Society. The expansion of the NSC Board has been necessary to accommodate the increasing needs of more programmatic offerings. For fiscal year 2015-2016, the NSC Board had 16 members, two co-chairing the committee and two former chairs serving as the review subcommittee. The remaining 12 members served as the treasurer and the staff for subcommittees, which include communications, dissertation and publication mentoring workshops, orientation, and the Essentials Series.

Accomplishments

With a central focus of supporting the interests and needs of the most junior members of the CIES, the NSC organizes and facilitates a wide breadth of programming to promote quality scholarship and to assist the careers of its most junior members. The NSC serves an increasing proportion of the Society. David Baker's (2013) President's Report revealed that 43% of the CIES members in 2013 were students. It is reasonable to assume that many of the other 57% are relatively early in their careers. These demographics illustrate that the professional field of CIE is changing rapidly, and with these changes come significant shifts in the needs and professional interests of the Society's membership that fall within the NSC purview. During his 2013/14 term, CIES President Gilbert Valverde established an Ad Hoc Committee for the Advancement of Early Careers in CIE that included one NSC member, but this committee did not meet during the year.

The NSC remains dedicated to addressing changing needs in the field of CIE. In her 2009 President's Report, Gita Steiner-Khamsi, who had served on the NSC Board prior to her presidency, stressed the importance of keeping abreast of these changes to develop a more active and engaged Society membership. The evolution of the Essentials Series and the mentoring workshops enhance the quality and engagement of new scholars. The Essentials Series creates programming that prepares junior researchers for employment outside academia in addition to more traditional offerings for the academic job market in order to address changing professional needs in CIE. The Essentials Series sessions are often filled to capacity; and the mentoring workshops have fostered substantive conversations between established scholars and those new to the field. The mentoring workshops have developed three travel grants to help fund scholars: for proposals displaying merit, from outside the majority world context, from institutions without CIE programs, from recently established CIE programs, and/or from small CIE programs. The travel grants encourage student participation at the annual conference and create an impetus to submit high quality papers. Financial support is part of a strategy to engage more students in the NSC and CIES activities, with awards comprising 64% of NSC's overall operating budget.

The NSC's use of new communication strategies to reach a broad audience has been instrumental in its success. The NSC uses its own website and Facebook and Twitter accounts to disseminate information about its offerings including financial aid. Webinars and live broadcasts such as New Scholars Google Hangout Sessions respond to the diverse needs of those new to CIE and remain accessible through CIES' YouTube channel. Increased collaboration between the NSC and various SIGs has also helped diversify its audience and encourage participation in both the standing committee and CIES.

The NSC has created a structure that has the capacity to adapt while remaining streamlined. The nature of NSC membership makes it one of the most dynamic standing committees in the Society, due to its high rate of turnover. By responding to new scholars' needs including providing important leadership opportunities as well as fostering their relationships with senior scholars, the NSC remains integral to the development of the field and the health of the CIES.

Note

[1] The authors relied on Elizabeth Sherman Swing's chapter in this volume for the earliest records of the NSC. Further, we are indebted to the impeccable record keeping of Rhiannon Williams, former NSC Co-Chair, who unearthed Klyburg et al.'s "Background on the New Scholars Committee" to inform the account of the early 2000s.

References

Baker, D.P. 2013. *2012-2013 Comparative and International Education Society President's Report*.

Comparative and International Educational Society. 2014. *Constitution of the Comparative and International Education Society*.

Comparative and International Educational Society. 2014. *Comparative and International Education Society Bylaws*.

Janigan, K. & Salto, D. (2014). *2014 New Scholars Committee Annual Report*.

Klyberg, S.F., Ortegon, N., Williams, R., Halabi, H., Leahy, P., Berzina-Pitcher, I. & Sobe, N. 2011. *Background on the New Scholars Committee*.

New Scholars Committee. 2009. *New Scholars Committee Annual Report*.

New Scholars Committee. 2015. *2015-2016 New Scholars Committee Members and Activities*.

Salto, D. & Tsagkaraki, V. 2015. *2015 New Scholars Committee Annual Report*.

Steiner-Khamsi, G. 2009. *2008-2009 Comparative and International Education Society President's Report*.

Swing, E.S. 2007. "The Comparative and International Education Society (CIES)." In V. Masemann, M. Bray & M. Manzon (eds.), *Common Interests, Uncommon Goals: Histories of the World Council of Comparative Education Societies and its Members*, CERC Studies in Comparative Education 21, Hong Kong: Comparative Education Research Centre, The University of Hong Kong, and Dordrecht: Springer, pp.94-125.

Internationalization

5
Inserting International Education into the Comparative Education Society

Louis BERENDS and Maria TRAKAS

Throughout the literature about comparative education, one fact seems quite apparent: no one focus, theory, or established method is solely responsible for driving scholarship in the field. Shifts between qualitative and quantitative emphasis, distinct ideologies of purpose, and variation in style of research have been part of the comparative education field since its inception. Naturally, as a result, there has been much discourse among scholars in the field about what constitutes "comparative education." This debate reached a peak in the 1960s when the professional society for comparative educators considered a proposal to change its name from the Comparative Education Society (CES) to the Comparative and International Education Society (CIES). Knowledge of the influences and factors that lead to this change along with the implications it has carried is vital to current members of the comparative education community not just as a piece of history but as a way to understand the debates that still ensue.

The Society was founded on the financing of study tours and the notion of international education in the service of comparative education.[1] The founders and subsequent members desired recognition of a scholarly and professional organization. Because study tours remained an integral part of the Society's activities, debates over the incorporation of "international" into the name of the Society snowballed over time. At the Board of Directors meeting on February 16, 1968, the Board "unanimously suggested that the name of the Society be changed to the

Erwin H. Epstein (ed.) (2016): *Crafting a Global Field: Six Decades of the Comparative and International Education Society*. Hong Kong: Comparative Education Research Centre (CERC), The University of Hong Kong, and Dordrecht: Springer. © CERC

'Comparative and International Education Society'," but unanimously passed a resolution "that the name of the Society's journal not be changed." The name change was officially announced in the September 1968 *CIES Newsletter*, which was the first to reflect the title change. The Society's official publication, the *Comparative Education Review* (CER), never changed its title to mirror the change made by the Society. This chapter investigates the name change from the CES to the CIES and analyzes internal and external influences contributing to the change.

Birth of the Society

Comparative education was a growing field before the formation of the Society in 1956. Scholars such as Freidrich Schneider, Joseph Lauwerys, Nicholas Hans, and Isaac Kandel were instrumental in influencing the establishment of the Society. They were active in teaching comparative education at the university level, and they attended and organized conferences to promote further analytic scholarship in the field. Dismayed with the descriptive level of research emerging from the field, Robert Templeton, Robert Ulich, and Isaac Kandel, among others, called for a more thorough understanding of foreign systems of education through direct observation and firsthand familiarity.

According to William W. Brickman, a founder and first President of CES, Kandel had time and time again stressed the need for personal field observation versus sole reliance on documentary analysis. In the venture to provide "adequate experiences for foreign observation," Gerald H. Read of Kent State University and Brickman of New York University joined forces in order to offer international study tour opportunities to educators (Brickman 1966). In 1954, Read and Brickman presented a plan to Dr. Bess Goodykoontz of the U.S. Office of Education to establish foreign school visitation programs, and after two years of correspond-dence, the first trip to study schools in Western Europe was scheduled for the summer, 1956. Read took responsibility for administration and logistics while Brickman oversaw academic programming for the trip. As Read looked into financing the study tour, he found travel expenses far less expensive for an organized group versus an unorganized group. Reflecting back 30 years later, Read stated, "Actually, the Comparative Education Society was formed as an organization to sponsor seminars and study tours" (Ohles 1986). As evidenced by Brickman (1966), he and

Read, among others, also felt it was necessary to form an organization in order to gain recognition as an academic and professional group.

In a letter dated June 28, 1956, Read explained that the Society thus was established on April 27, 1956, at the close of the Third Annual Conference on Comparative Education at New York University. Brickman assumed the role as President, William H.E. Johnson as Vice President (succeeding Robert B. Sutton who had resigned), Read as Secretary-Treasurer, and George Z.F. Bereday as Editor of the forthcoming journal *Comparative Education Review* (*CER*). By the time of publication of the first issue of the *CER* one year later, Johnson announced the many accomplishments of the Society to date. In its first year, CES had held five general meetings, hosted conferences for the Officers and Board of Directors of CES, conducted a 30-day tour of Western Europe, planned an upcoming tour of South America, and established an official publication (Johnson 1957).

Study tours were central to the establishment of the Comparative Education Society in its formative years, and they continued to be an integral part of the Society's activities. Read (1956) wrote in a letter, "Summary of the meeting to establish The Comparative Education Society":

> Foreign Study. The Society will undertake to sponsor programs of visitation to other lands for the purpose of on-the-spot studying of foreign educational systems by American educators. Members of the society, in turn, will serve as hosts to foreign educators visiting the United States. This summer (1956) the Society is sponsoring a European Comparative Education Study Program. It is contemplated that similar programs will be undertaken each year.

Read continued to spearhead these excursions. According to a Press Release dated February 26, 1963, Read collaborated with other organizations such as the American Association of School Administrators and the Ford Foundation, and he eventually expanded the trips in terms of geography, demographics of participants, and inclusion of cultural experiences. In time, Read's main focus became these trips. According to Brickman (1977), Read put so much time into study tours and placed so much value on them that the programs eventually took the place of his own scholarly studies and writing. However, Kim Sebaly (e-mail message, April 24, 2006), Read's protégé and student, expressed that

Read never abandoned his academic ventures. Read's original focus in forming CES was on international study tours, and he never wavered from that orientation. Although he continued to conduct tours to various places for various types of scholars, administrators, and professionals of education, he wove his scholarly work into these programs. Read may not have written academic articles for the *CER*, but he wrote numerous scholarly articles for *The Kappan* (the official journal of the Phi Delta Kappa organization), among others.

The dynamics that shape the founding of CES are important to understanding the debates surrounding the name change. As mentioned above, Kandel's emphasis regarding the importance of firsthand observation so impressed Brickman, a student of Kandel, that it led him to join forces with Read and establish the Society. Yet, Kandel himself never held an executive office of the Society. He was considered for a role on the Board of Directors at the April 1956 meeting, but he declined.[2] Kandel turned away from the Society feeling it was not scholarly enough due to the integral role study tours played in the organization's activities. On the other hand, Read, one of the founders of CES, eventually moved in a different direction from the organization in order to apply his scholarly work to international education opportunities and to collaborate with other organizations in the overall goal to provide study tours to educators. Whereas Kandel was concerned the Society was becoming less scholarly, Read was focused on the practitioner's role. The divide between academics of comparative education and practitioners of international education was widening while debates surrounding the purpose of the Society were increasing.

Twenty years after the formation of the Society, Brickman acknowledges, "In retrospect, the founding of the Society might be regarded as an act of rashness perpetrated by a relatively younger generation rather than as the outcome of deliberation by the outstanding experts in the field" (Brickman 1977, 399). Initially, he blames "the most experienced theoreticians and practitioners" (Brickman 1977, 398) for not having elevated the Society and, consequently, the field to higher standards, while acknowledging their many contributions such as joining the Board of Directors of CES and the Board of Editors of *CER*, contributing articles to *CER*, and preparing conference papers.

The Issue of Funds

This was a time that, in Liping Bu's words, "American educational institutions were active in exporting American democratic education abroad to promote world democracy and international understanding during the interwar years" (Bu 1997, 433). Even before the founding of the Society, Teachers College, Columbia University (TC) was at the forefront of the comparative education movement (for more on this, see the chapter by Gita Steiner-Khamsi in this volume). Well-known educators at Teachers College at that time included John Dewey, James Russell, William Kilpatrick, and Paul Monroe, who "was *the* activist for international education and world democracy" (Bu 1997, 415).

The International Institute at TC was established in 1923 with a $1 million grant from John D. Rockefeller, Jr. and the International Education Board (IEB) of the Rockefeller Foundation. According to Bu (1997, 413), the International Institute at TC began its role in promoting world democracy, the idea of wartime international understanding, and the exportation of American democratic education. "Trustees of the IEB approved Teachers College's proposal for an international institute for foreign students, authorizing a subsidy for 10 years of no more than $100,000 annually" (Bu 1977, 418). The International Institute staff included Monroe as Director, Russell as Associate Director, and Isaac L. Kandel, who was also a staff member at the Carnegie Foundation for the Advancement of Teaching (Bu 1977, 418). Also under Monroe's direction was the International Examination inquiry, a project sponsored by the Carnegie Foundation for the Advancement of Teaching and the Carnegie Corporation. The purpose of the project was "to instigate reform of educational systems worldwide" (Bu 1977, 427). It is interesting to note that both Kandel and Monroe, while working with the Institute, also worked directly with the Carnegie Foundation.

The International Institute was dedicated to providing the instruction needed for foreign students attending the university, to provide American students with an understanding of foreign educational systems, and to provide educational assistance abroad. While the International Institute received its funding, this mission was possible, but the Institute closed its doors in 1938 when the Rockefeller Foundation grant expired (Bu 1977, 432). Monroe's efforts in 1927 to receive permanent funding for the International Institute failed, as did Russell's in 1931.

Without proper funding, the International Institute's mission of educating and training future educational leaders could not be fulfilled.

However, the work of the International Institute was not for naught, as the scholarly research and collection of foreign materials that came out of the Institute sparked further interest in American educators. This interest paved the way for comparative education as a discipline in U.S. schools of education and new directions for American educators' work. The Institute showed that the areas of comparative education and international education were not only related but that each area improved because of the other. The foreign educational leaders and the comparative scholars that came out of the Institute were critical in the understanding of the world and its various educational systems, which led to a better understanding of the two fields (Bu 1977, 433).

The International Institute was one example of funding for comparative and international education. The Society also relied on external relationships for funding. In planning for the comparative education conference for 1964, correspondence between Cole S. Brembeck and C. Arnold Anderson (letter, January 13, 1964) reflects the hope that the meeting would be a stand-alone conference, provided that external funds could be raised to underwrite part of the conference costs. The organization identified as the source of this potential funding was the U.S. Office of Education. Interestingly, the Society had close ties to this government agency. As noted earlier, one of the original board members of the Society was Bess Goodykoontz, who worked in the U.S. Office when Read and Brickman proposed their first study trip. Later, in 1966, Kathryn Heath of the U.S. Office, while not an officer or board member of the Society, would chair the committee to revise the CES Constitution. Subsequently, letters from Claude A. Eggersten to Joseph Katz (March 6, 1964) and from Robert B. Sutton to Eggertsen (March 9, 1964) refer to the recent meeting of the Society in Chicago and infer that funding discussed in the letter from Brembeck to Anderson was approved. It was also discussed that expected funds from UNESCO were being delayed and that a 1964 conference may not be possible. According to a memorandum from Anderson to Members of the Consortium (March 25, 1964), the delayed funds could be carried over for a conference in 1965, and the U.S. Office of Education also agreed to reactivate the proposal for funding.

It was not only conference funding that was requested of the U.S. Office of Education. According to a letter from Eggertsen to Anderson (March 6, 1964) the Board of Directors of the Society requested that Anderson "consult with the people in the United States Office of Education about the fellowship project which has been discussed for some years." This letter also refers to the possibility of internships in comparative education through UNESCO. Aside from external funding sources, the Society also relied on such revenue as membership dues, advertisement revenue, royalties, bulk order revenue, bank interest, etc. (*CES Newsletter* March 1968).

Securing funding for an organization and its projects surely is part of the normal efforts of an organization, as evidenced by the International Institute example, and the Society was no different. The examples cited from the Society indicate that the Society worked closely with, and solicited funds from, organizations that were clearly more "international" than "comparative". As the Society was founded on the idea of international education, which then led to comparative education, it is surprising that the original name of the Society did not include the term "international", and that the name change did not occur until over 10 years after its founding.

External Pressures

The historical context of the Society's founding is quite significant. At the time of the Society's inception, the political environment of the world had been divided into two main ideological models: democratic and communist. With the Cold War in full swing, one aspect of American foreign policy looked to international education to bridge understanding between nations.

As the first director of the State Department's Division of Cultural Relations, established in 1938, Ben M. Cherrington declared, "cultural exchanges should involve the direct participation of the people and institutions concerned" (Lengyel 1947, 566). To further this point, the U.S. Advisory Commission on International Educational and Cultural Affairs noted, "in Europe, after World War I, exchange of students became a part of cultural relations programs promoted by governments to support their foreign policy" (U.S. Advisory Commission on International Educational and Cultural Affairs 1963, 18). Similarly, the birth of UNESCO in 1945, with the support of 20 countries, reflected the urgency for international understanding leading to peace between nations. Part of UNESCO's Constitution, signed on November 16, 1945, states, "since wars begin in the minds of men, it is in the minds of men that the defenses of peace must be constructed" (UNESCO Constitution 1946). Such "defenses of peace" are embedded in the philosophy of international education by the implicit notion that exposure to different cultures will lead to better understanding. To be sure, the events of World War II resulted in greater interest of study abroad programs (Ludden 2000), and in particular, the formation of the Fulbright-Hays program.

Introduced by Senator John W. Fulbright, the Fulbright Bill was designed to amend the Surplus Property Act of 1944.[3] Through the amendment, the U.S. Department of State assumed responsibility of all authorized sales to foreign governments in exchange for currency or credits. Specifically, the Secretary of State was given authority to make these exchanges for "financing studies, research, instruction and other educational activities for American citizens in other countries or of the citizens of such countries in American institutions overseas; and the financing of transportation for visitors from such countries to attend educational institutions in the United States" (Johnson and Colligan 1965, 13). The amendment, later known as the Fulbright Act of 1946, ingeniously disbursed profits from World War II surplus materials into an educational exchange program. In short, the Fulbright program aligned, in part, with American foreign policy that wanted to prevent the spread of communism from Eastern Europe to Western Europe.[4]

The founders of the Comparative Education Society recognized the prospect of considerable funding from U.S. government agencies to international education initiatives. As mentioned above, study tours were central to the establishment of the Society in its formative years, because travel expenses were far less for an organized group. As the Society continued to engage in study tours, other significant U.S. government legislation developed. For instance, in response to the Soviet launch of Sputnik, the National Defense Education Act (NDEA) was passed.[5] Similarly and perhaps more important to the Society, was the International Education Act of 1966. In his January 12, 1966 State of the Union Address, President Lyndon B. Johnson stated, "we will aid those who educate the young in other lands, and we will give children in other continents the same head start that we are trying to give our own children. To advance these ends I will propose the International Education Act of 1966." (See Lyndon B. Johnson, State of the Union Address, January 12, 1966.) Such legislation would undoubtedly impact the Society and its study tours.[6]

The month after President Johnson's State of the Union Address a draft to revise the Constitution was proposed by the Board of Directors of CES (*CES Newsletter*, December 1966). According to the December

Newsletter, "On Feb. 17 1966, the Board of Directors of the CES appointed a special Committee to draft a revision of the Society's Constitution in order *to make it responsive to current and anticipated future needs* (emphasis added).[7] Those serving on the Constitution Revision Committee understood the significance of this proposal in relation to the name change of the Society. The Committee included R. Freeman Butts, Teachers College, Columbia University, who went on to propose the name change; David G. Scanlon, a long-time time proponent and supporter of international education activities; John P. Lipkin, the Curry Memorial School of Education, University of Virginia; and Kathryn G. Heath, U.S. Office of Education, who was named Chairman (*CES Newsletter,* December 1966).[8] As a U.S. government official, Heath would have had information as to the particulars of the International Education Act, which may have led to her designation as Chairman of the Committee.

The revised draft of the Constitution contained significant use of the term *international* incorporated into the Purpose of the Society. For example, the December 1966 *CES Newsletter,* Article I, Section 2 states:

a) Promote teaching and research in comparative education *and international studies* in institutions of higher learning; b) Promote the study of education as a phase of the work of other comparative *and international disciplines,* area studies, *and centers of international studies*; c) Facilitate publication and distribution of comparative, cross-cultural, interdisciplinary, *and international studies* contributing to interpretation of developments in the field of education in their broad and interrelated political, economic, and social context; and d) *Encourage exchanges and other visits by educators.* (italics ours)

New Name, Renewed Focus

Assimilating *international* into the draft of the revised Constitution was the foundation for the subsequent proposal for the name change of the Society.[9] At the annual business meeting on February 16, 1967, the first official motion was made to change the organization's name from the Comparative Education Society to the Comparative International Education Society. The motion was presented to the membership by Butts who, initially, wanted to obtain a sense of how many members favored a name change. As shown in a draft of the meeting minutes (February 1967), he requested a "show of hands" vote that resulted in 24 members favoring a name change, 14 members opposed, and the remaining members abstaining. While the exact number of members present for the vote is unknown, minutes of the meeting indicate there were approximately 50 individuals present when the issue was brought to a vote. From this, one can deduce that roughly 12 members abstained from voting. It is interesting to note that the meeting minutes, as printed in the May 1967 *Newsletter*, indicated that the vote to consider the inclusion of "International" in the Society's name resulted in 24 for, 14 opposed, and only two abstaining (*CES Newsletter*, May 1967).

A second notable discrepancy exists between the May 1967 *Newsletter* and the February 1967 meeting minutes. The meeting minutes indicate there were 15 items of business discussed during the meeting. Fourteen of these were printed verbatim in the *Newsletter* as they appeared in the meeting minutes. Item 12, titled Change of Name, was the only item where wording differed. The meeting record suggests that there was a discussion that took place following the vote. Though there is no record of what specific arguments the debate entailed, the following brief statement was recorded in the Board of Directors meeting minutes (February 1967):

> In the ensuing discussion uneasiness was expressed that the report of the show of hands might exert unfair pressure on the membership on the issue of a change of name and might unduly influence any committee appointed to look into the matter. The observation was made that a change of name implied a change in function and direction and thus required careful study.

This statement was not included in the report of minutes sent to the Society's membership via the May *Newsletter*. While it is impossible to know the exact reasons these discrepancies exist, one can suppose a few possible explanations. The first is that in the final approval of meeting minutes by the Board of Directors, some or all members changed these items. The copy of the meeting minutes that has been referenced was obtained from the presidential files of Harold Noah. This copy was a draft that solicited either an "o.k. or corrections" to be sent to Franklin Parker, CIES Secretary. It is possible that the draft of the meeting minutes was returned to Parker with the request that the wording be changed, with the changes to be reflected in the May *Newsletter*. A second possible explanation is that Parker, as Editor of the *Newsletter*, removed this information himself because of relevance, space, accuracy or some other editorial reason. Regardless of why the text of the meeting minutes and *Newsletter* differ, the fact that a difference does exist can raise questions regarding what implications, if any, this may have had in the proceedings that followed.

As a result of a unanimously approved motion by Joseph Katz, former Society President, a name change was recommended for review by a committee to be assigned by incoming President William Brickman (*CES Newsletter* May 1967). It is unclear when or how Brickman formed the committee, but a letter by Franklin Parker in November 1967 indicated that the committee included R. Freeman Butts, Franklin Parker, Gerald Read, and Reginald Edwards who was appointed as chairman. Parker's letter suggested that there could perhaps be a statement from Edwards on behalf of the Committee that could be included in an early *CES Newsletter.* This apparently did not occur, as there is no record of a statement from Edwards or any member of the Change of Name Committee in the January 1968 *Newsletter.* The Committee submitted its report to the Board of Directors at their annual meeting on February 16, 1968. The report indicated that the Committee did not have any formal meetings but that each member had submitted an appraisal of the idea for a change of name of the Society. Three of the four appraisals advocated a change of name.

The first appraisal suggested that the name be changed to the International and Comparative Education Society. This suggestion was based on the belief that the academic discipline of the field had recently grown to include the international educational activities of government and non-government agencies, and the membership of the Society was representative of this changing focus. It was argued that to be influential in this emerging area, CES must become "a Society whose name and interests reflect a wider range of interests" (*CES Newsletter*, March 1968). The second and third appraisals both proposed that the name be changed to The Society for Comparative and International Education. The second, similar to the first, contended that there were a growing number of persons and agencies interested in becoming affiliated with organizations of an international dimension. It explained that a growing number of CES members were already involved in comparative analysis on a world-wide scale and that a change of name would be more descriptive of these members as well as "serve better special interests in comparative and international education" (*CES Newsletter* March 1968). The third proposal also argued that a change of name would better reflect the interests of the current membership. Specifically, this latter suggestion referenced the impact and national interest that had been generated in response to the International Education Act of 1966.

The final Committee member's appraisal was the only one that did not advocate a change to the Society's name. This assessment argued that the fields of comparative education and international education had very distinct natures. It explained that certain aspects of international education were attached to "opportunistic thinking" (*CES Newsletter* March 1968) and that if it were to be included as a focus of the society it could undermine the strides that had been made in comparative education to advance testable theories. The appraisal pointed out that the impact of the Department of International Education and the International Education Act was undeniable, but that without much knowledge of how these resources and funds would be allocated, "it would be difficult to judge which parts of the education enterprise are going to benefit" (*CES Newsletter,* March 1968).

Upon reviewing the appraisals that comprised the Change of Name Committee's report, the Board of Directors unanimously agreed to support the majority opinion of the Committee. They moved, as announced in the March 1968 *CES Newsletter*, that the following resolution be presented to the membership at the February 17, 1968 Business Meeting:

> The matter of a Change of Name of the Society having been under discussion for the past several years, and the Committee on Change of Name having recommended to the Board of Directors that the name of the Society be changed and that the Board of Directors having agreed, the Board had unanimously suggested that the name of the Society be changed to the "Comparative and International Education Society."

After it was agreed that the resolution would be brought to a vote of the membership at the business meeting, the Board recognized that to comply with the Society's Constitution there must also be a mail ballot sent to all members. Pursuant to CES Constitutional Article XII, if the issue were passed by both a majority vote at the business meeting and a two-thirds favorable response from the mail ballot, then constitutionally, the name could be changed (*CES Newsletter* December 1966). At this point, the Board addressed the issue of whether a name change should also apply to the *CER*. There appears to have been very little discussion regarding this possibility, because records later indicate simply that a unanimous motion was passed that the journal's name not be changed (*CES Newsletter* March 1968).

February 16, 1968, the members in attendance at the annual business meeting were presented with the Board's recommendation for the name change. No records were found showing the exact results of the members' vote, but apparently a majority ruled in favor of the change as the required mail ballot was subsequently mailed to the entire membership with the March 1968 *Newsletter*. Included with the ballot in the *Newsletter*, as per a suggestion at the business meeting, were all four of the Committee's appraisals as well as a statement giving reason for the Board's recommended name. This statement encouraged members to consider to what extent the current aims of the Society met their interests and desires. Members were asked whether their own interests had changed in emphasis and, since it most likely did, should this shift be representative in the name of the Society. The statement contended that the opinions of the four committee members covered a wide range of perspectives, leading to an implication of "a dual role for both Comparative and International Education, with recognition in the title of the origin of the Society" (*CES Newsletter* March 1968).[10]

The information that was printed in the March 1968 *CES Newsletter* appeared overwhelmingly in favor of a change of name. There was only a brief suggestion that opposition to the idea of a name change existed in the general membership of the Society. However, this may not have been the case. In March 1968, Erwin H. Epstein wrote a statement titled "On Renaming the Comparative Education Society – Or, Would a Rose by any Other Name Smell as Sweet?" In this statement, Epstein presented an argument against the name change of the Society, highlighting the fundamental differences between international education and comparative education. Epstein suggested that to change the name of the Society would suppose a change in its focus, something that could inevitably change the academic quality of the field. He contended that the academic prestige of the field was ultimately determined by the scholarly quality of its journal, noting that there was no consideration of changing the name of the *CER*.[10] Epstein apparently attempted to have this statement sent to the membership of the Society via the *Newsletter*'s editor, Barbara Yates. In a letter written to Professor C. Arnold Anderson on 16 April 1968, Epstein wrote that Yates was not willing to send the statement to the membership and was unwilling to provide Epstein with the list of members so that he could send it at his own expense.[11] Instead, Epstein indicated to Anderson that he submitted the statement to Harold Noah, Editor of the *CER*. Recognizing that the earliest the statement would go out to the general membership would be with the next edition of the *CER*, in the same April 1968 letter, Epstein told Anderson "it would not affect the vote, but I am confident that this will remain a live issue even after the ballots are cast." Epstein's statement was published as a letter to the editor in the October 1968 edition of the *CER*. The announcement of the official change of name to the Comparative and International Education Society was announced in the final (1968) *CES Newsletter*, that is, before the next issue became the *CIES Newsletter*.

Conclusion

Today, most members of the Society have only known it as the Comparative and International Education Society. While they may give little thought to the debates that created this title, most are probably keenly aware of the debate between "comparative" and "international" education. The issue has been the subject of the Society's journal articles, annual and regional conferences, and presidential addresses,[12] fueled by distinctions between research, practice, policies and basic activities that fall under this field's wide umbrella. As seen in this chapter, it is a discussion in which the comparative education community has engaged for decades, and there is no reason to believe that it will not continue for decades to come.

Most of us today, even if engaged in this discussion about the nature of the field, probably give little thought to how this debate carries through to the name of the Society in which we claim membership. The insertion of the word "International" into the Comparative Education Society was more than an aesthetic change to an organization's title; it marked a point in the history of this field when there was a concerted effort – be it historically, financially or externally influenced – to merge these two related ideas, *comparative education* and *international education*. It has subsequently affected the boundaries, focuses, and methodological approaches that characterize work in the field. Isaac Kandel (1955) believed that to truly understand a system of education, one must first understand its history. Similarly, if we as members of the comparative education community want to understand the debates that characterize the field, we must first understand the historical events that make up our professional organization, the Comparative and *International* Education Society.

Notes

1 For a detailed historical description of the origins of study tours, see Elizabeth Swing's chapter in this volume.

2 The first CES Board of Directors comprised: Harold R.W. Benjamin, George Z.F. Bereday, Claude Eggertsen, Bess Goodykoontz, Joseph Katz, David G. Scanlon, Robert Ulich, and Flaud C. Wooton.

3 The Surplus Property Act authorized the sale and orderly disposal of U.S. war materials to foreign governments. *See*, U.S. Department of State, *Regulations and Orders Pertaining to Foreign Surplus Disposal*, Publication 2704 (Washington: U.S. Government Printing Office, December, 1946).

4 Part of American foreign policy during the Cold-War era was to spread democracy to areas of the world that were most susceptible to communist influence. In attempting to do so, an increased understanding of America and its democratic principles were crucial. By extending the Fulbright Program to countries that were 'Cold War neutrals,' i.e. Austria, Finland, and Sweden, the program acted as a microcosm of U.S foreign policy. *See* Michael T. Ruddy, "U.S. Foreign Policy, the 'Third Force,' and European Union: Eisenhower and Europe's Neutrals," *Midwest Quarterly*, 42 no. 1 (2000): 61-80.

5 This federal legislation passed in 1958 provided aid to education in the United States at all levels, public and private. The NDEA was instituted primarily to stimulate the advancement of education in science, mathematics, and modern foreign languages; it has also provided aid in other areas, including technical education, area studies, geography, English as a second language, counseling and guidance, school libraries and librarianship, and educational media centers. *See*, *Columbia Encyclopedia*, Sixth Edition (New York: Columbia University Press, 2001-05).

6 If IEA was passed *and* funded, there stood a good chance of having the Society's study tours financed.

7 The Committee met in New York City on October 31, 1966 and had the advantage of having the Society's President, Davis G. Scanlon, present during most of its deliberations (*Comparative Education Society Newsletter*, December 1966. Comparative and International Education Society, Papers. Kent State University Libraries. Department of Special Collections and Archives. Box 9, folder 14 – CES Newsletter N. 6, December 1966).

8 Kim Sebaly adds, "I was at the Chicago meeting where the concept was presented. I recall an extended discussion, with Freeman Butts leading the initiative. I believe it was made in the context of the growing commitment of the U.S. to international assistance in response to competition from the Soviet Union and other western nations devising educational and other schemes to

influence the non-aligned nations of the world." Kim Sebaly, e-mail message to Lou Berends, March 26, 2006.

⁹ The difference between the use of "international" in the draft of the revised Constitution and the original Constitution is remarkable. See Gerald H. Read, "Constitution of the Comparative Education Society," *Comparative Education Review* 3, no. 2 (October 1959): 37-40. Article XII of the draft of the revised Constitution states: "This Constitution shall be amended when preliminary action on a proposed amendment shall have been taken at a duly constituted Business Meeting held during the Annual Meeting, a summary of the discussion and preliminary action together with an official ballot for voting on the proposed amendment shall have been sent to the active members along with any related recommendation by the Board of Directors or the Executive Committee, and two-thirds of those responding within three months to a mail poll of active members shall have voted in favor of the proposed amendment" (*Newsletter of CES*, December 1966).

¹⁰ As per Constitution Article XII, a statement regarding the Board's recommenddation was required to be sent with the mail ballot. This statement read,

"Members are being asked to consider one major question: 'Should the name of the Society be changed?' And if the answer is in the affirmative, they are being asked to consider what that new name should be. In coming to a decision members would have to consider the extent to which the Society meets, or fails to meet their desires as expressed when they became members; whether if their own interests have changed over the years, this change is likely to have been shared by others, and that being a majority of the members, this new emphasis should appear in the title of a Society to which they belong. It is always open to an individual, whose views and interests change, to cease membership of societies and groups which no longer cater to his new interests. It is also open to a group of such individuals to seek to change the character of the societies to which they belong; most societies protect themselves against too frequent exercise of this kind by requiring that a specified size of the majority of members should be in favor of any change of a major nature. It is apparent that changing the name of a society is a matter of major importance, and the decision to do so must be based upon a conviction that permanent rather than temporary benefits will accrue."

¹¹This statement was printed as a letter to the Editor but was originally submitted under the title "On Renaming the Comparative Education Society – Or Would a Rose by any Other Name Smell as Sweet?" *See* Erwin H. Epstein, "Letter to the Editor," *Comparative Education Review* 12 (October 1968): 376-378.

¹² Item not inventoried in archive collection at the time of writing. Retrieved April 7, 2006.

[13] See, e.g., David N. Wilson, "Comparative and International Education: Fraternal or Siamese Twins? A Preliminary Genealogy of our Twin Fields," *Comparative Education Review* 38 (November 1994): 449-486.

Correspondence and documents cited

Comparative Education Society Newsletter, No. 6, December 1966. Comparative and International Education Society, Papers. Kent State University Libraries. Department of Special Collections and Archives. Box 9, folder 14 – *CES Newsletter* N. 6, December 1966.

Comparative Education Society Newsletter, No. 7, May 1967. Comparative and International Education Society, Papers. Kent State University Libraries, Department of Special Collections and Archives. Box 9, folder 15 – *CES Newsletter* N. 7, May 1967.

Comparative Education Society Newsletter, No. 9, January 1968. Comparative and International Education Society, Papers. Kent State University Libraries, Department of Special Collections and Archives. Box 9, folder 17 – *CES Newsletter* N. 9, January 1968.

Comparative Education Society Newsletter, No. 10, March 1968. Comparative and International Education Society, Papers. Kent State University Libraries, Department of Special Collections and Archives. Box 9, folder 18 – *CES Newsletter* N. 10, March 1968.

Comparative and Education Society Newsletter, No. 11, September 1968. Comparative and International Education Society, Papers. Kent State University Libraries, Department of Special Collections and Archives. Box 9, folder 19 - *CIES Newsletter* N. 11, September 1968.

Constitution of the United Nations Educational, Scientific and Cultural Organization (London: UNESCO, 1946).

Draft of Meeting Minutes from February 1967 Board of Directors and annual business meeting. Kent State Archives, Box 15, folder 1 – CIES President's Files (Noah): Executive Committee, Board of Director Minutes, 1966-1969.

Kim Sebaly, e-mail message to Louis Berends, March 26, 2006.

Kim Sebaly, e-mail message to Louis Berends, April 24, 2006.

Letter from Brembeck to Anderson, January 13, 1964. Comparative and International Education Society, Papers. Kent State University Libraries, Department of Special Collections and Archives. Box 16B, folder 27 – CIES President's Files (Eggertsen): Miscellaneous, 1964-70.

Letter from Eggertsen to Anderson, March 6, 1964. Comparative and International Education Society, Papers. Kent State University Libraries, Department of Special Collections and Archives. Box 16B, folder 27 – CIES President's Files (Eggertsen): Miscellaneous, 1964-70.

Letter from Eggertsen to Katz, March 6, 1964. Comparative and International Education Society, Papers. Kent State University Libraries, Department of

Special Collections and Archives. Box 16B, folder 27 – CIES President's Files (Eggertsen): Miscellaneous, 1964-70.

Letter from Epstein to Anderson, April 16, 1968. Comparative and International Education Society, Papers. Kent State University Libraries, Department of Special Collections and Archives. Item not yet inventoried in archive collection, retrieved on April 7, 2006.

Letter from Parker to Anderson, Brickman, Fraser, Van Til, Goldstein, and Pomeroy, November 6, 1967. Comparative and International Education Society, Papers. Kent State University Libraries, Department of Special Collections and Archives. Box 15, folder 12 – CIES President's Files (Noah, Shafer & LeBelle): General Correspondence, 1968-72.

Letter from Read to Durnin, June 28, 1956. Comparative and International Education Society, Papers. Kent State University Libraries, Department of Special Collections and Archives. Box 15, folder 12 – CIES President's Files (Noah): General Correspondence, 1968-72, Financial Reports, Reginald Edwards.

Letter from Sutton to Eggertsen, March 9, 1964. Comparative and International Education Society, Papers. Kent State University Libraries, Department of Special Collections and Archives. Box 16B, folder 27 – CIES President's Files (Eggertsen): Miscellaneous, 1964-70.

Lyndon B. Johnson, State of the Union Address, January 12, 1966. Retrieved on March 30th, 2006 from: http://janda.org/politxts/State%20of%20Union%20Addresses/1964_1969%20Johnson/LBJ.66.html.

Meeting Minutes from Board of Directors meeting, February 15, 1967. Comparative and International Education Society, Papers. Kent State University Libraries, Department of Special Collections and Archives. Box 15, folder 1 – CIES President's Files (Noah): Executive Committee, Board of Director Minutes, 1966-1969.

Memorandum from Anderson to Members of Consortium on proposed world conference on comparative education, March 25, 1964. Comparative and International Education Society, Papers. Kent State University Libraries, Department of Special Collections and Archives. Box 16B, folder 27 – CIES President's Files (Eggertsen): Miscellaneous, 1964-70.

Press Release, February 26, 1963. Comparative and International Education Society, Papers. Kent State University Libraries, Department of Special Collections and Archives. Box 16B, folder 27 – CIES President's Files (Eggertsen): Miscellaneous, 1964-70.

U.S. Advisory Commission on International Educational and Cultural Affairs, *A Beacon of Hope: The Exchange-of-Persons* (Washington, D.C.: Department of State, 1963).

U.S. Department of State. *Regulations and Orders Pertaining to Foreign Surplus Disposal.* Publication 2704 (Washington: U.S. Government Printing Office, December, 1946).

References

Brickman, William W. 1977. "Comparative and International Education Society: An Historical Analysis." *Comparative Education Review* 21(2): 396-404.

Brickman, William W. 1966. "Genesis and Early Development of the Comparative and International Education Society." *Comparative Education Review* 10(1): 9-20.

Bu, Liping. 1997. "International Activism and Comparative Education: Pioneering Efforts of the International Institute of Teachers College, Columbia University," *Comparative Education Review* 41(4): 413-434.

Columbia Encyclopedia, Sixth Edition. 2001-05. New York: Columbia University Press.

Epstein, Erwin H. 1968 "Letter to the Editor." *Comparative Education Review* 12(3): 376-378.

Johnson, Walter and Colligan, Francis J. *The Fulbright Program: A History* (Chicago: University of Chicago Press, 1965).

Johnson, William H.E. 1957. "The Comparative Education Society." *Comparative Education Review* 1(1): 16.

Kandel, Isaac L. 1955. "The Study of Comparative Education." *Educational Forum* 20(5): 15-22.

Lengyel, Emil. 1947. "International Education as an Aid to World Peace." *Journal of Educational Sociology* 20(9): 562-570.

Ludden, David. 2000. "Area Studies in the Age of Globalization." *Frontiers: The Interdisciplinary Journal of Study Abroad 6*: 1-22.

Ohles, John F. 1986. "A Conversation with Gerald H. Read." *Kappa Delta Pi Record* (Winter): 53-56.

Read, Gerald H. 1959. "Constitution of the Comparative Education Society." *Comparative Education Review* 3(2): 37-40.

Ruddy, Michael T. 2000. "U.S. Foreign Policy, the 'Third Force,' and European Union: Eisenhower and Europe's Neutrals." *Midwest Quarterly* 42(1): 61-80.

Scanlon, David G. ed. 1960. *International Education: A Documentary History* (New York: Teachers College, Columbia University Press).

Sebaly, Kim. 2006a. e-mail message to Louis Berends, March 26.

Sebaly, Kim. 2006b. e-mail message to Louis Berends, April 24.

Swing, Elizabeth Sherman. 2007. "Comparative and International Education Society (CIES)." In Vandra Masemann, Mark Bray & Maria Manzon, eds. *Common Interests, Uncommon Goals: Histories of the World Council of Comparative Education Societies*. CERC Studies in Comparative Education 21. Hong Kong: Comparative Education Research Centre, The University of Hong Kong, and Dordrecht: Springer, pp. 94-115.

Wilson, David N. 1994. "Comparative and International Education: Fraternal or Siamese Twins? A Preliminary Genealogy of our Twin Fields." *Comparative Education Review* 38(4): 449-486.

6
The Society in the World Council of Comparative Education Societies

Vandra L. MASEMANN

The World Council of Comparative Education Societies (WCCES) is bound up almost inextricably in the history of the Comparative and International Education Society (CIES), because some of the same central figures were involved in their founding and development. The Comparative and International Education Society of Canada (CIESC) was also connected to these events because of the collegial relationships of scholars in the United States and Canada, and because of the hosting by the CIESC of the preliminary meetings in 1969 for the establishment of the WCCES in 1970. In this chapter, these relationships in several key time periods from 1956 to 2016 will be disentangled and discussed.

The central thesis of this account is that the early leaders of both organizations had personal characteristics of leadership and inspiration that led to the founding of the Comparative Education Society (CES/CIES) and the WCCES, which in time had to yield to more bureaucratic forms of organization in the process that Max Weber called "the routinization of charisma" (Gerth & Mills 1958, 54). In their introduction to Weber's essays, Gerth and Mills state that "the principle of rationalization is the most general element in Weber's philosophy of history" (1958, 51). With the passage of time, "Weber sees the genuine charismatic situation quickly give way to incipient institutions, which emerge from the cooling off of extraordinary states of devotion and fervor. As the original doctrines are democratized, they are intellectually adjusted to the needs

Erwin H. Epstein (ed.) (2016): *Crafting a Global Field: Six Decades of the Comparative and International Education Society*. Hong Kong: Comparative Education Research Centre (CERC), The University of Hong Kong, and Dordrecht: Springer. © CERC

of that stratum which becomes the primary carrier of the leader's message" (1958, 54).

The histories of both the CIES and the WCCES demonstrate the reliance at the outset on the personal and academic qualities of the founders, almost all of whom were men; the definition of the central goals of the organization; and the designation of eligible members. This was followed by the process of routinization in the creation of codified constitutions or statutes and by-laws, the setting up of financial accounts, the establishment of patterns of voting or appointment of executive and regular members, the choices of venues for meetings or Congresses, and the publication of regular newsletters and, in the case of the CIES, its own academic journal, the *Comparative Education Review*.

This chronological account will cover these various periods of development. It is based primarily on archival research carried out in October 2014 and February 2015 in the CIES collection at Kent State University, and more specifically in the files of CIES Past President Robert F. Lawson and the CIES Presidential Correspondence and CIES *Newsletter* files. Several files of Robert Lawson are also held by the CIESC as part of their archival founding papers.

1956-1970

William Brickman and Gerald Read were the two key players in establishing the New York conferences in Comparative Education from 1954-1956. They both had previous experiences which led them to value international understanding and to hope for peace in the world. Brickman had served in the U.S. army in World War Two, and Read was very concerned with the onset of the Cold War in the 1950s and with learning about Russia and Eastern Europe. They both thought that teachers and educators needed to learn more about education in other countries. In 1954 they met in Washington DC with Bess Goodykoontz of the United States Office of Education to establish study tours of education abroad. In order to meet the requirement that a group travel rate could be given only to pre-existing groups, Brickman and Read proposed at the 1956 New York conference that a Comparative Education Society should be formed. The first officers were William Brickman as President, Robert Sutton as Vice President, and Gerald Read as Secretary-Treasurer (Read in Swing 2007, 96).

It is noteworthy that the Canadian colleagues played a part in the newly fledged CES, and also were active in establishing the Comparative and International Education Society of Canada in 1967. In turn they would be influential in establishing the WCCES. Joseph Katz was President of the CES in 1960-61, and Reginald Edward was CES President in the period leading up to the first World Congress of Comparative Education, when the Canadians arranged for the Canadian International Development Agency to provide the funding for the pre-Congress organizational meeting in Ottawa and the Congress itself in 1970 (Masemann & Epstein 2007, 16). Joseph Katz and Gerald Read were notable for their participation in the founding of each of the CES, CIESC and WCCES.

An examination of the CES/CIES *Newsletter*s in the 1950s and 1960s, mainly edited by Gerald Read, dealt with the minutiae of setting up a viable CES with its journal and other internal organizational features. It was not until the late 1960s that the *Newsletter*s detailed the establishment of a routine structure to communicate with other groups, in the form of two committees. A key appointee was Suzanne Shafer as Chairman (sic) of the International Liaison Committee of the CIES. She reported in 1969 that the committee had been appointed to ask other international organizations and the U.S. Office of Education about their international activities. She would then pass on this information for publication in the *CIES Newsletter*. Another committee, the Overseas Liaison Committee chaired by Joseph Katz, communicated with other comparative education societies (*CIES Newsletter*, March 1969, no. 13, 6-7). Thus a regular conduit of information was established between the CIES and other societies.

The climate was building for the establishment of the World Council of Comparative Education Societies. International ties among academics in comparative education and among the nascent comparative education societies in Europe and Asia were increasing. The economic climate in Northern Europe and North America made funds for international travel increasingly available to tenured professors. The mandate of the societies was growing increasingly international, and in 1968 the Comparative Education Society became the Comparative and International Education Society (see Swing chapter in this volume).

By the late 1960s, the idea of a World Council was being talked about as a serious possibility. However, it was primarily individuals in the CIES, such as Joseph Katz and Gerald Read, who advocated it. Katz, in particular, had had this ambition ever since he had advanced the idea of the International Education Year in 1960 (Majhanovich & Zhang 2007, 173). He was indefatigable in the 1960s, campaigning for a wider international association of comparative education societies. On March 27, 1968, Joseph Katz wrote to Leo Fernig in Geneva that at the CES meeting in Chicago he had "explored the possibility of having a congress of Comparative Education Societies during 1970...." He had also sounded out Professors Brickman, Read and Holmes, and noted that "the American group, along with the Canadian, thought the idea worthwhile" (Lawson, *CIESC Founding Papers*, 1966-70). This letter was copied to Masunori Hiratsuka (Japan), Stewart Fraser and Gerald Read (USA), Sun Ho Kim (Korea), Brian Holmes and Joseph Lauwerys (UK), and Robert F. Lawson and Margaret Gillett (Canada), who had formed an International Committee of Comparative Education (Read 1985, 2 in Masemann and Epstein 2007, 15). By August 1968, Katz had prepared a proposal for the Congress and was soliciting funds of support from Canadian sources and foundations. Gerald Read personally donated US$1,000 to support the Congress.

In January 1970, Joseph Katz chaired a meeting at the University of Ottawa to plan and prepare for the First World Congress. The two CES representatives were Gerald Read (CES Secretary-Treasurer in 1957-1965) and Stewart Fraser (CES President in 1967-1968). There were four representatives from CIESC: Robert F. Lawson, Fred Whitworth, Antanas Paplauskas-Ramunas, and Andrew F. Skinner, as well as Philip Idenburg from CESE (Read 1985, 2 in Masemann & Epstein 2007, 15).

1970-1980

In 1970, the First World Congress of Comparative Education Societies was held in Ottawa, Canada. The registered participants included 36 based at American institutions. Canadians were the highest proportion of the 150 registrants, and participants from European, Asian and African countries also attended. There was one participant from each of Australia, Cuba, Jamaica and El Salvador. The two main themes were "The Place of Comparative and International Education in the Education of Teachers" and "The Role and Rationale for Educational Aid to Developing Countries" (Proceedings of the First World Congress of Comparative Education Societies, Ottawa, 1970). Of the 29 speakers on Teacher Education, six were from the United States; and of the 28 speakers on Educational

Aid, three were from the United States. The interest of the early CES/CIES members in teacher education was evident at this Congress, while international aid was not widely addressed.

In 1971, according to the Newsletters, it seemed as if the CIES committee structure was faltering, and the suggestion was made to rethink the structure and function of committees. The two committees involved in international liaison were among the ones mentioned for rethinking. Minutes of the March 21, 1971 meeting noted that in the *CIES Newsletter* Professor Philip Foster had reported on the World Congress of Comparative Education Societies held in 1970: "After discussion, the Board expressed general support for the idea of a Second World Congress in 1973. However in 1971, the Board felt it would be premature for CIES as a society to affiliate itself with the proposed World Council for Comparative Education. This position would not preclude individual CIES members from accepting appointment to the Council on an individual basis." (March 1971, no. 21, 3).

In June 1972, the World Council met in Paris to set up its Constitution, secretariat, consultative status with UNESCO, newsletter, membership, etc. Andreas Kazamias, who had been CIES President in 1970-71, attended. The precedent seems to have been set very early for Past Presidents of CIES to attend World Council meetings, whereas most societies sent their Presidents and still do so. Joseph Katz supplied an account of the meeting and its outcomes to the readers of the following issue of the *CIES Newsletter*. An announcement was made of the Second World Congress to be held in 1974 in Geneva, the new location of the WCCES Secretariat. Individual members of the constituent societies could subscribe to the new *WCCES Newsletter/ Bulletin* for news about the World Council and the member societies. There was still no announcement of the CIES having joined the WCCES. Elizabeth Sherman Swing noted in her account of the CIES history that "there was concern that ratifying the WCCES Constitution would mean endorsing a 'super-society' *(CIES Newsletter* No.34, December 1974). However, Robert Lawson and others successfully argued for ratification" (Swing 2007, 106).

The theme of the 1974 Second World Congress was "Efficiencies and Inefficiencies in Secondary Schools." It was smaller than the first Congress, organized along the European model with five working groups which dealt with various sub-themes of the main topic. Gerald Read organized a tour for the American and Canadian participants, via Hungary to Geneva. Then after the Congress, they would leave Geneva for France, Germany and Denmark. By 1975, there was still no notice about the CIES officially having joined the World Council, although the *CIES Newsletter* carried a column entitled World Council of Comparative Education Societies Report.

Suzanne Shafer, as Vice President of CIES, attended the WCCES meeting in Sèvres, near Paris, on May 29-June 1, 1975. In 1977, as CIES President (1976-77) she provided a report on the Third World Congress held in London, England, with the theme, Diversity and Unity in Education (*CIES Newsletter* 1977). In 1979, the *CIES Newsletter* contained an article entitled "WCCES Study Report" in which it was noted that Suzanne Shafer had distributed a memo to the CIES Board of Directors about membership in the WCCES, and the need for the CIES to join it. Even though she advocated that the CIES join the WCCES, she also presented alternatives, such as individual membership with a *WCCES/ CMAEC [Conseil mondial des associations d'éducation comparée] Newsletter/ Bulletin* subscription. The Board passed a motion that the next president of the Society explore ways to improve cooperation with WCCES member societies, either through WCCES or some other manner, and report back to the Board at the 1980 meetings (*CIES Newsletter* 1979).

During this period, there is a marked contrast between the newsletters of the CIES and the CIESC. In the latter, there are detailed accounts of World Council meetings during the 1970s as the CIESC was a founding member of the World Council. The CIES Board, on the other hand, was ambivalent about joining the WCCES. A revealing note is found in the November 1978 *CIES Newsletter* concerning a crisis in the World Council: they had to close the WCCES Secretariat office in Geneva because of cuts in funding by the International Bureau of Education and UNESCO (1978, 14). This may explain why the CIES Board was reluctant to become a member at that time, and it was exploring other ways of communicating with member societies. It may also explain the reference in Suzanne Shafer's report in 1979 to the alternative ways that a WCCES Secretariat could be operated: "by one member society on a permanent basis, or by the Society hosting the next world congress or by a designnated professor or a department at a designated university" (*CIES Newsletter* 1979). It was decided at a World Council meeting in Valencia, Spain in 1979 that the WCCES Secretariat be temporarily relocated to Japan, as Masunori Hiratsuka was WCCES President from 1977-1980 (Council Meeting of the World Council of Comparative Education

Societies, Valencia, July 26, 1979, in CIES Presidential Correspondence Files).

1980-1990

In 1980, the Fourth World Congress was held in Japan with a pre-Congress in Korea. When he attended that Congress, Erwin Epstein was Vice President of CIES. He was elected President of the WCCES at the Tokyo Congress after the joint CIES/UDEM (University of Monterrey) proposal for the Fifth World Congress in Mexico was accepted. The Congress was to take place in July 1983, sponsored by the CIES and hosted by the Universidad de Monterrey in Monterrey, Mexico.

Erwin Epstein had seen many advantages for the CIES in supporting the proposal to host the Congress, in that "CIES would fulfill an obligation to contribute its appropriate share to the World Congress movement.... Our members would have a unique opportunity to meet with their co-professionals from other comparative education societies.... International membership will grow as a result of increasing exposure of our society to people outside the U.S.... The opportunity for increased revenue other than from member subscriptions, would be very strong" (Letter from Erwin Epstein to Thomas La Belle, May 26, 1980, CIES Presidential Correspondence Files). This was one of the strongest statements about the perception of the relationship between the CIES and the WCCES in any of the CIES Presidential Correspondence files.

In the 1980s, after the World Congress in Japan, several letters in the CIES correspondence files address the CIES subvention for the WCCES. The matter under discussion was whether the CIES should levy US$1 per member to support the World Council (Philip Altbach to Tom LaBelle, August 13, 1980; and Erwin Epstein to Tom LaBelle, August 25, 1980, CIES Presidential Correspondence Files). There was an ongoing concern about the pros and cons of investing in the world body and the costs to the CIES itself when their own finances were not firm. Tom LaBelle wrote to Erwin Epstein on October 24, 1980, stating his opinion that the CIES Board would be split over the US$1 dues to support the World Council, and that a majority of the CIES Executive Committee "is not inclined to support the proposal." He hoped for a compromise proposal (Letter from Thomas La Belle to Erwin Epstein, October 24, 1980, CIES Presidential Correspondence Files).

Gerald Read was still active during this period and attended the planning meeting held in December 1980 in Monterrey. In addition to Erwin Epstein, CIES members who attended were Max Eckstein (who was President Elect) and Noel McGinn (who would become President in 1995). There were also eight Mexican representatives. Erwin Epstein has written in detail about the circumstances that brought about the non-acceptance of the plans for the Congress in Monterrey (Epstein 2007, 20-32). He was phoned by his Mexican colleague, Luis Quintero, telling him that the Mexican economy had collapsed and the University of Monterrey was compelled to withdraw its support (Epstein 2007, 30). As Erwin Epstein had been unable to procure other financing, the WCCES Executive Committee in New York in March 1982 accepted an offer from Michel Debeauvais and AFEC (the French-speaking Comparative Education Society) to host the Fifth World Congress in Paris in 1984.

The CIES members who were interested in the WCCES continued to support it. Suzanne Shafer chaired one of the Research Commissions at the Paris Congress. It had a very similar title to the proposed title of the Monterrey Congress: "Dependence and Interdependence in Educational Policies at the National Level: Sex, Regions, Minorities, Social, Ethnic and Cultural Groups" (*CIES Newsletter* 1984, 10), and several CIES scholars participated. By this period, the *CIES Newsletter* carried regular columns of information about the activities of other comparative education societies and the World Council, and has continued to do so until today.

Elizabeth Sherman Swing noted that in 1985 and 1986, the CIES explicitly committed itself to support the WCCES by attendance at Congresses, representation on committees, carrying WCCES news in the *CIES Newsletter*, the payment of WCCES dues, and individual members' assuming the costs of attending Congresses or serving on WCCES committees. She noted further that, in 1997, the practice was adopted of appointing the CIES Past President as the CIES representative to the World Council, with a duration of two years, thus skipping every other President (Swing 2007, 106).

Michel Debeauvais had been in contact with several Brazilian scholars in his work on UNESCO projects, and the Brazilian Comparative Education Society (SBEC) presented a proposal which was accepted to host the Sixth World Congress in Rio de Janeiro in 1987. He also made a point of inviting Martin Carnoy of Stanford University to head one of the Research Commissions at that Congress. It was very well attended and provided a strong support to the Congress (Masemann, personal recollection). The CIESC (Canada) and the CCES (Chinese) societies presented proposals to host the next Congress. They were accepted for 1989 and 1991. I had previously been President of CIESC from 1983-85 and was elected as President of the World Council at that meeting. As I also became President Elect of the CIES in 1987, the communications among the three organizations tended to flow through my office.

While the CIESC was very active in preparing for the Seventh World Congress in Montreal, the CIES remained somewhat aloof in pooling resources. For example, my proposal to have a joint CIES/World Congress in Montreal was soundly defeated at a CIES Executive meeting because of the proposed July date, which was seen as inconvenient for U.S. academics whose academic year ended in May. However, the Montreal World Congress in July 1989 was well attended by both Canadians and Americans as well as international CIES members. The major issue of significance in that June was the events in Tiananmen Square in Beijing, which had repercussions for the WCCES plans for the next Congress in Beijing in 1991. Many overseas Chinese students studying in North America contacted the CIESC and CIES Executive Committee members to urge them to take action in protest of the Tiananmen Square government crackdown. A decision was consequently made to defer the decision about the Congress until a subsequent meeting.

By the end of the 1980s, the attendance at World Congresses was increasing, and CIES members made their plans depending on the location and its attractiveness. Because the Congresses were usually held in July, summer holidays for scholars in the northern latitudes could be planned around them. The earlier WCCES conferences had been scheduled so as not to conflict with CESE (Comparative Education Society in Europe) meetings. A bias toward the global North was evident in these arrangements.

1990-2001

At a WCCES Executive Committee meeting in Madrid, a new proposal was accepted to hold the Eighth World Congress in Prague, Czechoslovakia in 1992. The Chinese proposal was to be considered for the Ninth World Congress but was later withdrawn (Masemann 2007, 47; Gu & Gui 2007, 236). By 1991, the President of the World Council was Wolfgang Mitter from Germany, who worked intensively with his European colleagues in preparing this Congress. The location of the

Congress was very attractive to Americans and Canadians, who attended in great numbers. Wolfgang Mitter remained in office until the Ninth World Congress in Sydney, Australia in 1996. At the Sydney Congress, David Wilson of the University of Toronto was elected as the new President of the World Council. He had also been a long-time member of the CIES and had become its President in 1993. Joseph di Bona, who worked closely with Suzanne Shafer, was Treasurer of the World Council from 1987-1996 (Mitter 2007, 51).

Through these overlapping links of the WCCES and CIES Executives from 1987 to 2001, the North American relationship between the two groups was strengthened. During this period, the process of routinization became firmly established, both in the CIES and the WCCES. The *CIES Newsletter*s still carried regular news about other comparative education societies. By the 1990s, the World Council had instituted a regular system of dues based on the numbers of members of constituent societies. Thus the CIES became one of the largest contributors to the World Council because of its many hundreds of members. In 1997, the CIES also set up a routine whereby past presidents represented it at meetings. In the 1990s, Mark Ginsburg attended meetings to represent CIES and carried on until the present day as a member of various WCCES committees. Several other CIES Presidents, notably Ruth Hayhoe, Robert Arnove, Heidi Ross and Karen Biraimah played key roles in the WCCES during the 1990s and 2000s. Carlos Alberto Torres, who was CIES President in 1997, also attended WCCES meetings in the 1990s and after 2000. Since the CIES has had a much swifter turnover of presidents than the WCCES, a new one being elected every year, this regular involvement of the CIES presidents stabilized the relationship and facilitated communication. As the attendance at CIES conferences had increased, especially after the 30th anniversary conference in Toronto in 1986, there was a more regular source of revenue and less overt concern internally about financial instability.

The Tenth World Congress was held in Cape Town, South Africa in 1998. David Wilson was re-elected President for a three years period until 2001. As much of his research since the 1960s had focused on Africa, he endeavored, along with the Congress organizers, to increase African participation in the World Congress. Since the Congress theme was "Education, Equity and Transformation," and the venue was South Africa, there was also greater participation of African-American scholars from CIES than previously. This Congress attracted nearly double the number of registrants overall than had been expected and was hugely successful.

The 1990s was also notable for the introduction of the computer and the Internet for both conference organization and routine communication. The 1989 CIES conference at Harvard University was the last one organized by hand (with paper mailings and telephone communication), with the computer being used only for word processing. The WCCES was still sending out its meeting materials by regular air mail until the 11th World Congress in Chungbuk, South Korea in 2001. However, increasingly, routine communication occurred electronically. These technological developments greatly increased the speed and number of messages between and among societies, and later led to the development of websites. "Linking member society webpages to the WCCES web page created a global network for the field of comparative education" (Wilson 2007, 67). By this time, CIES members had access to any information about the World Council that they wished and were not dependent on the notices created for the *CIES Newsletter*. This process of electronic communication was another part of the process of routinization.

2001-2016

The period from 2001 to 2016 has been one of greater differentiation and globalization for the World Council. In a parallel path, the same has occurred in the CIES. Attendance has increased at the meetings of both CIES and the WCCES. The committee structures of both have become more complex. The constitutions of both have had some revisions to adapt to changing circumstances, such as technological developments and the more complex organizational structure. Websites have been set up and revised, such that a great deal more information is available for the organization's members and the members of other comparative education societies. Conference proposals, registration, and payment of fees are now routinely carried out online. In CIES, there has been a proliferation of Special Interest Groups on many topics. There has been increasing involvement of practitioners from non-profit, government, and international agencies in the CIES conferences and World Congresses. For both organizations, the administration of finances has become much more complex. Financial reserves which can be used for student or Third World scholars' travel or for other uses have been established. In terms of size of conferences, the two organizations attract larger audiences than in earlier decades, although the World Congresses attract a more differentiated clientele, depending on their location in the world.

But there is still a distance between the two groups, exemplified most clearly in the fact that the CIES has not proposed to host a World Congress since the early 1980s. This lacuna is noticed and commented on by conference participants from time to time. My personal view is that many other countries have been able to count on financial support from their governments, but the CIES does not perceive that possibility as they are an entirely private organization. I have also heard CIES Executive Committee members say repeatedly over the years that CIES is an international organization and does not need to host an international meeting such as the World Congress when the international members of the CIES can attend the annual CIES conferences.

The 12th World Congress in Havana, Cuba in 2004 with the theme, "Education and Social Justice," attracted a large number of Americans who had not previously travelled to Cuba because of the U.S. trade embargo but who were able to travel under special academic arrangements. Anne Hickling-Hudson, WCCES President from 2001-2004, of Jamaican background and based in Australia, noted in her memories of her years on the World Council: "Another kind of imbalance I had noticed in the WCCES over the years of my association since 1992 was how few members from the USA were apparently active on the Council.... An exception was Erwin Epstein.... I cannot remember WCCES issues ever being an important agenda item of CIES Board meetings or conferences. In my term of office I wanted to see Americans – CIES members – from ethnically diverse communities active in the Executive and other committees of the World Council" (Hickling Hudson 2007, 71). She stated that she believed that three factors started "to bring about a more racially/globally balanced body" – the holding of the World Congress in Cuba, the restructuring of the standing committees, and the entry of several new societies from the global South (Hickling-Hudson 2007, 72).

Mark Bray, from the University of Hong Kong, became WCCES President in 2004. In 2005, at the 34th WCCES Executive Meeting in Bangi, Malaysia, the 13th World Congress was approved for 2007 in Sarajevo, Bosnia-Herzegovina. Again, there was a large attendance from the USA and Canada, as well as from Europe and Asia. Participation was also increasing from colleagues working in the international and multilateral agencies in comparison with the more traditional academic scholars. The recovery from the recent conflict in the area and the issue of ethnic pluralism were notable at this Congress, and it was the only Congress to my recollection where bullet-holes were still evident in the walls of the university buildings and the hotel.

The next President of the WCCES was Wing-On Lee from the National Institute of Education in Nanyang Technological University, Singapore. He was elected at the 14th World Congress in Istanbul, Turkey in 2010. Diane Napier of the University of Georgia, USA was also elected Secretary General. She was the first U.S. based scholar to take on this position. Wing-On Lee organized a high-level meeting in Singapore to consider the future of the World Council. Several CIES members participated, notably Diane Napier, Gita Steiner-Khamsi, Mark Bray, and Suzanne Majhanovich among others, along with various international colleagues.

The 15th Congress was held in Buenos Aires, Argentina in 2013. This Congress drew in many scholars from Latin America and increased their representation on the academic program and on the committees of the World Council itself. At that meeting, Carlos Alberto Torres from the University of California at Los Angeles was elected President. For the first time, and until late 2014, the WCCES had a President and Secretary General who were both based in the United States. During this recent period, CIES members have been playing more of a role in the consultations and operation of the World Council. The World Congress for 2016 is planned for Beijing, China. The goal of spreading the geographic reach of the World Council has been, to a great extent, realized.

Conclusion

The 60th anniversary conference of the CIES, in Vancouver, Canada, brought the link between CIES and WCCES closer again, as Mark Bray, former Secretary-General and President of the World Council, who was elected Vice-President of the CIES in 2014 and became President-Elect in 2015, was its organizer. Thus the relationship of the CIES and the WCCES has grown more complex over the years as more CIES members play a part in the Executive and the Standing Committees. The original thesis of this chapter was that the process of routinization in the establishment of rational and bureaucratic ways of administration had occurred over a long period of time. The founders of the CIES and the

WCCES mainly acted on the basis of their personal qualities and interests. They attracted members to their meetings and to their professional activities. Over the years, the processes of organizational development took over, and personal attributes and relationships lessened in importance. The structure of each organization and its increasing complexity gave each a form of stability which, it is hoped, will cause it to endure.

References

Comparative Education Society/Comparative and International Education Society. *Newsletters*. CIES Collection, Special Collections and Archives. Kent State University, Ohio.

Comparative Education Society/Comparative and International Education Society. *Presidential Correspondence Files*. CIES Collection, Department of Special Collections and Archives, Kent State University Library, Kent State University, Ohio.

Epstein, Erwin H. 2007. "The World Council at the Turn of the Turbulent 80s." In Vandra Masemann, Mark Bray, & Maria Manzon, eds. *Common Interests, Uncommon Goals: Histories of the World Council of Comparative Education Societies and its Members*. CERC Studies in Comparative Education 21. Hong Kong: Comparative Education Research Centre, The University of Hong Kong, and Dordrecht: Springer, pp. 20-32.

Gerth, H.H., & C. Wright Mills. 1958. *From Max Weber: Essays in Sociology*. New York: Oxford University Press.

Gu Mingyuan, & Gui Qin. 2007. "The Chinese Comparative Education Society (CCES)." In Vandra Masemann, Mark Bray, & Maria Manzon, eds. *Common Interests, Uncommon Goals: Histories of the World Council of Comparative Education Societies and its Members*. CERC Studies in Comparative Education 21. Hong Kong: Comparative Education Research Centre, The University of Hong Kong, and Dordrecht: Springer, pp. 225-239.

Hickling-Hudson, Anne. 2007. "Improving Transnational Networking for Social Justice." In Vandra Masemann, Mark Bray, & Maria Manzon, eds. *Common Interests, Uncommon Goals: Histories of the World Council of Comparative Education Societies and its Members*. CERC Studies in Comparative Education 21. Hong Kong: Comparative Education Research Centre, The University of Hong Kong, and Dordrecht: Springer, pp. 69-82.

Lawson, Robert. 1966-70. *Comparative and International Education Society of Canada, Founding Papers*, CIESC Archives.

Lawson, Robert. 1969-1975. *Comparative and International Education Society of Canada [including WCCES Origins]. Correspondence*. CIESC Archives.

Majhanovich, Suzanne, & Lanlin Zhang. 2007. "The Comparative and International Education Society of Canada (CIESC)." In Masemann, Vandra,

Mark Bray, & Maria Manzon, eds. 2007. *Common Interests, Uncommon Goals: Histories of the World Council of Comparative Education Societies and its Members*. CERC Studies in Comparative Education 21. Hong Kong: Comparative Education Research Centre, The University of Hong Kong, and Dordrecht: Springer, pp. 170-182.

Masemann, Vandra, & Erwin H. Epstein 2007. "The World Council from 1970 to 1979." In Vandra Masemann, Mark Bray, & Maria Manzon, eds. *Common Interests, Uncommon Goals: Histories of the World Council of Comparative Education Societies and its Members*. CERC Studies in Comparative Education 21. Hong Kong: Comparative Education Research Centre, The University of Hong Kong, and Dordrecht: Springer, pp. 13-19.

Mitter, Wolfgang 2007. "Turmoil and Progress: 1991-1996." In Vandra Masemann, Mark Bray, & Maria Manzon, eds. *Common Interests, Uncommon Goals: Histories of the World Council of Comparative Education Societies and its Members*. CERC Studies in Comparative Education 21. Hong Kong: Comparative Education Research Centre, The University of Hong Kong, and Dordrecht: Springer, pp. 116-127.

Read, Gerald 1985. "The World Congress of Comparative Education Societies." Mimeo, 6pp.

Wilson, David N. 2007. "From Sydney to Cape Town to Chungbuk: 1996-2001." Vandra Masemann, Mark Bray, & Maria Manzon, eds. *Common Interests, Uncommon Goals: Histories of the World Council of Comparative Education Societies and its Members*. CERC Studies in Comparative Education 21. Hong Kong: Comparative Education Research Centre, The University of Hong Kong, and Dordrecht: Springer, pp. 62-68.

World Council of Comparative Education Societies, 1970. *Proceedings of the First World Congress of Comparative Education Societies*. WCCES: Ottawa.

Intellectual Currents

7
Shaping the Intellectual Landscape

José Cossa

The shape of the intellectual landscape of any given scholarly field can be attributed to a variety of factors, not least of which are the thoughts and acts of its early leaders. In this chapter, I focus on the role played by some early editors of the *Comparative Education Review* (*CER*).

Cook, Hite, and Epstein (2004) argue that:

> Although we value epistemological analysis, we believe that a field's contours and boundaries are best discerned through assessing the thoughts and actions of the field's practitioners. Those who seek to alter comparative education cannot do so on their own; they must convince other comparativists of the need for change. (125)

Following Cook et al.'s argument, I contend that *CER* editors have played a critical role in shaping the intellectual landscape of the field of Comparative and International Education (henceforth referred to as "the field"). Perspectives about how a field is influenced, and how boundaries and contours are established, are shaped by how comparativists think about educational research and practice.

Until 1994, the *Review*'s volumes had been produced by staffs headed by a single editor: George Z.F. Bereday with 27 issues (June 1957-1964 and 1966), Hu Chang-tu with three issues (1965), Harold J. Noah with 13 issues (1967-February 1971), Andreas M. Kazamias with 22 issues (June 1971-1978), Philip G. Altbach with 36 issues (1979-1988), Erwin H. Epstein with 40 issues (1989-1998), and John N. Hawkins with 20 issues

Erwin H. Epstein (ed.) (2016): *Crafting a Global Field: Six Decades of the Comparative and International Education Society*. Hong Kong: Comparative Education Research Centre (CERC), The University of Hong Kong, and Dordrecht: Springer. © CERC

(1999-2003). For these early editors, ample files exist in the Comparative and International Education Society (CIES) Archive at Kent State University only for Bereday, Altbach and Epstein, and I therefore examine the correspondence for these editors alone, except for a brief description of Noah's editorship as a transition between Bereday and Kazamias.

This chapter seeks to understand how Bereday, Altbach and Epstein, who collectively produced more than 100 issues of the *Review*, contributed to shaping the intellectual landscape of the field. It does so by scrutinizing their editorial correspondence, without neglecting their editorials. Furthermore, the chapter addresses variations in the rejection modes of these *CER* Editors. The goal, then, is to inform the Comparative and International Education community about how perceptions reflected in such correspondence can influence the field's landscape, particularly as displayed in epistemological propensities and individual preferences regarding methods of research, and in what constitutes critical subject matter in the field.

Methodology

Hill (1993) claims that "clues to the temporal rhythm of an individual's domestic work and professional chores may be uncovered in letters written to friends, colleagues, and relatives" (60) and cautions against 'concealment channels' in that "an author inadvertently (or purposefully!) might carry concealment to an extreme, such that letters never sent to their intended recipients reside now in an archive to be misframed by us as communications" (66). In this study, I established validity by means of two main stages of hermeneutical inquiry, i.e., internal and external criticism. *External criticism*, which is also known as lower criticism, is a tool used by historians and exegetes to determine the validity of a document, particularly a document with some sort of historical significance. It is the first of two stages of inquiry and pursues inquiry regarding (a) authorship; (b) originality and accuracy of copy; and (c) the nature of errors. *Internal criticism*, which is also known as higher criticism, is the stage of inquiry in which the researcher engages with the meaning of the text rather than the external elements of the document. More than in external criticism, engaging in internal criticism requires domain specific knowledge. In this stage, the researcher and exegete engage in *positive criticism*, which attempts to restore the meaning of statements, and *negative criticism*, which places doubt on what external and positive criticism have established as reasonable findings. Here the researcher and exegete combat both *aesogesis*, i.e., reading unintended meaning into text, and untrustworthiness. While positive criticism simply attempts to ascertain what the text means by analyzing its statements within a context, i.e., literary, historical, geographical, etc., in negative criticism, the historian (a) conducts tests of competence; (b) identifies gossip, humor and slander; (c) identifies myths, legends and traditions; (d) conducts tests of truthfulness; and, (e) discredits statements.

I scrutinized editors' correspondence files and employed the conceptual historical method, as described by Leedy (1997), by assessing the impact of an idea or concept on perceptions. Cropley and Harris (2004) argue that the conceptual historical method is used to research the history of concepts, since ideas and concepts can influence people and events. For Leedy and Ormrod (2001), this method is distinct from conventional historical research in that its focus is on the description of ideas and their dynamics rather than on the description and interpretation of events. Hence, this research focuses on the dynamics of perceptions displayed in editors' correspondence found in the Comparative and International Education (CIES) Archive, located in the Special Collections Department of the Kent State University Libraries.

Findings and Discussion
Bereday (June 1957-1964 and 1966)
Bereday (Teachers College, Columbia University) played a key role in the creation of the *CER*. Other key players were Gerald Read (Kent State), Kenneth Holland (Institute of International Education), William Johnson (University of Pittsburg), and Harold Benjamin (George Peabody College for Teachers). Bereday's choice of Editorial Board members as well as associate and contributing editors extended beyond scholars from North America to those in Europe. As the pioneer editor, Bereday had autonomy in deciding what articles got published in the *CER*. Furthermore, most of Bereday's decisions seem haphazard as they were sometimes guided by an emotional leaning towards the author (e.g., someone he liked, knew or knew someone in the person's immediate intellectual circle); at times based on epistemological preference, particularly in regards to what he deemed appropriate methods and analysis; and, at times it was hard to tell whether his decisions were based on space constraints (e.g., when another article addressing the same region or

country was already accepted for publication in an upcoming issue) or on not liking what he read. Bereday's early decision-making practice may have also been the result of the fact that the Board of Editors was only created in the *CER*'s third year of existence. Nonetheless, this autonomy might have allowed him to define the field in his own way.

It is evident in the correspondence that he intended to nurture a field that is "empirical scientific", characterized by cross-national comparisons and with "adequate scholarly analysis". Such intention led him to coordinate, along with Read, visits to foreign countries and to instruct travelers to take notes in order to get them published in the *CER*, though not necessarily by the travelers themselves. Travelers should "concentrate on presenting eyewitness point by point accounts which will be respected as vital primary sources by more specialized scholars" (Bereday 1958a). In other words, unless they were deemed "more specialized scholars," they would only serve as field data collectors. The concept of "more specialized scholars" is evidence that Bereday and Reed had conceptualized a hierarchy of scholarship for the field. Given Bereday's emphasis on the importance of research methods, the key criterion for reaching a high level of scholarship would best be characterized by requiring methodological expertise viewed as scientific by Bereday and his intellectual allies.

Bereday's intellectual preference is reflected in both his association with like-minded people, as evidenced by his invitations to Joseph Lauwerys and Robert Ulich to submit papers for publication in the first CER issue, and his decisions to accept and reject manuscripts. The rejection of one manuscript (Bereday 1958b) on the basis that "it was not comparative enough" is evidence of how the journal starts to referee materials submitted and, in some way, starts to shape the comparative nature of the field. Nonetheless, Bereday's preference for some sort of methodological rigor as against simple description was not without exceptions or, at times, an apparent uncertainty about rejecting descripttion altogether, or to accommodating descriptions based on some random criterion. His request for an article from Walter Merk (Bereday 1957a), University of Hamburg, that would describe the work in Comparative Education at Hamburg or "to write on any comparative subject that you feel disposed to treat, such as the recent developments in German education as a whole, or description of the present work in pedagogy at the university level, or a good overview of the work of the Volkschule, or some such" seems counter-intuitive to Bereday's foundational argument when rejecting or accepting articles for publication in the CER.

In 1960, in a letter to John Searles (Bereday 1960a) pertaining to his potential article, "Assessing Education in Newly-Developing Countries," Bereday urged that the awaited article for revision should not deal exclusively with one country. On the other hand, the rejection of one manuscript (Bereday 1958c), "Training of Technicians in England," was on technical merits rather than its one-country focus, i.e., the rejection was on the basis that it was entirely unsupported by references as well as its inadequate and (at times) careless writing of the theme. As such, Bereday seemed to show bias in favor of certain country-studies over others. For instance, he rejected a manuscript (Bereday 1959a) on the basis that the article is unsuitable for *CER*: "Its contents are exhortatory while Comparative Education as now understood deals with facts and the analysis of facts. As this article is addressed to Nigerians I feel it should be published in Nigeria." Bereday (1959b) rejected a manuscript, "The Struggle Against the Brazilian Public School," on the basis that it "having been written for the Brazilian audience it is naturally more exhortative in nature.... we are interested in descriptive and analytical article [sic].... we are particularly keen to have articles which apply the methods of social science or liberal art to education." On the other hand, Bereday (1960b) requested that Fabre-Luce write his "comments on the recent church and state dispute on the subject of French education" for publication, noting that such publication would make him "overjoyed". Other one-country studies that Bereday seemed happy to consider for publication were on England by Edmund King (Bereday 1960c); one on Italy by Lamberto Bhorghi (Bereday 1960d) of the University of Florence, commissioned by Bereday, and another on that country (Bereday 1960e); one on a university in Moscow by Burton Rubin (Bereday 1960f); and one potential study on Pakistan by John Owen (Bereday 1959c), of which his only reluctance was that a "survey of the overall problem of Pakistani education" may not fit the short space allocated for articles.

Bereday (1959d) rejected conditionally a manuscript on Bolivia – sponsored by William T. Meyer, Dean of the Division of Graduate Studies at Adams State University – on the basis that it is "completely descriptive". In Bereday's words, "Comparative Education uses descriptive statements if concerned with more analytical treatment of education and its problems." Here Bereday displays a standard to accommodate a certain level of description, provided it pairs-up with analysis. Bereday's advice to Richard R. Renner (Bereday 1960g) to submit a manuscript about his college program seemed a radical accommodation leading to the eventual acceptance of ideographic, and largely descriptive, studies.

Bereday's (1959e) rejection of a manuscript, "The Role of the Educated Man in a Free Society," on the basis that the "CER deals by and large with education in foreign countries" presents a seeming contradiction, or at least some evasiveness, in regards to the field's geographic scope. He (Bereday 1959f) rejected a manuscript, "The Background Culture," on the basis that "we are interested in the treatment of countries other than the United States"; rejected a manuscript, "The Persian Culture," on the basis that "such studies would have to be much more closely related to how an education system reflects the character or its people" (Bereday 1959g); and rejected a manuscript, "United Nations University Centers: A Proposal to Extend International Educational Understanding Through Education," on the basis that "this article deals with a proposal for the future, rather than an example of present day educational system" (Bereday 1959h).

The justifications used to reject these articles are not altogether consistent. One is not sure if Bereday's concern with a proposal for the future, for instance, is a concern based on the fact that it is hard, if not impossible, to analyze the future or if it is merely a random rejection, since futuristic studies can be based on analysis of present-day educational systems.

Bereday (1960h) rejected one manuscript on the basis that "it is almost a chronology... yet your paper is serious, scholarly, and well written ... it seems better that I commission you to write an article for us on Rumanian education past and present, with emphasis on the present." Here he seems to lean more towards the idea that a single country paper needs to be more thorough in terms of critical analysis and historical background; if a general report, it would be more appropriate to target readers interested in Eastern Europe overall than a single country. Further evidence of apparent arbitrariness can be seen in the rejection of a manuscript on the "comparison of Texas children" (Bereday 1959i), because "its length and somewhat informal treatment makes it unsuitable" for the *CER*, and rejection of another manuscript as purely historical (Bereday 1959j).

Inconsistencies in review feedback raise suspicions of arbitrariness, yet one is able to gauge a sense of Bereday's intention to gain academic respect for the *CER* by applying a standard worthy of being considered a "scientific journal". Another revealing review is the rejection of DL's article, "A Note on the Relevance of the Sociology of Knowledge" (Bereday 1964a) based on a reviewer's passionate objection. While the analysis of the sociological conceptualizations of "classification-oriented" and "action-oriented" might have appealed thematically to Bereday, his rejection seems to have been tied to his strategy to enhance the scientific nature of the field and the *CER*.

Some letters reveal a remarkable power dynamic between editor and author. In Bereday's energetic rejection of a manuscript on "Native Education in Sub-Saharan Africa" (Bereday 1960i), he berates the author for "your inexperience in dealing with editors" as displayed by her/his "rather unbelievable letter of August 3rd ..." Bereday had pointed out that the author had written on Africa without ever having been there. In response, the author contended that "the article is based on official documents and backed by the African Project at the Center for International Studies at MIT."

One can characterize Bereday's editorial tenure as a search for a clear method for the field, enhancing the quality of articles by complying with method requirements, and an editorial team that exhibited strong ties in a club-like fashion and a leaning at times toward arrogant scholarship: in rejecting manuscripts, comments would occasionally be demeaning rather than constructive. However, Bereday's concern with method became increasingly more flexible, as reflected in some of his later years' responses (Bereday 1964b, 1964c).

In a eulogy for Bereday, Philip Altbach (1983a) described Bereday as one whose strengths included "a commitment to reflect a broader parameter of the field rather than to shape the journal in the image of one scholarly approach or ideology." If this statement was accurate about Bereday's latter years as an editor, it can be attributed to a long journey from a rigid stance on what he considered to be adequate methodology to an understanding that the field was bigger than his commitment to specific methods he deemed empirical scientific.

Altbach (1979-1988)

To put the review process on a more systematic and objective footing, Altbach adopted a "Manuscript Evaluation Form," which contained instructions for reviewers to type their evaluations, sign, and date (Altbach 1983b). While Altbach's tenure cannot be characterized as driven by methodological orthodoxy, it shows a continued effort to root the journal in methodological rigor and introduces a more robust theoretical layer. Altbach's editorship seemed more concerned than in the past with structure (e.g., length of articles) and somewhat with a concern for data interpretation and presentation.

By the time of Altbach's editorship, the *CER*'s Editorial Board was to be nominated by the editor and approved by the CIES Board of Directors, strengthening the relationship between the Society and the journal (Altbach 1978). This practice enhanced diversity in gender and specialization in terms of region and methodology, Altbach's Board comprised the following members: Erwin Epstein, University of Missouri at Rolla, specialist on Latin America and Sociology; Hans Weiler, Stanford University, specialist on Africa and Political Science; Vandra Masemann, Ontario Institute for Studies in Education (OISE), specialist on Africa and Anthropology; Remi Clignet, Northwestern University, specialist on Africa and Sociology; Rolland Paulston, University of Pittsburgh, specialist on Europe; Douglas Windham, University of Chicago, specialist on Latin America and Economics; Ursula Springer, Brooklyn College, specialist on Europe; John Hawkins, UCLA, specialist on China and East Asia; and, Joseph Farrell, OISE, specialist on Latin America and Planning.

Epstein (1988-1998)

Epstein presented the most explicit criteria until that point for evaluating manuscripts. He announced that the following elements need to be present in order for an article to be published in the *CER*: (a) originality, (b) relevance to Comparative Education, (c) use of data, (d) clarity of expression, and (e) contribution to the advancement of knowledge. As an example, Epstein rejected the manuscript, "The Impact of Impact: A Study of the Dissemination of an Educational Innovation in Six Countries," on the grounds that (a) it lacked objectivity; (b) was a-theoretical, i.e., "authors need to drench themselves in theory"; and (c) was limited to functionalist case studies. His letter of rejection stated that "we believe that your material is interesting and relevant to the field, but it is not theoretically well grounded as it should be" (Epstein 1989a).

Epstein introduced double-blind peer reviews. Evidence of the difficulty in holding to this procedure is found in a letter from Gail Kelly to Epstein of November 14, 1989 (Kelly 1989), raising issue with the mistake that a reviewer's name had been left on the manuscript and Epstein's acknowledgement to Kelly and to the author in the rejection letter of November 17, 1989 (Epstein 1989b). In addition to blind peer reviews and review criteria comprising theoretical and methodological clarity, there was a shift toward including more articles on gender and inclusion of women in the editorial and review teams. In particular, a special issue guest edited by Joel Samoff during Epstein's tenure had diversity at the core of its criteria (Samoff 1990), as exemplified by the expectation that articles be diverse in authorship, geographical focus, substantive concern, theoretical or empirical mix, and analytical approach. One shortcoming in this particular issue, however, was in regards to diversity in the list of reviewers, as all of them were California educators – Nelly Stromquist, University of Southern California; Richard Fagen, Stanford University; and, Joaquim Samayoa, Stanford University.

Epstein's rejection letters display an emphasis on the importance of "prevailing comparative theory and perspectives," exemplified in his comments on an accepted manuscript titled, "Transfer of Knowledge in Educational Innovation: A Case Study of Curricular Reform in Brazil." When reviewers varied in their application of the criteria for strong theory and research methods, Epstein exercised subjective decision-making in accepting or rejecting manuscripts, as editors of scholarly journals conventionally do. For instance, in a letter to Young Pai (Epstein 1988), a reviewer, Epstein notes that Pai's unfavorable review of "Education for Authentic African Development" was not consistent with that of other reviewers, yet he decided to reject the article because Pai's review was more credible and reflected a leaning toward high standards for the *CER*.

Prior to becoming the editor of *CER*, Epstein (1983) had engaged the issue of ideology, as it relates to inherent epistemological and ontological orientations, in comparative and international education by calling into question the extent to which comparativists are willing and able to problematize theories and methods employed in comparative research. Later, Epstein (Epstein 1998) observed that, when positivism permeated the field as a dominant epistemology, endorsing positivism meant that only statements about education that were considered empirical were scientific. He warned that much theory and adequate research could be neglected in favor of a range of quantitative methods deemed more scientific. Given that Epstein had strong positivistic tendencies early in his career, his caveat against taking an extremist stance in the field augured an eclectic epistemological orientation for the journal.

Conclusion

Cook et al. (2004) claim that boundaries are indispensable for any field because lack of such would undercut teaching the field to new generations, engaging in meaningful discourse about the field, and ensuring appropriate scholarly material in journals and other fora. Bereday's contribution was critical in that it drove scholars to think about how the field was to be conceptualized. His tenure set a platform to force scholars to engage in discourse to shape how future scholars were to view research in the field as well as launch *CER* as a reputable scholarly journal. While one may not agree with the idea of "scientific" as being solely quantitative, and even more so statistically grounded, and while acknowledging that his tenure was marked by a subjective and club-like decision-making process, his influence is to be appreciated for having laid the foundation for defining the field as distinct from other fields in education. The subjectivity and club-like gathering of like-minded scholars on the editorial board and review network are perhaps justifiable in the context of a time when there was scant knowledge about the field.

Later editors built on the foundation laid by Bereday. Altbach shifted towards influencing the field via a structured approach to assessing manuscripts. This structured review process seems to have been a reaction to the absence of a clearly defined structure in the past for reviewing manuscripts. Thus, Kazamias' files show original edits on manuscripts under review, but the files, scarce as they are, contain no review forms. The creation of a more structured process might have inspired reviewers to think more carefully about the field and to influence it (intentionally or unintentionally) in a much clearer way. Noah's stance on comparative analysis is characterized by an emphasis on the need to establish generalizations that can apply across contexts (Noah 1988; Noah & Eckstein 1969). Marginson and Mollis (2001) argue that Noah provided revealing insight into positivism and charge him with holding a position that constitutes a "clear statement of the homogenizing effects of positivism, its deep desire to mirror the natural sciences, and its deliberate occlusion of national specificities and the dynamics of difference" (592). Thus, Noah's editorship amplified Bereday's commitment to a rather rigid methodology that he deemed scientific. Indeed, Nordtveit (see his chapter in this book) and Silova and Brehm (2010, 24) argue that "the principles of 'scientific rationality' increasingly became more visible in the journal's publications" under Noah.

By contrast, the archival documentation suggests that Epstein's was the most influential post-Bereday editorship among the single-editor editorships. Epstein's influence was undoubtedly aided by the fact that he produced more issues than the others. He stood on the threshold of methodological eclecticism and promoted the indispensable role of theory, thus launching a definition of the field as an application of theories and methods from history and the social sciences. What Bereday aimed to achieve through a rather rigid methodological approach to educational issues, Epstein achieved through the insistent inclusion of comparative context and the application of cogent theories and methods.

Since Epstein's tenure, the field has changed considerably. Yet his influence is still prevalent, notwithstanding current tendencies toward a less strict theoretical and methodological grounding in favor of more pragmatic applications of educational solutions to educational and development issues, showing that Epstein's eclecticism has its limits. Epstein had a deep appreciation for Bereday's creative genius, yet nevertheless reacted against Bereday's methodological narrowness, at least as displayed in the early years of Bereday's editorship, in stressing the "scientific" approach as an indispensable condition for acceptance into the field's network of reputable scholars.

Archived Correspondence and Documents Cited

Altbach, Philip. 27 October 1983a. "Eulogy for George Z. Bereday." *Comparative and International Education Records. Kent State University Libraries. Box 1. Special Collections and Archives*.

Altbach, Philip. 1 July 1983b. "Letter to W. Acherman." *Comparative and International Education Records. Kent State University Libraries. Box 8, folder 21. Special Collections and Archives*.

Bereday, George Z.F. 17 August 1959a. "Letter to A. A. C. E." *Comparative and International Education Records. Kent State University Libraries. Box 1. Special Collections and Archives*.

—. 19 January 1959e. "Letter to AB." *Comparative and International Education Records. Kent State University Libraries. Box 1. Special Collections and Archives*.

—. 24 July 1959h. "Letter to AB." *Comparative and International Education Records. Kent State University Libraries. Box 1. Special Collections and Archives*.

—. 5 January 1960b. "Letter to AF." *Comparative and International Education Records. Kent State University Libraries. Box 1. Special Collections and Archives*.

—. 21 September 1960f. "Letter to Burton Rubin." *Comparative and International Education Records. Kent State University Libraries. Box 1. Special Collections and Archives.*

—. 22 September 1958c. "Letter to CA." *Comparative and International Education Records. Kent State University Libraries. Box 1. Special Collections and Archives.*

—. 5 October 1964a. "Letter to DL." *Comparative and International Education Records. Kent State University Libraries. Box 1. Special Collections and Archives.*

—. 15 January 1960c. "Letter to Edmond King." *Comparative and International Education Records. Kent State University Libraries. Box 1. Special Collections and Archives.*

—. October 1958a. "Letter to Gerald Read." *Comparative and International Education Records. Kent State University Libraries. Special Collections and Archives.*

—. 8 September 1964b. "Letter to GR." *Comparative and International Education Records. Kent State University Libraries. Box 1, folder 12Special Collections and Archives.*

—. 5 August 1960i. "Letter to HS." *Comparative and International Education Records. Kent State University Libraries. Box 1. Special Collections and Archives.*

—. 3 July 1959j. "Letter to JE." *Comparative and International Education Records. Kent State University Libraries. Box 1. Special Collections and Archives.*

—. 15 May 1959f. "Letter to JF." *Comparative and International Education Records. Kent State University Libraries. Box 1. Special Collections and Archives.*

—. 6 October 1958b. "Letter to JKF." *Comparative and International Education Records. Kent State University Libraries. Box 1. Special Collections and Archives.*

—. 20 October 1959c. "Letter to John Owen." *Comparative and International Education Records. Kent State University Libraries. Box 1. Special Collections and Archives.*

—. 28 November 1960a. "Letter to John Searles." *Comparative and International Education Records. Kent State University Libraries. Box 1. Special Collections and Archives.*

—. 10 April 1959i. "Letter to JS." *Comparative and International Education Records. Kent State University Libraries. Box 1. Special Collections and Archives.*

—. 1960d. "Letter to Lamber Bhorghi." *Comparative and International Education Records. Kent State University Libraries. Box 1. Special Collections and Archives.*

—. 22 February 1960e. "Letter to MB." *Comparative and International Education Records. Kent State University Libraries. Box 1. Special Collections and Archives.*

—. 7 January 1957b. "Letter to MG." *Comparative and International Education Records. Kent State University Libraries. Box 1. Special Collections and Archives.*

—. 25 August 1959d. "Letter to MR." *Comparative and International Education Records. Kent State University Libraries. Box 1. Special Collections and Archives.*

—. 15 July 1959g. "Letter to PO." *Comparative and International Education Records. Kent State University Libraries. Box 1. Special Collections and Archives.*

—. 31 May 1960h. "Letter to RF." *Comparative and International Education Records. Kent State University Libraries. Box 1. Special Collections and Archives.*

—. 21 March 1960g. "Letter to Richard R. Renner." *Comparative and International Education Records. Kent State University Libraries. Box 1. Special Collections and Archives.*

—. n.d. "Letter to Robert Ulich." *Comparative and International Education Records. Kent State University Libraries. Box 1. Special Collections and Archives.*

—. 2 June 1964c. "Letter to RW." *Comparative and International Education Records. Kent State University Libraries. Box 1. Special Collections and Archives.*

—. 19 October 1959b. "Letter to SK." *Comparative and International Education Records. Kent State University Libraries. Box 1. Special Collections and Archives.*

—. 20 November 1957a. "Letter to Walter Merk." *Comparative and International Education Records. Kent State University Libraries. Box 1. Special Collections and Archives.*

Epstein, Erwin H. n.d. "Letter to David Plank." *Comparative and International Education Records. Kent State University Libraries. Box 21:B. Special Collections and Archives.*

—. 17 November 1989b. "Letter to Gail Kelly." *Comparative and International Education Records. Kent State University Libraries. Special Collections and Archives.*

—.27 June 1989a. "Letter to TL." *Comparative and International Education Records. Kent State University Libraries. Special Collections and Archives.*

—. 29 September 1988. "Letter to Young Pai." *Comparative and International Education Records. Kent State University Libraries. Box 22, Folder 34. Special Collections and Archives.*

Kelly, Gail. 14 November 1989. "Letter to Erwin H. Epstein." *Comparative and International Education Records. Kent State University Libraries. Special Collections and Archives.*

Kent State University Archives. "Comparative Education Review, Editors' Files." *CIES Records: Series 1.*

Paulson, Roland. 21 March 1978. "Letter to Philip Altbach." *Comparative and International Education Records. Kent State University Libraries. Box 8, folder 21. Special Collections and Archives.*

Samoff, Joel. 15 February 1990. "Comparative Education Review Special Issue." *Comparative and International Education Records. Kent State University Libraries. Special Collections and Archives.*

References

Cook, Bradley J., Steven J. Hite, & Erwin H. Epstein. 2004. "Discerning Trends, Contours, and Boundaries in Comparative Education: A Survey of Comparativists and Their Literature." *Comparative Education Review 48*(2): 123-149.

Cropley, D.C., & M.B. Harris. 2004. "Too hard, too soft, just right ... Goldilocks and three research paradigms in SE." *Fourteenth Annual International Symposium of the International Council on Systems Engineering.* Toulouse, France.

Epstein, Erwin H. 1983. "Currents Left and Right: Ideology in Comparative Education." *Comparative Education Review* 27(1): 3-29.

Epstein, Erwin H. 1998. "The Problematic Meaning of 'Comparison' in Comparative Education." In K. Kempner, M. Mollis & W. Tiernay, eds. *Comparative Education.* New York: Simon & Schuster, pp. 31-40.

Hill, Michael R. 1993. *Archival Strategies and Techniques: Qualitative Research Methods Series.* Vol. 31. Thousand Oaks, California: Sage Publications.

Leedy, Paul D. 1997. *Practical Research: Planning and Design.* 6th edition. Upper Saddle River, NJ: Prentice-Hall.

Leedy, Paul D. & J.E. Ormrod. 2001. *Practical Research Planning and Design.* New Jersey, NJ: Merrill Prentice-Hall.

Marginson, Simon & Marcela Mollis. 2001. "The door opens and the tiger leaps: Theories and Reflexivities of Comparative Education for a Global Millennium." *Comparative Education Review* 45(4): 581-615.

8
The Comparative Education Review

Bjørn H. NORDTVEIT

The launch of a new journal

The first headline in the *Comparative Education Review (CER)*, "A new journal in comparative education," appeared just four months ahead of the Soviet Union's launch of Sputnik 1, the world's first artificial satellite. The quasi-simultaneous takeoff of the Sputnik and the *CER* was coincidental, but the impact of the former would be conspicuous in the latter for over 15 years to come. The post-World War II rise of the Soviet Union stirred U.S. worries of being "left behind" in the sciences and mathematics, and led to increased interest in comparative education as a field of research and as a perceived necessary part of educators' training.

In line with these needs, the *CER* was launched as an outlet for research and as a resource for teaching comparative education. William Brickman, author of the aforementioned headline, was President of the Comparative Education Society (CES) in 1957 and summarized the *raison d'être* of the *CER* as follows:

> Professors, students, and others who work in this area will now have a regular, systematic publication containing up-to-date information and interpretative analysis of educational developments and problems all over the world.... It [also] aspires to be a clearing house of basic data and resources for the effective teaching of comparative education in the colleges and universities (Brickman 1957, 1).

Brickman had since 1954 gathered annually at the New York University with a group of people "interested in the teaching of Comparative

Erwin H. Epstein (ed.) (2016): *Crafting a Global Field: Six Decades of the Comparative and International Education Society*. Hong Kong: Comparative Education Research Centre (CERC), The University of Hong Kong, and Dordrecht: Springer. © CERC

Education" (Johnson 1957, 16), and at its third meeting, in 1956, the CES was formed. In a very real sense the birth of the journal accompanied that of the Society; the two were interrelated institutions. Elizabeth Sherman Swing, a student of Brickman, noted that the creation of the journal was discussed by William Brickman, David Scanlon, George Bereday and William Johnson "on April 25, 1957, a few months after the first annual meeting [of the Society]." The first issue appeared in June that same year "with George Bereday as Editor and Gerald Read as Business Editor" (Swing 2006, 4).

George Z.F. Bereday, whose editorship lasted from 1957 to 1966, played a key role in the formative years of the journal. In Philip G. Altbach's words:

> No one has had as much influence in shaping this journal and in making it an internationally respected voice for a field of inquiry.... [Bereday] encouraged both established scholars and novices to write for the journal and provided an outlet for scholarship of different viewpoints and perspectives. The Review has been marked by an eclecticism and by a willingness to publish new and sometimes controversial ideas. One of its strengths has been a commitment to reflect the broad parameters of the field rather than to shape the journal in the image of one scholarly approach or ideology (1984, 6).

A strength and perhaps the *niche* of the journal was − and still is − this effort to publish new and controversial pieces, and also to accept papers from students and practitioners in comparative and international education as well as from established scholars from all over the world. Other important policies of the *CER* included Bereday's hallmark "effort to make scholarship relevant to broader issues of educational theory and practice" (Altbach 1984, 6). In the present day, authors are still encouraged to submit "Studies that have a command not only of the relevant literature but place the topic at hand into broader debates within the field" (*CER* Website).

In addition to publication of comparative and international education research pieces, a key feature of the journal consists of regular reviews of publications in the field. In Vol. 1(1) appeared an article titled "A note on textbooks in comparative education" (Bereday 1957, 3). Later, Bereday would systematically review papers and books in his editorials. In 1960, a special issue made by the Comparative Education Center at the

University of Chicago contained short reference lists on "Recent Books of Interest to Comparative Educators" and "Recent Articles of Interest to Comparative Educators." The former contained 23 references and the latter 27. The effort evolved into a yearly bibliography, with over 3,000 references in a recent addition. Also, each *CER* issue still contains reviews of recent books and media reviews.

In view of the exponential growth of knowledge production and publication in the field (as evidenced by the aforementioned increase in the size of the annual bibliographies), the *CER* has remained remarkably stable. Already in 1984 (p. 6), Altbach wrote, "Journals are fragile enterprises," and attributed the success of the *CER* to "scholarly quality and relevance." In an ever-expanding field, its success may more modestly lie in authors', readers' and peer reviewers' trust in the journal as an outlet of research and a source for information.

CER management

On January 25, 1957, a noteworthy exchange between Bereday and Gerald Read took place, setting the stage for the future journal:

> My dear Gerald,
>
> I want to report what I have done to date as regards our quarterly publication, which you have asked me to edit. 1) I have tentatively arranged with Teachers College Publications Bureau to have this printed for us ... 3) I should like to call this publication Comparative Education Review, even though it is a small publication. It would be thus possible to retain the same letter and title format when we switch to a magazine. I was advised that Newsletter would not sound well. 4) I should like to ask you, if at all possible, to use your already established machinery for mailing purposes. I would ship to you every three months a postal parcel containing 250 or 300 copies of the Review.... What are your and Bill's (Dr. W.W. Brickman) reactions to these proposals. [sic] I am sending Bill a copy of this letter.
>
> Yours ever, George Bereday.
>
> (Bereday 1963, 3).

The journal's name was thus set at its conception, but instead of being a quarterly, it first appeared three times a year (June, October and February). Since it was launched in June, Volume 1 covered 1957 (2 issues) and 1958 (1 issue); Volume 2 covered 1958 (2 issues) and 1959 (1 issue) and so forth. This was changed in 1964, which saw four issues (1 issue of Volume 7 and 3 of Volume 8). The pattern with 3 issues per volume, and each volume covering one calendar year continued until 1984 (Volume 28) when the CER moved to a quarterly "to publish a larger number of articles and to plan occasional theme-based issues" (Altbach 1984, 10). The journal was at first self-published, and its launch was made possible by private subsidies (Bereday 1958).

The first issue of the *CER* contained a "draft" of the "aims of the Society" (Johnson 1957, 16), but the CES was still at that time without a formal constitution. This latter only appeared in Vol. 3(2) of the journal, and institutionalized the function of *CER's* relationship with the Society insomuch as Article V.1 promulgated that "The Society shall publish a professional journal which shall be distributed to members without further cost other than membership dues" (Read 1959, 40). Further, the Constitution ratified *post hoc* the editor's place on the Society's Board of Directors and on its Executive Committee, as an "appointed executive officer" ... "responsible to the Board of Directors for the publication of the Society's professional Journal" (Section 3; Read 1959, 39).

The international aspect of the journal was visible from the beginning, not only in its content, but also in its authorship, readers, and Editorial Board. Concerning this last, Brickman noted with a trace of humor that of the three first editors, George Z.F. Bereday, Harold J. Noah, and Andreas M. Kazamias, "not one of this trio was born in the U.S." He added, "nor should one forget the editorial activity of the China-born Professor C.T. Hu of Teachers College [in] 1961-1962" (Brickman 1977, 400). Bereday actively pursued the institutional internationalization of the journal, and, in addition to American and U.S.-based personalities such as James Bryant Conant (former President of Harvard), and Robert Ulich (then at Harvard), he persuaded Franz Hilker and Friedrich Schneider of Germany, Pedro Rosselló of Switzerland, and Torsten Husén of Sweden to join his Editorial Board (Swing 2007, 100). Bereday thus convened well-known international academics in the field of economics and education to join his team. Torsten Husén stayed on the Editorial Board well beyond Bereday's term. Bereday joined the Editorial Board at the end of his term as editor, and both stayed on until Altbach changed the administrative structure of the *CER,* and, among other changes, turned the Editorial Board into an "Advisory" Board.

During Altbach's editorship (1979-1988), the affiliation with the University of Chicago Press (UCP) was established by Philip Foster. Altbach noted in February 1983 (p. 1) that "Under a new agreement, the University of Chicago Press (UCP) is taking full fiscal responsibility for the Review" whereas "Editorial control remains in the hands of the Comparative and International Education Society." By the end of his editorship, the agreement with UCP was "giving the society a guaranteed financial base" (Epstein 1989, 1).

Erwin H. Epstein's editorship (1989-1998) made the jump into the digital area, with a Web site and an online editorial tracking system:

> The Review now has its own web page, under the supervision of the University of Chicago Press, with plans to include tables of contents. Most important, I assisted technicians at the University of Chicago Press in developing the Journal Office Tracking System (JOTS), a proprietary database software program that allows every phase of the editorial tracking process to be placed on computer. This was a large undertaking, especially during the first 2 years of my editorship, when we established the protocols for our database and refined its operation. With the use of JOTS [Journal Office Tracking System], my successor will have ready access to the records we processed of almost 1,000 manuscripts, about 1,400 manuscript reviews, and more than 1,200 people serving as authors and reviewers (Epstein 1998, 418).

The following editorship, under John Hawkins (1999-2003), expanded the online presence. Also, with an expanding number of submissions, Hawkins made use of co-editors, sharing management responsibilities of the journal. This was a departure from earlier editors. Under the editorships of Bereday (1957-1966), Harold Noah (1967-February 1971), and Andreas Kazamias (June 1971–1978), the *CER* functioned with an editor, associate editor(s), and advisory editors, as well as a business editor (or business manager) and an Editorial Board. The Altbach and Epstein editorships functioned similarly, but still without co-editors.

The David Post (2004-2013) and Bjorn H. Nordtveit (July 2013 – present) editorships further increased the co-editors' role. Hence, David Post and Mark Ginsburg made a combined and successful bid for the *CER* editorship in 2003, and initially shared responsibilities for the journal. A similar system is currently in place, in which the editor shares the editorship with six co-editors (one of whom is specifically in charge of book and media reviews, and another having responsibility for an annual bibliography of the field). Whereas the editor and co-editor team are responsible for the content of the journal, managing editors are in charge of the actual processing of the manuscripts and for keeping the editors "on track."

During the Epstein, Hawkins and Post editorships, many of the current editorial practices were set up. Similarly to other journals, the *CER* uses a combination of editorial selection and peer review. On a rotating basis every month, two of the editors are "on duty," reading all of the manuscripts that are submitted that month. If they agree that a manuscript does not conform to the journal's policies (available on *CER's* web page, under "instruction for authors"), they write a notice to the author(s) explaining the reason for rejecting the manuscript. In 2008, the *CER* shifted to using Editorial Manager software, making paper sub-missions obsolete. With an increasing number of submissions (partially due to costless e-submissions) and increasing pressure for fast turn-around, this pre-selection has become stricter: when the editors are doubtful that a manuscript will make it to the publication stage, it is normally rejected before peer review. Under the former editorship, the editors sent out for peer review about 50 per cent of manuscripts. The current team, prioritizing quicker processing of papers – and taking into consideration peer reviewers for whom time is an increasingly scarce resource – sends out about 25 per cent.

The papers that are not rejected are sent out for double blind peer review. Depending on the peer review, a paper may go forward, i.e., ordinarily upon being revised and re-reviewed, or it may be rejected. If it goes forward, the editor in charge of the manuscript will write a "decision letter" pointing out the needed revisions to be made, based on the peer reviewers' suggestions. The editors' and peer reviewers' decisions aim at making publishing part of a scholarly conversation (even with pieces that are rejected without peer review). Hence, the editors try to provide *all* authors with quality feedback, those whose papers are rejected as well as those who are asked to revise their submission. Presidential addresses (one per year) by tradition are accepted, though subject to revision.

A spatial expedition from Sputnik 1 to Shenzhou 5

Analysis of the content of the *Comparative Education Review* has shown a great deal of diversity as well as shifting connections to debates in the field and to political and societal events at large. Changing thematic, geographic and epistemological foci therefore appear regularly, following societal concerns. Charl C. Wolhuter (2008) in a content analysis of 1,157 articles covering 50 years of the *CER* (1957-2006) demonstrated that the key thematic focus of the first 15 volumes of the journal covered aspects of the education system in the former USSR, reflecting "the interest in the Soviet school system in the cold-war era after the launching of Sputnik" (Wolhuter 2008, 329). Gita Steiner-Khamsi (2006, 21) noted how admiration for the Soviet Union abruptly changed:

> For comparative education researchers in the United States, Soviet education was first an object of admiration, and in the following two decades a counterreference for all that U.S. education was not supposed to be or never wished to become.

Wolhuter demonstrated that the interest of *CER* authors shifted from the USSR to Europe and that in "Volumes 21 to 25, Greece was the focus of more articles than any other country" (2008, 329). The attention to Greece was largely a response to the reestablishment of democracy in that country, and *CER* editor Andreas Kazamias also stimulated contributors' and readers' interest by featuring, in Vol. 22(1), "a symposium on various aspects of the recent reform measures in Greek education" involving "statements by individuals who actually participated in the reform" (Kazamias 1978, 2).

According to Wolhuter, the USA moved into the top geographic position in Volumes 26-45, which he thought might be due to a "trend towards an inward orientation in the post-Vietnam years" (2008, 329). Yet, although North America figured prominently in comparative pieces, single-case studies largely focused on non-U.S. countries, suggesting that Wolhuter's data and interpretation from this period over-estimated the salience of the USA. The focus again moved in the nineties, this time towards a greater attention to South Africa in Volumes 46-50 "as interest grew in the post-1994 societal reconstruction project" (Wolhuter 2008, 329). More recently, writings and publication on Chinese education have increased for multiple reasons, including the country's evolution towards "Socialism with Chinese characteristics," the new ideology of the Chinese Communist Party, and the emergence of Chinese scholars who know

English and have incentives to publish in English-language journals. Similarly to the impact of Sputnik 1 in 1957, the economic performance of China since its "opening up" policies, together with spectacular scientific successes such as the space flight of Yang Liwei in Shenzhou 5 in 2003, as well as the 2008 Summer Olympics, have generated further interest. The current surge of papers *submitted* and published on China is also due to the increasing internationalization of Chinese universities. In this regard, higher education institutions in China (including Hong Kong and Macau) have a double goal: attracting high-caliber international faculty and students who are encouraged to publish in international journals such as the *CER*, and many Chinese institutions attach monetary prizes to faculty who publish in these journals.

Geographic areas of interest for *CER* contributors also include Latin America and especially Mexico. Some regions, such as the Middle East (with the exception of Israel), are conspicuously absent (or nearly absent) from a journal that is otherwise proud of its diversity. The "Arab Spring" and its aftermath will perhaps lead to more scholarly interest and knowledge production related to that particular geographic area. *CER*'s various editorial teams have as a matter of policy tried to maintain and even enhance the journals' representation of geographical diversity, while at the same time preserving its reputation for quality and fairness in consideration of *all* manuscripts submitted regardless of their region of origin.

Epistemological excursions

At the same time as seeking geographic diversity, the *CER* also has a historic reputation of seeking pieces with epistemological diversity. One of Brickman's trademarks, a "vision for a vibrant epistemological diversity of the field" (Silova & Brehm 2010, 24), was largely implemented by Bereday. The epistemological foundation of comparative education has been the subject of much debate. The first issue of *CER* contained an article on philosophy of education, "An Educational Philosopher Looks at Comparative Education" (McClellan 1957), and Bereday himself contributed a piece on "Some Discussion of Methods in Comparative Education," where he discussed the distinction between single-case and "comparative" approaches. The former, which he called "area studies in comparative education," were characterized as "not only legitimate but indispensable." The latter, "comparative branch of the discipline is of necessity more complex and hence rare" and could be divided into two types, the "total approach," or "the comparison of the total socio-educational system," and the "problem approach," which "takes one aspect, one part, one theme in education and it traces its variations under foreign conditions" (Bereday 1957, 14).

Wolhuter, in his analysis of *CER* articles, found that the most constant characteristic of the journal's content had been its focus on the "nation-state or national education system," which "tenaciously remains the principal level of focus of articles" (2008, 325), and "at all levels and at all times there is a preponderance of single-unit [or 'problem approach'] studies" (326). Most of the early studies were based on historicism, which was seen as a foundation of comparative education rather than individualist epistemologies such as empiricism or rationalism. Val D. Rust *et al.* (1999) analyzed three data sets drawn from a subsample of articles published by the *CER* from 1957 to 1995, as well as from its British analogue, *Comparative Education* (1964-95), and from the *International Journal of Educational Development* (1981-95). The majority of articles from the *CER* sample used literature reviews and historical analysis, and relatively few were based on project reviews or field research:

> ... those publishing in the field [of comparative education] during the 1960s ... relied heavily on contemporary and historical literature, which we might describe as interpretive studies, and rarely adopted other data-collection strategies (1999, 97).

The content of the *CER* subsequently saw an evolution towards more field-based studies which Steiner-Khamsi labeled "The Development Turn in Comparative Education," suggesting that the cold war and development initiatives in the 1960s "entirely transformed the field of U.S. comparative and international education" (2006, 30). Two indications of change in the field had implications for the *CER*. Theories of national development underpinned hopes to make comparativism useful (and fundable), as seen most clearly with the 1965 establishment of the Stanford International Development Education Center (SIDEC). During the same period, the Comparative Education Society added the words "and International" to its name in hopes of benefiting from the (unsuccessful) Bill in the U.S. Congress to create an "International Education Act." (See especially chapters by Swing and Berends and Trakas in this volume.)

This "turn" also was characterized by wider epistemological diversity in the *CER*, and Rust *et al.* found that comparative education contained most methods in social sciences, but not comparative education methods as "reflected in the work of Bereday, Noah and Eckstein, Holmes, and other scholars" (1999, 102). Bereday seemed to be open-minded, even curious, about new approaches: "The incorporation into total analysis of the structural-functional approach of sociology and the cross-cultural methods of anthropology awaits future treatment. Such integration is always needed" (Bereday 1957, 14).

Epistemological traditions and values of a journal are developed by its editorship as well as by trends in epistemological discourses. After 10 years of Bereday's stewardship of the journal, Harold Noah's team took a different approach and sought to move comparative education from its historicist base to a more positivist and empirical foundation. As described by Silova and Brehm (2010): "When Harold Noah took over the editorship of *CER* in 1967, the principles of 'scientific rationality' increasingly became more visible in the journal's publications," thus to an extent dividing "the debate on theory and method ... into two extremes, with new approaches on one end of the spectrum and 'old' ones on the other" (24). However, despite a "scientific turn," papers published in the *CER* remained diverse. The "two extremes" in the past as in the present thus function more like a continuum from post-positivist to mixed-methods and qualitative/constructivist methodologies, as well as a number of manuscripts making use of the emancipatory and/or critical methodologies. In a special issue on the "State of the Art" for the celebration of the 20 years of the *CER*, editor Andreas Kazamias and Karl Schwartz (1977, 151) noted that:

> There is no internally consistent body of knowledge, no set of principles or canons of research that are generally agreed upon by people who associate themselves with the field [of Comparative and International Education]. Instead, one finds various strands or schools of thought, theories, trends or concerns, not necessarily related to each other.

The "State of the Art" issue's front page depicted a puzzled-looking Humpty Dumpty behind a broken wall of bricks on which were written buzzwords of the day (see the chapter by Wiseman and Matherly in this volume), such as "structural functionalism", "pedagogy", "cost-benefit", "development", and "mankind." Humpty Dumpty's perplexity over comparative education and much of the "state of the art" 40 years ago still lingers in our current interrogations on the field. For example, the *CER* has generally relied on well-established discourses in the social sciences, and on looking at "the other," often through the well-meaning lenses of the *academic practitioner* (see Wilson 1994; Nordtveit 2015). A recurrent question is how such investigation may be experienced by the *studied*. As noted by Takayama, Sriprakash & Connell (2015, v):

> A particular challenge for the field [of Comparative and International Education] is to engage in intellectual projects that interrogate the field's own modernist and colonial foundations and, in doing so, shift what is recognized as legitimate educational knowledge, beyond a guided tour of the South.

Hence, in its search for epistemological diversity, the *CER* is also trying to avoid publishing papers that are deemed to represent good "quality" only in a technical (methodological) sense. In particular, the editorship is encouraging scholarship that does not perpetuate a patronizing Western attitude towards "other" societies depicted as static and undeveloped, ready for the academic practitioners' analysis and "intervention." Instead, the journal is seeking epistemological diversity and is especially sensitive to research using critical and decolonizing methodologies (see, for example, Takayama, Sriprakash, & Connell 2015).

The *Comparative Education Review* at 60

To most CIES members, the *CER*'s red cover with the black stripe is a familiar sight, and some may wonder what has changed over the years. The questions posed in the very first issues of the *CER* regarding the nature and epistemologies of comparative education, as well as the "state of the art" of the field (represented by the puzzled anthropomorphic egg) could lead to an easy answer: that "not very much has changed." Many of the challenges of defining comparative and international education have remained the same over the years. Kathryn G. Heath reviewed key questions for the field in her 1958 article, "Is Comparative Education a Discipline?" Specifically, she asked:

- Have comparative educators defined their specialized body of knowledge?
- What is the educational foundation for work in comparative education?

- What type and how much specialized training is required to become a comparative educator?
- What in-service learning process is required in the field of comparative education?
- What are the paths of entry into comparative education? Who recognizes the standards?

Over the years, many scholars have tried to answer her questions, but rather than becoming more defined, the delineations of the field seem fuzzier. Bradley J. Cook, Steven J. Hite, and Erwin H. Epstein asked similar questions in a 2004 article, "Discerning Trends, Contours, and Boundaries in Comparative Education: A Survey of Comparativists and Their Literature" and concluded that:

> Comparative education exhibits little or no consensual references or orientations. Those entrusted to transmit the field do it in widely disparate ways, both in subject matter and in method of approach. Within this fragmented characterization of comparative education, what does the future hold? (p. 148)

If the "future" of 1958 or 2004 is "now", there is still no answer to these questions, no unifying theme or epistemology of the field. However, this is not to say that nothing has changed. On the contrary, some things *have* changed. Perhaps, the anthropomorphic egg is broken and we can start appreciating that there is and can be no definition of the field of comparative education, and in that lies both its weaknesses and its strength. Instead then of being a journal characterized by a specific field, with a subset of rules and guidelines, the *CER* is open to a wide variety of articles. At the same time, the *context* of knowledge production and consumption has shifted, and *CER* has grown to being an established journal prized as an outlet for research.

However, despite the shifting context, and academic careers that are increasingly linked to production of knowledge, *CER* is still striving to maintain a policy of academic dialogue instead of being, as David Post put it, merely an outlet of "Rank Scholarship" (2012, 4), referring to the devices used to weigh the quality of research published in journals. Scholarly journals face pressures that over the years have transformed from media of communication for communities, to become largely manufactories of items for CVs and for the "currency" of academia: publication. This transformation is accomplished with the eager support from commercial publishing that profits richly from the increased demand. Commercial publishing now vastly outnumbers scholarly publications by non-profit university presses (such as the University of Chicago Press). Against these trends (Post 2012), the *CER*, as do many scholarly journals, has promoted scholarship and dialogue by relying on peer reviewers and in an iterative process of manuscript development (as opposed to making gatekeeping editorial decisions only by editors). In this sense, the *CER* project resists ranking pressures.

As an indication of this resistance, the editors decided to publish a special issue on the *CER*'s 60th anniversary, labeled "Rethinking Knowledge Production and Circulation in Comparative and International Education: Southern Theory, Postcolonial Perspectives, and Alternative Epistemologies." This title epitomizes Bereday's legacy as described by Harold Noah (1984, 2):

> George was dedicated to scholarship in the service of humane values, not to scholarship which served only a narrow circle. He wanted all men and women to be admitted to the charmed circle offered by knowledge and understanding. Inclusiveness, friendly outreach, giving the benefit of the doubt were his watchwords. He abhorred exclusiveness, cliquishness, and differentiation. The leitmotiv of his work was enlightenment for all, with equal emphasis to be placed on "enlightenment" and "all."

Such scholarship in the service of humane values is at the heart of the *CER*, and is the very *raison d'être* of the journal.

Acknowledgement

I thank Professor David Post, former editor of the *Comparative Education Review*, for his useful comments and suggestions on various stages of this chapter.

References

Altbach, Philip G. 1983. "Editorial Introduction." *Comparative Education Review* 27(1): 1-2.

Altbach, Philip G. 1984 (1). "Editorial." *Comparative Education Review* 28(1): 10.

Altbach, Philip G. 1984 (2). "Farewell to a Founder." *Comparative Education Review* 28(1): 5-7.

Bereday, G.Z.F. 1957 (1). "A note on textbooks in comparative education." *Comparative Education Review* 1(1): 3-4.

Bereday, G.Z.F. 1957 (2). "Some discussion on methods in comparative education." *Comparative Education Review 1*(1): 13-15.

Bereday, G.Z.F. 1963. "From Comparative Education Review History." *Comparative Education Review 7*(1): 3.

Brickman, William W. 1957. "A New Journal in Comparative Education." *Comparative Education Review 1*(1): 1.

Brickman, William W. 1977. "Comparative and International Education Society: A Historical Analysis." *Comparative Education Review 21*(2/3): 396-404.

Comparative Education Review Website. Downloaded April 5th 2015, from: http://www.press.uchicago.edu/ucp/journals/journal/cer.html

Cook, Bradley J., Steven J. Hite, & Erwin H. Epstein. 2004. "Discerning Trends, Contours, and Boundaries in Comparative Education: A Survey of Comparativists and Their Literature." *Comparative Education Review 48*(2): 123-149.

Epstein, Erwin H. 1989. Editorial. *Comparative Education Review 33*(1): 1-2.

Epstein, Erwin H. 1998. Editorial. *Comparative Education Review 42*(4): 417-420.

Heath, Kathryn G. 1958. "Is Comparative Education a Discipline? *Comparative Education Review 2*(2): 31-31.

Johnson, William H.E. 1957. "The Comparative Education Society." *Comparative Education Review 1*(1): 16.

Kazamias, Andreas M. 1978. "Introduction." *Comparative Education Review 22*(1): 1-2.

Kazamias, Andreas M., & Karl Schwartz. 1977. "Intellectual and Ideological Perspectives in Comparative Education: An Interpretation." *Comparative Education Review 21*(2/3): 153-176.

McClellan, James E. 1957. "An Educational Philosopher Looks at Comparative Education." *Comparative Education Review 1*(1): 8-9.

Noah, Harold J. 1984. "A Colleague's Reflections." *Comparative Education Review 28*(1): 1-3.

Nordtveit, Bjorn H. 2015. "Knowledge production in a constructed field: reflections on comparative and international education." *Asia Pacific Education Review 16*(1): 1-11.

Post, David. 2012. "Rank Scholarship." *Comparative Education Review 56*(1): 1-17.

Read, Gerald H. 1959. "Constitution of the Comparative Education Society." *Comparative Education Review 3*(2): 37-40.

Rust, Val D., Aminata Soumaré, Octavio Pescador, & Megumi Shibuya. 1999. "Research Strategies in Comparative Education." *Comparative Education Review 43*(1): 86-109.

Silova, Iveta. 2009. "The Changing Frontiers of Comparative Education: A Forty-Year Retrospective on *European Education*." *European Education 41*(1): 17-31.

Silova, Iveta, & William C. Brehm. 2010. "For the Love of Knowledge: William W. Brickman and His Comparative Education." *European Education 42*(2) 17-36.

Steiner-Khamsi, Gita. 2006. "The Development Turn in Comparative Education." *European Education 38*(3): 19-47.

Swing, Elizabeth Sherman. 2007. "Comparative and International Education Society (CIES)." In Vandra Masemann, Mark Bray, & Maria Manzon, eds. *Common Interests, Uncommon Goals: Histories of the World Council of Comparative Education Societies*. CERC Studies in Comparative Education 21. Hong Kong: Comparative Education Research Centre, The University of Hong Kong, and Dordrecht: Springer, pp. 94-115.

Takayama, Keita, Arathi Sriprakash, & Raewyn Connell. 2015. "Rethinking Knowledge Production and Circulation in Comparative and International Education: Southern Theory, Postcolonial Perspectives, and Alternative Epistemologies." *Comparative Education Review 59*(1): v-viii.

Wilson, David N. 1994. "Comparative and International Education: Fraternal or Siamese Twins? A Preliminary Genealogy of Our Twin Fields." *Comparative Education Review 38*(4): 449-486.

Wolhuter, C.C. 2008. "Review of the Review: Constructing the Identity of Comparative Education." *Research in Comparative and International Education 3*(4): 323-344.

9
The Mobilization of Knowledge

Iveta SILOVA, Robyn READ and Karen MUNDY

Driven by a growing awareness of the need to better understand complex problems in the era of globalization, the shift towards a knowledge-based economy has resulted in a common interest to strengthen the value of research among governments, research producing agencies, funders, and the broader public. Rising demands on limited resources and a general culture of accountability have produced, at least in much of the industrialized world, a political climate emphasizing the need for "evidence-based" policy and practice in all public service sectors. The result has often been to integrate research into policy and practice across various disciplines and public service sectors, including education.

Many terms are used to encapsulate these efforts, including knowledge mobilization in education (Cooper 2014; Lingard 2013; Fenwick & Farrell 2012); knowledge sharing and knowledge management in international development (Court & Young 2003; Hovland 2003); knowledge transfer and knowledge management in business (Argote & Ingram 2000; Inkpen & Dinur 1998); as well as knowledge transfer, knowledge translation, and knowledge exchange in health (Grimshaw et al. 2012; Mitton et al. 2007). Some argue that the subtle differences between various terminologies do impact understanding of the phenomena; for example, the term "knowledge transfer" implies linear movement from research to practice, whereas terms such as "knowledge exchange" or "mobilization" highlight the multi-dimensional, purposeful, and interactive nature of these efforts (Sa, Li & Faubert 2011). Others believe that the considerable overlap in definitions make it worthwhile to push for an

Erwin H. Epstein (ed.) (2016): *Crafting a Global Field: Six Decades of the Comparative and International Education Society*. Hong Kong: Comparative Education Research Centre (CERC), The University of Hong Kong, and Dordrecht: Springer. © CERC

all-encompassing term – the symbol K* (K star) – to describe the various interfaces between knowledge, policy, and practice (Shaxson et al. 2012).

Just as there is no agreement on the terminology used to describe efforts linking research, policy and practice, the term "knowledge" itself is highly contested. While the scope of this chapter does not allow a full discussion of the debates, the labeling of particular types of knowledge as "evidence" is not merely a matter of technical expertise but also of positional power. As Nutley and Davies (2007) point out, "the attaching of labels such as evidence or research to particular types of knowledge are political acts" (p. 3). The role of determining what evidence counts and what does not falls under the control of those in power (Nutley & Davies 2010), and in a global climate of limited resources, there are no value-free ways for those in power to define what counts as evidence.

In the field of education, knowledge mobilization (KMb) is a commonly used term to describe this work. While most scholars in the KMb field limit their definition of "knowledge" to knowledge gained through empirical research (Cooper 2014; Nutley & Davies 2010), we would like to use a broader definition by the Social Science and Humanities Research Council of Canada, which describes knowledge mobilization as a process of "... moving knowledge into active service for the broadest possible common good." In this conceptualization, knowledge implies any or all of the following: "(1) findings from specific social sciences and humanities research, (2) the accumulated knowledge and experience of social sciences and humanities researchers, and (3) the accumulated knowledge and experience of stakeholders concerned" (SSHRC 2008, para 5). Considering the complex realities of various practice and policy contexts, this definition acknowledges the importance of less formal ways of knowing (such as experience) and non-Western forms of knowledge production (such as indigenous knowledges) (Jones, Datta & Jones 2009). It also opens up opportunities for multi-directional flows of knowledge across various geographical areas and disciplinary fields, and for the reconstitution of power relationships among different stakeholders.

Knowledge Mobilization and CIES

While the term KMb has only recently joined the lexicon of the Comparative and International Education Society (CIES), the principles of knowledge mobilization are embedded in the DNA of our Society and can be traced back to the beginning of recorded history of the field. Even before the generally recognized founders of the field, such as César Auguste Basset (1808) and Marc-Antoine Jullien (1817), "travelers have described aspects of education in countries they visited, with the notion that the educational structures and practices they examined might be useful for adoption and adaptation in their own countries" (Wilson 2003, 19). These "travelers' tales" were perhaps a precursor to what we now know as the study of education transfer (or educational policy borrowing and lending), which has become one of the central, yet at the same time one of the most contested areas of research in the field (Silova 2012; Steiner-Khamsi 2004; Steiner-Khamsi & Waldow 2012).

On the one hand, educational borrowing is seen as a pragmatic tool for identifying and transferring "best practices" from one context to another with the goal of improving national educational systems. Often drawing on the cross-national student achievement studies (such as the Programme for International Student Assessment, or PISA, and the Trends in International Mathematics and Science Study, or TIMSS), such research is facilitated by the emphasis on empirical data about "what works" in education elsewhere and rests on the assumption that there exists a legitimate "blueprint" of educational policies and practices, which could be used to increase education opportunities and improve education quality worldwide. On the other hand, many scholars have continuously warned that mass "policy pilgrimage" by policy makers from low ranking countries to countries ranking the highest on student achievement tests could lead to uncritical, de-contextualized education transfer. Pointing to the political nature of the process, they suggest that education transfer could become a "cargo cult" (Cowen 2000) and lead to the "the tyranny of league tables" (Robinson 1999) in comparative and international education research.

In a similar vein, long before "knowledge mobilization" became the technical term to describe connections between research, policy and practice, members of our Society engaged in heated debates over the apparent divide between researchers and the practitioners in the field of comparative and international education. More than a decade before Carol Weiss (1979) penned *The Many Meanings of Research Utilization,* a seminal piece for those who study knowledge mobilization, our Society had been debating a name change from the Comparative Education Society (CES) to the Comparative and International Education Society (CIES). A proposal to change the Society's name was introduced in 1967 and aimed to bridge the division between researchers and practitioners in the field of comparative and international education. As Wilson (1994) explained in his presidential address, "the apparent dividing line" between international and comparative education was "the distinction between researchers (either descriptive or analytic) and practitioners directly concerned with policy and practice" (p. 454). Further, Epstein (1994) summarized:

> Comparativists ... are primarily scholars interested in explaining why educational systems and processes vary and how education relates to wider social factors and forces.... International educators use findings derived from comparative education to understand better the educational processes they examine and thus to enhance their ability to make policy relating to programs such as those associated with international exchange and understanding. (p. 918)

As the field grew and diversified during the post-World War II Cold War era to include international educational activities of government and non-government agencies, the membership of the Society needed to become more representative of this changing focus (Berends & Trakas, in this volume). In 1968, the Society members voted to formalize the name change from the CES to the CIES, officially including 'international' (and by implication practice- and policy-oriented work) in the name of the Society. This "marriage between comparative and international educators" (Wilson 1994, 450) signaled an institutional attempt to identify the ways in which research could inform policy and practice and vice versa. The debate over how to strengthen the collaborative relationships between researchers and practitioners in the field has continued throughout the decades (Reimers & McGinn 1997; Ginsburg & Gorostiaga 2001; Sutton and Levinson 2001; among others) and has been the focus of many CIES presidential addresses (e.g., Masemann 1990; Wilson 1994; Arnove 2001; Carnoy 2006; Kobayashi 2007; Klees 2008 for example). In his CIES presidential address, Wilson (1994) ultimately captured this idea in his characterization of the "research-practitioner" who embodies the fusion of the two fields and engages in both basic and applied research at various points over time.

However, despite a long history of sharing knowledge about education across different geographical and disciplinary borders, knowledge sharing and dissemination efforts of CIES have remained somewhat limited. They have been mostly confined to academic publication outlets and conferences. And while academic publications are an important venue for research dissemination, KMb requires sharing research beyond the (pay) walls of academic publishing. KMb requires sustained effort over time to develop connections between research, policy, and practice; practical knowledge and skills in communicating research in clear language that targets the practical needs of a wide variety of audience groups; as well as the skills required to conceptualize, develop, and implement innovative products, events, and networks that engage busy academics, policy makers, and practitioners.

In 2014, under the leadership of CIES President Karen Mundy, CIES rose to this challenge by institutionalizing the concept of KMb through the creation of the Ad Hoc Committee on Knowledge Mobilization, New Media, and Member Communications. The KMb Committee is responsible for (1) developing a knowledge mobilization strategy for the Society and (2) proposing a set of investments and activities for "moving the Society forward into a digital age" – both to increase knowledge accessibility, usability, and impact, and to improve internal networking and communication among the CIES members. One of the first initiatives of the KMb Committee was to survey CIES members in order to identify needs and areas of critical concerns around knowledge sharing and networking. While only about 10 percent of the Society members participated in the survey (a total of 326 CIES members), the respondents reflected the diverse fabric of our Society and included those who self-identified as researchers (69 percent) and those self-identifying as practitioners (31 percent), females (67 percent) and males (32 percent), as well as graduate students (31 percent). Sixty three percent of the respondents self-identified themselves as Caucasian, 15 percent as Asian, 9 percent as Hispanic/Latino, 3 percent as Black or African American, and 4 percent as "other," while 6 percent preferred not to answer. Most of the respondents (56 percent) had been members of CIES for 1-5 years, while 18 percent had belonged to CIES for 6-10 years and 26 percent for more than 11 years; and most of the respondents (74 percent) belonged to one or more Special Interest Groups (SIGs).

As one of the respondents aptly noted, and as the findings of the survey clearly reveal, comparative and international education is "very out of date compared to other fields" in the area of knowledge mobilization. While the majority of the respondents believed that their knowledge was easily or somewhat accessible to scholars/academics (87 percent) and graduate students (82 percent), it is considerably less so for other stakeholders, including educators/practitioners (66 percent), policy-makers (48 percent), non-governmental organization (NGO) representa-tives (47 percent), and general public (42 percent). Importantly, only 65 percent of the surveyed CIES members evaluated their own experience of accessing academic knowledge and publications as "easy" or "very easy," pointing to obstacles ranging from language to financial costs. This holds true for the larger field of education research, which has been slow to embrace the principles of KMb compared to other public services such as health or criminal justice (Cooper 2014; Cooper, Levin & Campbell 2009).

Our field's hesitation to jump onto the KMb bandwagon has not been unfounded. While the principle of KMb may be woven into the fabric of CIES, so too are the tensions surrounding knowledge mobilization initiatives. One certainly does not need to be an expert in the field of KMb to be able to identify some of the many issues that CIES must address in order to develop a KMb strategy of its own. As the initial findings from our KMb survey make clear, while many of our members would like the Society to provide avenues for research dissemination beyond the walls of academia and create meaningful opportunities for interaction between members, they are also acutely aware that this is more easily said than done. The following section highlights some of the key challenges the Society faces as it moves forward with the development of a KMb strategy.

Barriers to Knowledge Mobilization

Article 27 of the Universal Declaration of Human Rights (United Nations 1948) illustrates one of the most challenging dilemmas of KMb work. Clause one of the Article states that, "Everyone has the right ... to share in scientific advancement and its benefits." This clause frames scientific knowledge as a global public good, one which enables everyone to participate in the production of "scientific" knowledge, and benefit from the application of this knowledge. However, clause two of this article states that "everyone has the right to the protection of the moral and material interests resulting from any scientific, literary or artistic production of which he [sic] is the author." Based on the findings of our KMb survey, the tension between the public vs. private good of knowledge is one with which many members of our Society (and indeed academia as a whole) struggle.

Despite increasing expectations from some important research funders for research impact beyond academia (e.g., SSHRC mobilization requirements, Research Impact framework in the UK, Research Impact framework in Australia), academic tenure and promotion continue to favor research dissemination through traditional academic venues (especially peer reviewed journals) over research products which target non-academic audience groups (Cooper 2014; Sá, Li & Faubert 2011). While members would like to see the Society's KMb strategy include free, open access publications translated into clear, attainable language, and made available in some of the many languages spoken by the members of our Society, it is also clear that our members would like the Society to create more publishing opportunities that count towards tenure and promotion in their respective institutions. As one respondent put it, "we can use more publication venues, but if they aren't peer-reviewed ... then they are of little utility for academic careers." Unfortunately, despite leaps forward in open access publications, the top-tier peer reviewed journals in our field (including our own *Comparative Education Review*) continue to be locked behind paywalls and difficult for those without a highly developed research literacy to understand.

However, while CIES members are clearly concerned about meeting requirements for tenure and promotion, our KMb survey results demonstrate that members are acutely aware of how limiting academic outputs can be. Respondents to the KMb survey listed a set of concrete obstacles that prevent various stakeholders from accessing their knowledge. In particular, 68 percent mentioned a lack of awareness among policymakers and practitioners about their research, pointing to the inaccessibility of academic publication outlets to the broader public. Importantly, 57 percent pointed to the high costs associated with obtaining publications and approximately 40 percent listed language – both in terms of translations and professional jargon – as the main obstacles to accessing and sharing knowledge. While these are all important issues that will require specific interventions in order to advance knowledge mobilization within the CIES context, collectively they point to the larger debates in the field of comparative and international education, problematizing what counts as knowledge in the first place, and questioning how the current academic system recognizes and rewards (as well as discourages) the production and dissemination of particular knowledge(s).

Though academic tenure and promotion practices continue to be misaligned with new norms of mobilizing academic knowledge, studies show a positive correlation between research dissemination through non-academic and academic mechanisms. In other words, scholars who produce the most non-academic publications also tend to produce the most academic publications (Cooper et al. 2011; Jensen et al. 2008). Thus, while traditional academic publishing continues to be a barrier to KMb, it is possible to be productive in both academic and non-academic outputs. Unfortunately, possible does not always mean easy. Just as high quality academic outputs require a highly specialized, technical language which is often at odds with the desires and needs of those in policy and practice (Ward et al. 2010), KMb requires researchers to be able to write and speak of their work in plain language using a variety of formats that target the specific needs of diverse audience groups. In the context of CIES, this is complicated further by the wide range of languages our members speak and use in their research. Our KMb survey found that while 80 percent of respondents conduct research in non-English language countries, only 40 percent responded that they publish (at least some of the time) their research in languages of the country in which they conducted research.

To add to this complexity, the field of KMb is increasingly interested in the ways communications technology and social media can vastly expand our reach. Despite the arguments in support of knowledge mobilization via social media (which tend to mirror the arguments for knowledge mobilization in general), many CIES members remain skeptical of the opportunities they offer. In fact, some respondents were wary of "too much reliance on social media" by suggesting, as one respondent put it, that "it is bound to go away and be replaced by something else. Forget it!" Others echoed: "I do not think that electronic communication really works to enhance knowledge mobilization. I do not want CIES to turn into a 'virtual society.' Funds should be invested in more opportunities for interpersonal knowledge sharing," and, "Keep it fairly conservative and it will not go out of style. How long will blogs and twitters be around before we are inundated with something new?" These three respondents were not alone. Our survey found that only 35 percent of the respondents use Twitter, and of those that do only 12.5 percent are active users. While 60 percent of respondents reported using Facebook, only 20 percent claimed to be frequent users.

CIES scholars are certainly not the only late adopters of these communications technologies. Studies show that uptake of social media by scientists is low, especially on platforms such as Twitter, Facebook or Google+ (McClain & Neeley 2015), and our failure to engage with these new modes of social networking could be significantly limiting our reach. While there is a dearth of studies empirically evaluating the benefit of using social media to disseminate research, those studies which have been done demonstrate that these technologies can significantly speed the pace at which scholars are developing and sharing knowledge, both within academia and with the general public (Darling et al. 2013; Terras 2012; Fenner 2012).

While academics may be slow to adopt new methods of communication, many colleagues in policy and practice are not. Organizations such as the World Bank, the UK's Department for International Development, and the Overseas Development Institute all have well defined KMb strategies and critical evaluations of their KMb work, and contribute to an empirical understanding of this emergent field of research. Additionally, organizations such as the Global Partnership for Education and the Education for All Global Monitoring Report provide rich examples of how to translate complicated research into easily attainable language and well developed strategies for communicating their knowledge products through various channels, including social media. There is much to learn from the ways in which these organizations translate and disseminate academic research, and many good reasons for researchers to actively seek partnerships with organizations that serve as intermediaries between researchers and those in policy and practice (see Cooper 2014; Lingard 2013).

Looking forward

As we continue to explore the barriers as well as develop potential solutions to enhancing knowledge mobilization within the field of comparative and international education, it is clear that there is no one KMb strategy, skill, or tool that can take us towards the goal of "... moving knowledge into active service for the broadest possible common good" (SSHRC 2008, para 5). As the results of the CIES KMb survey suggest, knowledge mobilization is a complex process that requires a multi-faceted approach, including investments in the KMb initiatives (rated as somewhat or very important by 86 percent of the respondents), development of skills among the CIES members for effectively sharing their knowledge with different audiences (86 percent), provision of dedicated staff and institutional structures (80 percent), and the creation of a (free) online hub for sharing digital content generated by CIES members, including blogs, videos, photos, and other social media (71 percent). Ultimately, the CIES KMb strategy should aim to overcome, in a logical and staged manner, the different barriers related to the production, sharing, and mobilization of knowledge across different academic disciplines, global sites, languages, and stakeholders in the pursuit of new knowledge. For this, the Society will need dedicated expertise and resources.

Thus, while there are many ways CIES can support its members in their KMb efforts, there is much its members must continue to do in order to ensure that the Society remains "a house in which there is space for many points of views, disciplines and vocations ... a house in which the doors between the different rooms are open – inviting us to move around, explore different approaches, concepts; build linkages, and experiment with and learn about new ideas, programs and interventions going on in all corners of the world" (Mundy forthcoming). Through their research and practice, CIES members have the power to ensure that our Society remains a space where all stakeholders take responsibility for continuously questioning what types of knowledge counts, and the privilege to participate in extending the reach of the knowledge we produce as a global public good.

References

Argote, Linda, & Paul Ingram. 2000. "Knowledge Transfer: A basis for competitive advantage in firms." *Organizational Behavior and Human Decision Processes 82*(1): 150-169.

Arnove, Robert F. 2001. "Comparative and International Education Society (CIES) Facing the Twenty-First Century: Challenges and Contributions." *Comparative Education Review 45* (4): 477-503.

Basset, Cesar Auguste. 1808. *"Essais sur l'organisation de quelques parties d'instruction publique."* Paris: Hazard.

Carnoy, Martin. 2006. "Rethinking the Comparative – and the International." *Comparative Education Review 50*(4): 551-570.

Cooper, Amanda. 2014. "Knowledge Mobilisation in Education across Canada: A cross-case analysis of 44 research brokering organizations." *Evidence & Policy 10*(1): 29-59.

Cooper, Amanda, Ben Levin, & Carol Campbell. 2009. "The Growing (but still limited) use of Evidence in Education Policy and Practice." *Journal of Educational Change 10*(1&2): 159-171.

Cooper, Amanda, Joelle Rodway Macri, & Robyn Read. 2011. "*Knowledge Mobilization Practices of Educational Researchers in Canada.*" (Paper presented at conference of the American Educational Research Association, New Orleans, Louisiana, April 8-12).

Court, Julius, & John Young. 2003. *Bridging Research and Policy: Insights from 50 case studies* (August). Retrieved October 2009, from Overseas Development Institute: http://www.odi.org.uk/resources/details.asp?id=148&title=bridging-research-policyinsights-50-case-studies.

Cowen, Robert. 2000. "Comparing Futures or Comparing Pasts?" *Comparative Education 36*(3): 333-342.

Darling, Emily S., David Shiffma, Isabelle M. Côté, & Joshua A. Drew. 2013. "The Role of Twitter in the Life Cycle of a Scientific Publication." *PeerJ PrePrints* 1:e16v1 https://dx.doi.org/10.7287/peerj.preprints.16v1.

Epstein, Erwin H. 1994. "Comparative and International Education: Overview and historical development." In T. Husén, & T.N. Postlethwaite, eds. *The International Encyclopedia of Higher Education*, Volume 2. Oxford: Pergamon.

Fenwick, Tara, & Lesley Farrell, eds. 2012. *Knowledge Mobilization and Educational Research: Politics, languages and responsibilities*. London and New York: Routledge.

Fenner, Mark. 2012, February 9. "Do More Tweets Mean Higher Citations? If so, Twitter can Lead us to the 'Personalised Journal'; pinpointing more research that is relevant to your interests". *LSE Impact Blog*. Retrieved from http://blogs.lse.ac.uk/impactofsocialsciences/2012/02/09/more-tweets-more-citations/.

Ginsburg, Mark B., & Jorge M. Gorostiaga. 2001. "Relationships between Theorists/ Researchers and Policy Makers/Practitioners: Rethinking the Two Cultures Thesis and the Possibility of Dialogue." *Comparative Education Review 45*(2): 173-196.

Grimshaw, Jeremy M., Martin P. Eccles, John N. Lavis, Sophie J. Hill, & Janet E. Squires. 2003. "Knowledge Translation of Research Findings". *Implement Science 7*(50): 1-17.

Hovland, Ingie. 2003, August. *Knowledge management and organizational learning: An International Development perspective*. Retrieved August 7, 2010, from Overseas Development Institute: http://www.odi.org.uk/resources/download/143.pdf.

UN General Assembly. 1948. *The Universal Declaration of Human Rights*. United Nations, Paris. Retrieved from http://www.un.org/en/documents/udhr/.

Inkpen, Andrew C., & Adva Dinur. 1998. "Knowledge Management Processes and International Joint Ventures". *Organization Science 9*(4): 454-468.

Jensen, P., J-B Rouquier, P. Kreimer, & Y. Coissant. (2008)." Scientists Who Engage with Society Perform Better Academically." *Science and Public Policy* 7(35): 527-541.

Jones, N., A. Datta, & H. Jones. (2009). Knowledge, Policy and Power: Six dimensions of the knowledge-development interface. Retrieved November 2009, from Overseas Development Institute: http://www.odi.org.uk/resources/download/3790.pdf.

Klees, Steven J. 2008. "Reflections on Theory, Method, and Practice in Comparative and International Education." *Comparative Education Review* 52(3): 301-328.

Kobayashi, Victor. 2007. "Recursive Patterns That Engage and Disengage: Comparative Education, Research, and Practice." *Comparative Education Review* 51(3): 261-280.

Lingard, Bob. 2013. "The Impact of Research on Education Policy in an Era of Evidence-based Policy." *Studies in Education* 54(2): 113–131.

Jullien, Marc-Antoine. 1817. "Esquisse et vues préliminaires d'un ouvrage sur l'éducation compare." *Paris: Société Établie à Paris pour l'Amélioration de l'Enseignement Élémentaire.* Reprinted in 1962: Geneva: Bureau International d'Éducation.

Masemann, Vandra L. 1990. "Ways of Knowing: Implications for Comparative Education." *Comparative Education Review* 34(4): 465-473.

McClain, Craig, & Liz Neeley. 2015. "A Critical Evaluation of Science Outreach via Social Media: Its role and impact on scientists [v2; ref status: indexed, http://f1000r.es/5ey]". *F1000Research* 3:300. Retrieved from http://f1000research.com/articles/3-300/v1.

Mitton, Craig, Carol E. Adair, Emily McKenzie, Scott B. Patten, & Brenda Waye Perry. 2007. "Knowledge Transfer and Exchange: Review and synthesis of the literature". *The MillBank Quarterly* 85(4): 729-768.

Mundy, Karen. Forthcoming. "Leaning in on Education for All". *Comparative Education Review.*

Nutley, Sandra, & Huw Davies. 2010, April 21. *Using Research to Provide Stronger Services and Programs for Youth: A Discussion paper for the William T Grant Foundation.* Retrieved November 14, 2010, from http://www.nekia.org/files/DP1_Promoting_research_use_v2_6.doc.

Nutley, Sandra, Isabel Walter, & Huw Davies. 2007. *Using Evidence: How Research Can Inform Public Services.* Bristol: The Policy Press.

Reimers, Fernando, & Noel McGinn. 1997. *Informed Dialogue: Using Research to Shape Education Policy Around the World.* Westport, Conn.: Praeger.

Robinson, Peter. 1999. "The Tyranny of League Tables: International Comparisons of Educational Attainment and Economic Performance." In R. Alexander, P. Broadford, & D. Phillips, eds. *Learning from Comparing: New Directions in Comparative Education Research.* Vol. 1. Oxford: Symposium Books.

Sá, Cresso, Sharon Li, & Brenton Faubert. 2011. "Facilities of Education and Institutional Strategies for Knowledge Mobilization: An Exploratory Study." *Higher Education 61*(4): 501-512.

Shaxson, Louise, Alex Bielak, Ibrahim Ahmed, Derek Brien, Bernadette Conant, Catherine Fisher, Elin Gwyn, et al. 2012. *Expanding our understanding of K*(KT, KE, KTT, KMb, KB, KM, etc.). A concept paper emerging from the K* conference, Hamilton, ON, Canada, April, 30.* Hamilton, ON, Canada: UNU-INWEH. Retrieved from http://inweh.unu.edu/archive/River/KnowledgeManagement/ documents/KStar_ConceptPaper_FINAL_Oct29_WEBsmaller.pdf.

Silova, Iveta. 2012. "Contested Meanings of Educational Borrowing". In G. Steiner-Khamsi, & F. Waldow, eds., *World Yearbook of Education 2012: Policy Borrowing and Lending in Education.* New York: Routledge.

Social Sciences and Humanities Research Council. 2008. *SSHRC's Knowledge Mobilization Strategy.* Ottawa: SSHRC.

Steiner-Khamsi, Gita, ed. (2004). *The Global Politics of Educational Borrowing and Lending.* New York: Teachers College Press.

Steiner-Khamsi, Gita, & Florian Waldow, eds. 2012. *Policy Borrowing and Lending: World Yearbook of Education 2012.* London and New York: Routledge.

Sutton, Margaret, & Bradley Levinson. 2001. *Policy as Practice: Toward a Comparative Sociocultural Analysis of Educational Policy.* Westport, CT: Praeger.

Terras, Melissa. 2012, April 19. "The Verdict is in: Is blogging or tweeting about research papers worth it?" *LSE Impact Blog.* Retrieved from http://blogs.lse.ac. uk/impactofsocialsciences/2012/04/19/blog-tweeting-papers-worth-it/.

Ward, Vicki, Simon Smith, Robbie Foy, Allan House, & Susan Hamer. 2010. "Planning for Knowledge Translation: A researcher's guide." *Evidence & Policy 6*(4): 527-541.

Weiss, Carol H. 1979. "The Many Meanings of Research Utilization." *Public Administration Review 39*(5): 426-431.

Wilson, David. 1994. "The Institutions of Comparative Education: Fraternal or Siamese Twins?" *Comparative Education Review 38*(4): 449-486.

Wilson, David. 2003. "The Future of Comparative and International Education in a Globalised World." *International Review of Education 49*(1-2): 15-33.

10

The Social Organization of
CIES Special Interest Groups

Oren PIZMONY-LEVY

At the 2005 Comparative and International Education Society (CIES) Conference, held at Stanford University, the CIES Board of Directors approved the creation of Special Interests Groups (SIGs). SIGs are small communities within a larger professional organization that provide a forum for the involvement of individuals with shared interests in advancing a field of study. SIGs are a feature in some other professional associations such as the American Educational Research Association (AERA) and the American Sociological Association (ASA). The CIES Bylaws (Article V) outline the purpose of SIGs: "[to] promote new research and mentor educational researchers." The Bylaws stipulate that "any group of 15 or more active CIES members may petition to establish a SIG" and that membership dues must be similar across all SIGs and across all members (US$10). As observed by Williams (2008), the Bylaws leave the definition and delineation of the focus of a proposed SIG to the petitioners.

SIGs vary in their level of activity and interaction throughout the year, but all of them are active during the annual CIES conference. During the conference they organize and sponsor highlighted sessions that provide a platform for continuing, long-term discussion on shared research interests. These sessions are often given preferred time slots on the program and are visually highlighted in the printed version of the program. SIGs also hold business meetings that focus on organizational and governance aspects of the SIGs and create a space for networking

Erwin H. Epstein (ed.) (2016): *Crafting a Global Field: Six Decades of the Comparative and International Education Society*. Hong Kong: Comparative Education Research Centre (CERC), The University of Hong Kong, and Dordrecht: Springer. © CERC

among members. Additionally, throughout the year, SIGs disseminate information about new scholarship by members, calls for papers for journals and edited volumes, and funding opportunities.

An important factor behind the creation of CIES SIGs was the immense growth of the annual conference, especially since the early 2000s. At that time, many members expressed the need for more intimate groups to discuss matters of common interest and to develop more robust working relationships with likeminded colleagues. SIGs were seen as a means to better integrate individuals within CIES by reducing anonymity and facilitating a sense of belonging. Finally, SIGs were seen as an opportunity for professional development and mentoring, and as an avenue for engaging members in leadership positions (e.g., Chairperson, Program Officer, Secretary, etc.).

Although individual members have discussed the matter of forming SIGs since the early 2000s, the CIES Board was hesitant to introduce this organizational feature.[1] The main concern was that SIGs would fragment the society into silos of scholarship areas and would undermine collaboration on issues in the field that affect multiple countries, regions, and disciplines. Other concerns focused on whether CIES rules and regulations were adequate to deal with the rapid growth of SIGs. These concerns are clearly reflected in the creation of two CIES ad hoc committees on SIGs (Jacob and Hunt 2011; Williams 2008).

Over the years, however, CIES leadership worked to better incorporate SIGs into the Society. Several documents were crafted to guide the work of CIES SIGs, including Policies and Procedures for Development and Activities of CIES SIGs (CIES 2011) and Handbook for CIES SIG Chairpersons (CIES 2013). Further, starting in 2008/9, SIGs were fully integrated in the submission system for the annual conference. That is, members were given the option to submit their papers to the SIGs or to the general pool. The byproduct of this move was the decentralization of the review process to the SIGs. Indeed, submission statistics for the 2015 annual conference show that more than three-fifths of the total number of papers submitted (62.3 percent) were reviewed by SIGs.

Growth and Expansion of SIGs

Figure 10.1 presents the number of new SIGs approved annually (bars) and the cumulative number of SIGs (line).[2] The first six groups were established in 2005/2006 and were included in the 2006 annual conference in Honolulu, Hawai'i. One group had a regional focus – Africa – whereas the rest had a thematic focus: Citizenship and Democratic Education, Globalization and Education (originally named: Comparative Study of Globalization and Education), Cultural Contexts of Education and Human Potential (originally named: Cultural Issues), Language Issues, and Peace Education.

Figure 10.1: Number of Special Interest Groups Established Every Year and Cumulative Number of Special Interest Groups

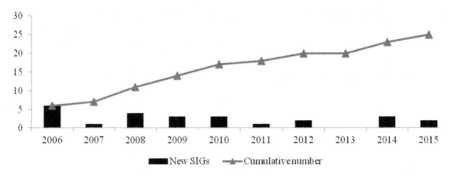

Interestingly, the themes and regions identified in the *Comparative Education Review 2006 Bibliographic Essay* (Raby 2007) as central to the field were not necessarily those reflected in the names of the first set of SIGs to be approved. For example, Raby (2007) points to the dwindling references to English-language articles on education in Africa and to the growing interest in Europe and Asia. Yet the Africa SIG was created before other regional SIGs.

By 2015, there were 25 active groups. Five new groups had a regional focus: East Asia (originally named: Japan; est. 2008), Middle East (est. 2008), South Asia (est. 2009), Eurasia (est. 2010), and Latin America (est. 2010). Fourteen new groups had a thematic focus: Indigenous Knowledge and the Academy (est. 2007), Early Childhood Development (est. 2008), Information and Communications Technology for Development (est. 2008), Higher Education (est. 2009), Inclusive Education (est. 2009), Global Literacy (est. 2010), Education for Sustainable Development (est. 2011), Teaching Comparative Education (est. 2012), Teacher Education and the Teaching Profession (est. 2012), Global Mathematics Education (est. 2014), Large Scale Cross National Studies (est. 2014), Religion and Education (est. 2014), Contemplative Inquiry and Holistic Education (est.

2014), and Post-Foundational Approaches to Comparative and International Education (est. 2015).

The development of new SIGs is a continuous process. At the time this chapter was written, five additional groups were being considered by the CIES Board of Directors. All of them had a thematic focus: African Diaspora; Education Policy and Program Evaluation; Education, Conflict and Emergencies; Learning Economics and Global Education Finance; Youth Development and Education.

Currently, the full roster of SIGs (i.e., those currently active or in formation) corresponds to trends in scholarship, as reflected in the *Comparative Education Review 2013 Bibliographic Essay* (Easton 2014). All of the common regions, with the exception of North America and Australia and the Pacific Basin, are also represented by a SIG. Most of the common themes are also represented by a SIG. However, some themes, such as Adult Education/Lifelong Learning, Special Education, and Research Methods, are still not represented on the roster of SIGs.

Another window by which to examine the link between advances in the field of Comparative and International Education and the emergence of new SIGs are the petitions for establishing new SIGs. For example, the petitioners for the Education, Conflict and Emergencies SIG made the case for their group by recounting the growth and activity in their sub-field:

> In the past two decades, the field of education and conflict/ education in emergencies has grown tremendously, as evidenced by the increase in academic research, as well as networks of organizations such as the Inter-Agency Network for Education in Emergencies and the USAID Education in Conflict and Crisis Network.... With the creation of the new SIG, we aim to bring together a range of academics, researchers, and practitioners from many organizations ranging from academic institutions, think tanks, non-governmental organizations, and large multi-lateral, and bi-lateral organizations.

Petitioners for the African Diaspora SIG, however, presented a different argument. Rather than reacting to advances in the field, they frame the purpose of their group as a way to enhance research and to offer new perspectives:

> What does a comparative analysis of the Black Diaspora afford researchers and practitioners, particularly as it relates to educa-

tion participation generally and more specifically community and community engagement? ... (1) An historical context can provide an examination of similar and different educational challenges to better determine different and new paths; (2) a broader examination of the educational experiences of Black populations outside of the United States offer the opportunity to rethink new and different solutions; and (3) a review of similarities and lessons learned across groups, using history and cultural contexts as lenses, can lead broader and more generalizable possibilities.

Finally, petitioners for the Learning Economics and Global Education Finance made their case by highlighting the limitations of the domestic nature of spaces dedicated to explore issues of finance:

> We aim to contribute to the perception of Learning, Economics, and Education Finance as a global issue and not just a national issue.... Currently there are only three conferences for scholars in the field ... and most of these conferences focus on the domestic aspects of Education Finance.

Membership in SIGs

In order to explore membership and the social organization of SIGs, I use data from the CIES membership database, which is managed by the University of Chicago Press. In addition to basic demographics (e.g., gender, country of residence, and academic degree), the database also includes information about membership in SIGs. The analysis is limited to individuals who were members of the Society in 2014. That is, individuals who attended the 2015 annual meeting and joined SIGs without being a member of the Society are excluded from this analysis. The analytical sample includes 3,059 individuals. The analytical strategy consists of descriptive statistics, multivariate analysis, and social network analysis.

About two-fifths of CIES members (39.3 percent) are affiliated with at least one SIG. In other words, a large majority of the Society do not view SIGs as necessary and/or as addressing their needs. One-fifth of CIES members (21.6 percent) are affiliated with one SIG, one-tenth (10.6 percent) are affiliated with two SIGs, and the rest (2.6 percent) are affiliated with three or more SIGs. The tendency to join only one SIG could be explained perhaps by having to pay an annual per SIG membership fee (US$10). As I demonstrate below, members affiliated with multiple SIGs are important because they facilitate connections between groups.

Membership in SIGs varies across individual characteristics, as illustrated in Table 10.1. CIES members affiliated with an academic institution and those who hold a doctorate degree are more likely than others to be a member of a SIG. This pattern aligns with the initial purpose of SIGs to promote new research and mentor researchers. Further, it echoes findings regarding the importance of research interests and enhance research capabilities as motivations to join SIGs (Jacob and Hunt 2011). We could speculate that this pattern is a result of SIGs activities – such as awards for "best paper" and/or "best book" – that resonate with academics. Also, SIGs are commonplace in other professional associations, thus academics might be more cognizant of their importance.

Table 10.1: Unstandardized Coefficients for Logistic Regression Predicting Membership in any Special Interest Group (1=yes, 0=no)

	Model 1	
Years of CIES membership	.143***	(.021)
Years of CIES membership squared	-.005***	(.001)
Location: North America	.323***	(.089)
Academic affiliation (yes)	.370***	(.095)
Doctorate degree (yes)	.517***	(.103)
Student (yes)	.066	(.090)
Female	.139	(.090)
Intercept	-1.333***	-1.333***
N	3,059	
pseudo R^2	.041	

Standard errors in parentheses
$^* p < 0.05, ^{**} p < 0.01, ^{***} p < 0.001$

CIES members who reside in the U.S. and Canada, whose incomes are generally higher than others, therefore making dues more affordable for them, are more likely to be a member of a SIG. Membership fees make SIGs more affordable for scholars in North America. Also, the relative proximity to the location of CIES meetings, where SIGs hold their business meetings and host other events, plausibly makes SIGs more attractive to scholars in North America.

With regard to tenure in CIES, measured by number of membership years, there is a curvilinear association (inverted U shaped relationship).

The likelihood of membership in SIGs increases with tenure in CIES, but then declines among those who have members for more than 15 years. Drawing on the perspective of innovation diffusion, SIGs are more likely to be joined by new members who entered the Society after the introduction of these groups. In contrast, SIGs are less likely to be adopted by members who joined CIES before SIGs were created and thus do not see their necessity.

SIGs vary in size of membership. Table 10.2 presents the list of SIGs that were approved before 2014, sorted by their membership size. Four

Table 10.2: Special Interest Groups, by Membership (N=3,059)

SIG Code	SIG Name	Membership	
		Number	Percent
GLE	Globalization and Education	235	7.7%
HED	Higher Education	226	7.4%
AFR	Africa	193	6.3%
TEP	Teacher Education and the Teaching Profession	154	5.0%
CDE	Citizenship and Democratic Education	123	4.0%
LAI	Language Issues	96	3.1%
LAM	Latin America	96	3.1%
GLI	Global Literacy	83	2.7%
EAS	East Asia	81	2.6%
IED	Inclusive Education	79	2.6%
PED	Peace Education	78	2.5%
ECD	Early Childhood Development	74	2.4%
SAS	South Asia	73	2.4%
CEH	Cultural Contexts of Education and Human Potential	71	2.3%
SDV	Education for Sustainable Development	64	2.1%
MIE	Middle East	62	2.0%
LSC	Large Scale Cross National Studies	60	2.0%
EUR	Eurasia	54	1.8%
ICT	Information and Communication Technology for Development	53	1.7%
TCE	Teaching Comparative Education	48	1.6%
IKA	Indigenous Knowledge and the Academy	36	1.2%
RLE	Religion and Education	29	0.9%
GME	Global Mathematics Education	25	0.8%
IHE	Contemplative Inquiry and Holistic	11	0.4%

groups attracted a significant number of CIES members (more than five percent): Globalization and Education (7.7 percent), Higher Education (7.4 percent), Africa (6.3 percent), and Teacher Education and the Teaching Profession (5.0 percent). These groups hold discussions and debates that are central to the field of Comparative and International Education.

SIGs as Social Structure

One of the concerns surrounding SIGs is their effect on the cohesiveness of the Society. In order to assess this issue, I conducted a social network analysis of SIGs, as illustrated in Figure 10.2 SIGs (represented in grey squares) are connected to the extent they have members in common. In other words, individuals with multiple SIG memberships create connections between groups. The thickness of the line reflects the strength of the link between SIGs. For the sake of robustness and clarity, this analysis includes only SIGs that share at least 10 members.

Figure 10.2: Social Network of Special Interest Groups

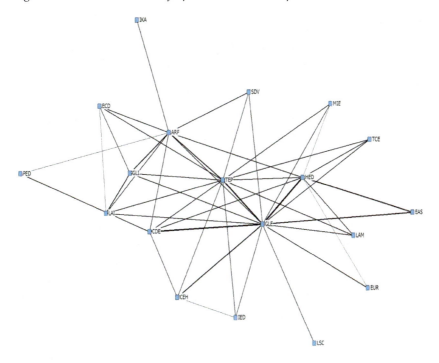

As Figure 10.2 indicates, the network of SIGs is coherent, with many connections between SIGs (i.e., many SIGs share at least 10 members). The network measure suggests that almost half (47.8 percent) of all possible connections between SIGs exist. The network centrality measures indicate that, on average, SIGs have ties to just over three other groups (M=3.76; SD=2.03; range=0-15). The core of the network includes mostly theme-oriented SIGs, with the exception of the Africa SIG. CIES members are affiliated with multiple theme-oriented SIGs, but not with multiple regional SIGs.

Three SIGs have connections to nine or more other groups: Globalization and Education (GLE), Teacher Education and the Teaching Profession (TEP), Africa (AFR), and Higher Education (HED). These SIGs also share many members. This network structure suggests that these groups (and the topics they represent) are central in CIES and hold the Society together. One possible implication is that ideas (broadly defined) discussed in SIGs with many connections to other groups (e.g., Globalization and Education) are more likely to "travel" across groups.

The network of SIGs also presents clusters of interests among CIES members. Many members are interested in Globalization *and* International Large-scale Assessments, or many members are interested in Global Literacies *and* Early Childhood Education. Conversely, the network hints to missing connections as, for example, Education for Sustainable Development *and* Middle East, or Indigenous Knowledge *and* Latin America.

In sum, using social network analysis, I presented the social structure of CIES SIGs. The evident network of SIGs should allay some of the initial concerns regarding the consequences of creating SIGs. The structure, however, also points to holes and gaps in the network of SIGs.

Conclusion

Ten years after their approval by the CIES Board of Directors, SIGs are flourishing. As this chapter demonstrates, SIGs cover progressively more topics and regions of the world. They engage a significant portion of CIES members. Moreover, many SIGs do not function independently of others; they have connections to other groups through individuals with memberships in multiple SIGs.

Nevertheless, as the early SIGs enter their second decade, it is time to reevaluate their operation and to consider changes to the Bylaws. For example, it might be valuable to increase the minimum number of petitioners for establishing a new SIG from 15 to 30. Comparing the minimum requirements for establishing SIGs in other professional associations, CIES has a relatively low minimum: AERA requires 75 members (out of 25,000 members) and ASA requires 200 members (out of 13,000 members). Increasing the minimum number of petitioners would guarantee that SIGs represent significant numbers of members interested in the topic of the SIG. Also, it might be useful to standardize the leadership and governance structure across SIGs to assure engagement of members in the life and stability of the SIGs.

Future research on SIGs could shed light on their impact. One possible direction is to examine whether SIGs create two types of members in CIES: those who view Comparative and International Education broadly as a field and thus identify with the Society overall, and those who see the field in terms of particular topics/regions and thus are more likely to identify with specific SIGs. Another possible direction is to examine the contribution of SIGs to scholarship and production of knowledge. Research on SIGs would not only inform the organizational practice, but also provide new perspectives on CIES and the field of Comparative and International Education.

Notes

[1] Jacob and Hunt (2011) cite leaders of one SIG indicating that informal meetings of SIGs were held in 2001 as a "networking platform and to coordinate our efforts at conference to avoid time conflicts and organize coherent panels ..." (65).

[2] In order to examine the growth of SIGs over the past decade, I use the program of the Annual Conferences of CIES to construct the timeline in which SIGs were introduced. Digital copies of most programs are available on the Society website and on the Internet Archive (https://archive.org/web/). Other programs became available through colleagues.

[3] Based on the available documents, and to my knowledge, only one petition for a new SIG did not developed into a fully active SIG: Cross-National Educational Transfer.

References

Comparative and International Education Society. 2008. Handbook for CIES SIG Chairpersons.

Comparative and International Education Society. 2011. Policies and Procedures for Development and Activities of CIES SIGs.

Easton, P.B. 2014. "Documenting the Evolution of the Field: Reflections on the 2013 Comparative Education Review Bibliography." *Comparative Education Review 58* (4): 555-574.

Jacob, W.J., & P.F. Hunt. 2011. CIES Special Interest Groups – Review Commit-tee Final Report. Comparative and International Education Society.

Raby, R.L. 2007. Fifty years of comparative education review bibliographies: reflections on the field. *Comparative Education Review 51*(3): 379-398.

Williams, J. 2008. Report of the CIES Ad Hoc Committee on Special Interest Groups. Comparative and International Education Society.

Focusing on Gender and Education

Nelly P. STROMQUIST, Halla B. HOLMARSDOTTIR &
Caroline MANION

Introduction

Established in 1989 and in operation since 1990, the Gender and
Education Committee (GEC) is one of the largest standing committees in
the Society. It was initiated by Vandra Masemann – one of her first
actions as CIES president – who had been prompted by the absence of
women's issues and gender concerns within the Society. The overarching
objective of the GEC has been to introduce a greater awareness of the role
of gender in education in our professional organization. The GEC has
grown to become a valuable referent within the CIES, as it not only gives
the issue of gender greater visibility and oversees the situation of gender
issues within the Society, but also serves as a venue for intense practical
and theoretical debates.

Contributions to the Society

In its early years, the GEC undertook a basic stocktaking of the presence
of women in the Society. Through several iterations, the GEC mapped
the status of women in the CIES as reflected in conference participation
and in publications in the Society's journal, the *Comparative Education
Review*. Early activities also called for an exchange of gender and
education syllabi and, in 1991, a directory of scholars and practitioners
that was updated in 1993. A "Comparative Analysis of CIES
Participation 1992-1998" was presented at the CIES conference in 1999.

Erwin H. Epstein (ed.) (2016): *Crafting a Global Field: Six Decades of the Comparative
and International Education Society*. Hong Kong: Comparative Education Research
Centre (CERC), The University of Hong Kong, and Dordrecht: Springer. © CERC

Monitoring gender parity issues in multiple forms (e.g., as Society leaders, keynote speakers, *CER* authors, conference participants) within the CIES remains on the GEC agenda. Tracking conference presenters by sex over time has been very useful in showing the changes in the Society and to ensure that progress is maintained. Our Society today is more sensitive to gender, and gender has made it to the forefront of the minds of more members than ever before.

One of the most significant contributions of the GEC Committee has been the provision of workshops through one-day pre-conference sessions, a practice started at the beginnings of the GEC, in 1990. These workshops have addressed a variety of issues, from enhancing feminist dialogues to building a career in practice and helping new scholars to refine their doctoral dissertation work. The pre-conference sessions have provided a positive space within the CIES as younger scholars are seeing more women as role models and mentors by established members of the Society. The one-day event has included an informal lunch period, affording very beneficial social conviviality and professional exchanges among GEC members.

Since 2005, the GEC has organized an annual symposium within the conference to present the ideas of prominent scholars working on gender in various parts of the world. Symposium presentations have reflected the breadth, depth, and quality of the research, programming, and advocacy in the field of gender and education. Recent topics have included: gender as a cross-cutting theme in research, policy, and advocacy; family life and academic stress; men and masculinities; gender and peace education; and globalization, gender, and education. Symposium events have often included lunch, which again has created a climate for informal academic exchanges. The GEC has thus played an important role in the development of academic networks covering several issues, including improving educational quality, combatting sexual harassment in universities, and strengthening professional organizations. Efforts have also been made to promote the development of successful careers in comparative and international education.

By virtue of its active performance over the years, the GEC has lent legitimacy to women's perspectives and ways of knowing in the CIES. Further, the GEC has served as a pathway for junior scholars to interact actively with pivotal people in the field of gender in education and development. The symposia and workshops have deepened our collective knowledge and thinking about gender in the field, and simultaneously enabled the GEC to play a substantial role in agenda-setting within the Society and the work of its members.

The creation of networks enabled by the GEC has supported the continuing ascent of junior scholars to positions of leadership and critical service, from which they have been able to serve the larger society as well. Active performance in the GEC has served as a path for several women to become CIES presidents and to foster gender-sensitive performance from that position. In the words of a former president, "My involvement in GEC most assuredly instilled in me the need to be aware ... to reflect the breadth, depth, and quality of the research, programming, and advocacy occurring in the field of gender and education."

It was through a GEC initiative in 1992 that the CIES board created the Gail P. Kelly award to recognize outstanding doctoral dissertations. Initially focused on issues related to gender, the Kelly award was expanded by the awards sub-committee at that time to apply to broader issues of social justice and equity. The first award was presented at the annual CIES conference in 1994. Many of its recipients have gone on to academic positions, from which they continue their work on social inclusion. Other tangible contributions to the Society include the GEC's participation in the evaluation of gender-related paper presentations and panels submitted for the annual CIES conferences. The GEC was active in providing input to the CIES Constitution revision in 2003, at which time it upheld the importance for gender in the Society to function in a standing committee.

As members of the GEC have gained representation in the CIES Board of Directors and the presidency, they have used their positions to advance gender issues in the society. For instance, when serving as *CER* book review editor, one former GEC member who later became CIES president, made a deliberate effort to include both male and female reviewers, a measure that brought the critical appraisal of male and female scholars to the knowledge produced.

CIES women presidents have in notable instances been extremely supportive of the role of the GEC as a standing committee and have provided generous support for the GEC's efforts to organize its different events during the conference and bring the message of the committee out to the membership. Up to the present, among the 58 CIES presidents, 15 have been women. Momentum has built in the election of women presidents to the point that during the past 16 years there has been a numerical parity. This has not yet been reflected in the naming of honorary fellows, however, as only five of the 27 fellows have been women. This shows that despite the achievement in parity, in some areas the work of the GEC is still important in order to bring about parity along with gender equity in other areas.

A special note must be made of the development of the *Gender and Education Manifesto*, which sets objectives and parameters of work on gender and education. This document was inspired by a GEC symposium in Puerto Rico (2012), where the keynote speaker described a *Gender in Science Manifesto* as part of a European initiative to promote the presence of women in scientific fields. The refinement of the *Gender and Education Manifesto* and its formal adoption by the GEC took place at the CIES meeting in New Orleans in March 2013. This event was followed by a wide distribution of the *Gender and Education Manifesto* in five languages (English, Spanish, Portuguese, French, and Chinese) at the World Congress of Comparative Education Societies held in Buenos Aires in June 2013. Signed by over 100 congress participants, this document offers substantive points that should serve as a standard for policies and behavior within the field of international and comparative education. A similar standard could also be applied in a number of areas in the CIES, such as the choice of committee chairs and in the publication arms of the CIES.

The support of Board of Directors members (both female and male) has been instrumental in providing GEC financial support, which has permitted the participation of several women scholars from various parts of the world in its annual symposia. Men have long been involved in the GEC, attending and participating in GEC-sponsored sessions, although in small numbers. The GEC has counted on the support of several men scholars who have been constant allies. They include Steven Klees, Robert Arnove, Mark Ginsburg, Joel Samoff, David Baker, and the late David Wilson. Noah Sobe, from his position as treasurer at that time, supported the work of the GEC by setting a procedure whereby the committee makes a yearly budget request to the Board. This means the work of the GEC is supported today more robustly [and predictably] than it had been in the 2000s. A small group of men in the Society equate the much greater representation of women in the CIES programming and positions of leadership as indicative that gender issues no longer affect either the CIES or the field of international and comparative education.

This notion that the work of gender is "done" hides a number of social justice issues with regard to gender that go beyond simple parity.

Facilitation of Gender-Related Knowledge

The GEC has played a crucial role in the dissemination of gender-related knowledge and in reminding researchers that the GEC's concern is not only with numerical parity between women and men but also – and perhaps more – with gender dynamics and relations. Several GEC chairs have been concerned with linking policy, scholarship, and practice, after observing the gap between development projects and published scholarly research. To reduce this gap, GEC chairs have attempted to showcase in annual gender workshops the work of colleagues who largely work in non-university organizations and development agencies. As attested by its outreach to the rest of the CIES and beyond, the GEC has been able to create important bridges across educators, researchers, and practitioners. Among its close ties is another CIES standing committee – the Underrepresented Ethnic and Abilities Group (UREAG) – with which it has developed considerable synergy, leading both committees to consider more intensely the interaction between gender and race and other categories of differentiation. Gendered experiences are often compounded by the intersectionality of other identity categories, and this underscores the need for continued collaboration between the GEC and UREAG, along with the New Scholars Committee.

Methodological and Theoretical Contributions

Feminist methodologies are not marginalized in comparative and international education research, and many researchers who use feminist methodologies can talk about them and find others who share similar perspectives. The GEC has reflected ongoing developments in the field and has maintained itself attuned to recent global policies such as Education for All (EFA) and the Millennium Development Goals (MDGs). For instance, panels organized by the GEC on girls' right to education and on empowerment and gender justice using the capabilities approach have provided the Society with knowledge from other disciplines that is being applied toward the transformation of education policy and practice globally. Contributions from post-modern theory through deconstruction and discourse analysis have been incorporated in the analysis of texts produced by international development agencies to show that such discourses, based on of modernization theory and neoclassical economics, re-create hierarchies of gender and race closely connected to the global capitalist system that leave many women in the Global South without access to education, economic, and political resources.

The concepts of intersectionality, fluid identities, and both the use and rejection of binary categories such as women and men have brought a lively debate into the GEC conversations and served to challenge as well as enrich methodological and theoretical perspectives. Some fields, such as development studies (notably, gender and development) and the social sciences generally (especially anthropology and sociology) have developed their thinking about gender to a greater degree than has the field of comparative and international education. The GEC will continue to introduce innovative theories and analytical perspectives to bring the CIES and the CIE field in general to the forefront of gender-related research.

Persistent Challenges

Within the CIES leadership, the GEC has resisted occasional calls to classify itself as a SIG rather than a standing committee. A SIG by definition is a special interest group around a certain education theme. The GEC as a standing committee has instead a broader mission that provides a collective space to engage in systematic knowledge production and dissemination as well as in ongoing assessments and reflections on society's ex/implicit actions that manifest patterns of power, inclusion, and advocacy regarding gender. Fortunately, the challenge to remain a standing committee has by now become weak.

There is consensus among former and current GEC leaders that efforts must be constantly present to improve the quality of educational research – an effort that will benefit from greater incorporation of key social markers such as gender and race/ethnicity. There is also widespread consensus on the need to link our research to action. To date, the development specialists (USAID, World Bank, etc.) have taken the lead in describing the results of their "work on the ground." This has been possible, of course, given the abundant resources of these agencies. Yet, the application of research to subsequent policy design and implementation remains a challenge to feminist scholars. Further, feminist activists, too, need to explain the contributions that they have been able to make at both local and national levels.

In the policy/practice arenas, gender concern is "stuck" on access – counting bodies on seats in schools. Significant progress has been made in getting girls into school, and with the 2015 adoption of the Sustainable Development Goals that will guide worldwide policy until 2030, access is now being targeted to secondary schooling. However, the focus on quality, equality, and equity is not as well supported, and dealing with them will need questioning the content of the curriculum, the nature of schools as protective spaces. It will also need training in gender issues for teachers, administrators, and education authorities. The dominant use of quantitative indicators does not foster attention to more complex and dynamic aspects of schooling.

Finally, a challenge that remains is the participation of men in GEC activities. Efforts have to be made to incorporate more men as members. Likewise, discussions about masculinities in the construction of gender in both workshops and symposia are to be intensified.

Conclusions

As an autonomous space, the GEC has gone beyond anti-discrimination approaches to explore deeper causes of gender asymmetries. The number of CIES conference sessions dealing with gender issues has been increasing, a clear sign that the gender dimension is affecting the conceptualization of much of the research in comparative and international education. As a result, the CIES now has a healthier social and academic environment that encourages multiple ideas and approaches to scholarship and intellectual exchange that are rooted in multiple experiences. The GEC has also helped to bring more horizontal and thus more democratic decision making to the Society as a whole.

It has become a matter of great pride to serve as the GEC chair (and, during the past eight years, as co-chair), and each leader has brought her own contributions, some emphasizing the link between theory and practice, others highlighting new perspectives in methods or in theory. The GEC is cognizant of its mission to prepare new generations to a full understanding of gender as a key dimension affecting social development. It will persevere in this task in the years ahead.

Table 11.1 GEC Chairs and Co-Chairs (1990-Present)

Name	Institutional Affiliation	Years in Office
Caroline (Carly) Manion	OISE, University of Toronto	2014-Present
Halla Holmarsdottir	Oslo and Akershus University College	2013-Present
Supriya Baily	George Mason University	2011-2014
Vilma Seeberg	Kent State University	2011-2013
Regina Cortina	Teachers College, Columbia	2011
Karen Monkman	DePaul University	2008-2010
Nancy Kendall	University of Wisconsin	2008-2010
Shirley Miske	Miske Witt & Associates	2005-2007
Mary Ann Maslak	St. John's University	2002-2004
Margaret (Peg) Sutton	Indiana University	2000-2001
Heidi Ross	Indiana University	1997-1999
Karen Biraimah	University of Central Florida	1993-1996
Nelly Stromquist	University of Maryland	1990-1992

Acknowledgment: This account of the history of the Gender and Education Committee builds upon comments made by multiple respondents, listed here alphabetically: N'Dri Assié-Lumumba, Supriya Baily, Regina Cortina, Ratna Ghosh, Beverly Lindsay, Vandra Masemann, Mary Ann Maslak, Karen Monkman, Heidi Ross, Vilma Seeberg, Gita Steiner-Khamsi. Of course, it also relies on the views of the authors of this chapter.

Distinguished Shapers and Doers

12
Shaping Leadership

Ratna GHOSH and Mariusz GALCZYNSKI

Going "International"

Reflecting on the Society's first ten years, William W. Brickman noted that the Board of Directors had included "truly international" represent-atives from countries including Switzerland, England, and Chile. At the same time, he contrasted this to the domesticity of the Society's elected leadership, which he attributed to the expense of attending meetings in the United States and the formation of the Comparative Education Society in Europe five years earlier (Brickman 1966, 11). Several years later in a historical analysis of the Society – by that time called the Comparative *and International* Education Society (CIES) – Brickman (1977) defended his interpretation of international representation:

> At this point, it becomes important to emphasize the fact that the CES, from its very inception, was an international, not a strictly American, organization. The conferences always attracted representatives from other countries. Both the board of directors of the Society and the editorial board of the *Review* included not only scholars from several European countries, but also some from Canada, South America, and Asia. Some from other nations have served as officers of the Society. Thus, Professor Philip J. Idenburg of the Netherlands, Professor Pedro Rosselló of Switzerland, Professor Irma Salas of Chile, and Professors Edmund J. King and Vernon Mallinson of Great Britain were members of the board of directors. During 1966-1967, the eight-person editorial board included Professors Friedrich Schneider

Erwin H. Epstein (ed.) (2016): *Crafting a Global Field: Six Decades of the Comparative and International Education Society.* Hong Kong: Comparative Education Research Centre (CERC), The University of Hong Kong, and Dordrecht: Springer. © CERC and Franz Hilker of Germany, Professor Pedro Rosselló of Switzerland, and Professor Joseph A. Lauwerys of England. As early in the history of the Society as 1961-1962, the presidency was graced by Professor Joseph Katz of Canada. Since then, Professors Philip J. Foster and Harold J. Noah (originally from Britain), Andreas M. Kazamias (born in Cyprus), and Reginald Edwards and Joseph Farrell (Canada) have occupied the presidential chair; in addition, Professor Mathew Zachariah (Indian) is currently the Society's president-elect. Without proclaiming one's self-perception of virtue at the lack of ethnocentrism in the Society, we can point to objective data testifying to the international character of the CES. Accordingly, it is not strictly sporting for some European specialists to refer, both in speaking and in print, to the "Comparative Education Society of the U.S." (399).

Yet the above interpretation of "international" was limited to membership of people, most of whom originated from European countries, rather than on development and global issues. And strangely enough, Mathew Zachariah was identified as Indian rather than Canadian, although Reginald Edwards and Joseph Farrell were listed as Canadians.

Regardless, the Society was headed in a decidedly more international – and younger – direction going into the future. Even as early as the mid-1970s, the Society began "the policy of electing students as members of the Society's board of directors" (Brickman 1977, 400). By the mid-1990s, Society "viability" was embodied by a membership approaching 1,000 persons (about a quarter of whom were international) and including nearly 1,400 institutions. Of course, CIES benefitted from the increasing contributions of students in particular, among them the ever-growing numbers of international students (Wilson 1994, 460). The trend towards younger and more international membership represented the Society's "continued vitality" well into the turn of the century – most notably with student membership between 1989 and 2000 increasing over twofold for American students and more than fourfold for international students (Arnove 2001, 493).

The Nominations Committee

With the first constitution of the Comparative Education Society, ratified on June 1, 1959, both the offices of President and Vice President were henceforth to be elected annually by the membership. To be eligible, candidates had to have been Society members for at least one year. They were elected to one-year terms, with the possibility of re-election for an additional year. In contrast, the offices of Secretary-Treasurer and Editor of the *Comparative Education Review*, which rounded out the Executive Council to manage Society business between meetings, were to be appointed.[1] Among the President's duties, "*He* [emphasis added] shall appoint committees other than the Nominations Committee" (Read 1959, 38).

As it turned out, it took nearly 20 years to elect a President who was not male. Susanne Shafer (Arizona State University) became the Society's first female President in 1976, nineteen years after Brickman's inaugural presidency in 1957. The next women presidents were elected seven and ten years later, respectively: Barbara Yates (University of Illinois-Champaign/Urbana) in 1983 and Gail Kelly (State University of New York at Buffalo) in 1986. Around this period, board members such as Vandra L. Masemann called for revision of the Constitution and Bylaws to ensure regional, gender, and ethnocultural equity in the composition of the CIES Executive and Board. In 1988, Beverly Lindsay (University of Georgia) became the first minority female President; she was succeeded the next year by Masemann (University of Toronto), who became the first non-American female President. In 1994, Nelly Stromquist (University of Southern California) became the first female of Latin American origin to hold the position. Following Ruth Hayhoe's (University of Toronto) term in 1999, women held the presidency three years in a row between 2001-2003: Heidi Ross (Colgate University), Karen Biraimah (University of Central Florida), and Kassie Freeman (Vanderbilt University). The same happened from 2009-2011, with Gita Steiner-Khamsi (Columbia University), Maria Teresa Tatto (Michigan State University), and Ratna Ghosh (McGill University). Most recently, Karen Mundy (University of Toronto) and N'Dri Assié-Lumumba (Cornell University) respectively served as CIES Presidents in 2014 and 2015. The increased nomination and election of women is among manifestations of the Society's diverse character.

Originally, the Board of Directors itself would "serve as the Nominations Committee to receive nominations from members for elective posts, prepare the slate, and submit it to the Secretary-Treasurer in time for inclusion with the notice to members concerning the next Annual Meeting" (Read 1959, 39). Board members would serve their terms on a staggered basis. To ensure this, the first cohort consisted of three members serving for just one year, another three serving two years, and the final three serving a full three-year term. Directors would likewise be eligible for re-election for an additional term. "Provision in the first Constitution for election by the membership of the President, Vice-President, and the Board of Directors, rather than their appointment by a group in power, reflected the political traditions in which the founders of the society were acculturated. The fact, moreover, of term limits for officers, board members, and appointed officers ensured that no clique would dominate the society for long" (Swing in this volume).

The Nominations Committee was established as a separate entity from the Board of Directors with ratification of the 1998 Constitution of the CIES. Today, the Nominations Committee continues as a standing (permanent) committee as indicated in Article VI, Section 2 of the Constitution:

> The Nominations Committee shall be appointed from among the members who are not holding office in the Society and who shall have been members for at least one year. The committee shall consist of not less than three members including the Chair. (CIES 2015a).

Currently, the CIES President appoints the Nominations Committee annually. Whereas the functions of the Nominations Committee remain similar to their origins, specific duties are delineated in the CIES Bylaws. In preparing to present a slate of candidates to the Society Membership, the Nominations Committee must receive nominations from members, obtain consent from nominees themselves, narrow down the slate to two candidates for each elected office, and submit a draft ballot with candidates' biographical sketches "in time for communicating to all members" (CIES 2015a). The work of the Committee begins with elaboration of the call for nominations, including the criteria to determine candidates for each position. The Committee's goal is to ensure a broad slate that mirrors the diversity of the Society. All CIES members are invited to make nominations including self-nominations.

Candidates for Vice President must demonstrate long-term CIES membership (at least ten years); significant involvement in Society activities, such as previous terms on the Board of Directors or as Chair of a Special Interest Group (SIG); and a record of scholarly attainment within comparative and international education. Guidelines for identifying candidates for the Board of Directors are similar and require at least five years of Society membership and leadership. Every three years, a student representative is also nominated for the Board of Directors. Potential candidates must demonstrate CIES involvement for at least two years, and attendance and participation in at least two national or regional CIES conferences. Each candidate must also provide a letter of recommendation from a faculty member active within the Society. As of 2014, the offices of Secretary, Treasurer, and Historian – all serving three-year terms – were also to be elected by the membership. While constitutional amendments for these roles were pending, the Nominations Committee accepted nominations and selected candidates.[2]

In a typical year, the call for nominations is disseminated by the Secretariat through the Society's list-serv in August/September. Nominees are evaluated by the Nominations Committee and a slate of candidates is determined in October/November. The slate is then shown to the Board of Directors as a courtesy while candidates are given time to submit photos, brief biographies, and plans for CIES. The Secretariat disseminates candidates' information online in December, and voting begins in January. Balloting procedures are carried out according to the CIES Bylaws and conclude two weeks prior to the Society's annual meeting. As identified by databases overseen by the University of Chicago Press (publisher of *Comparative Education Review*), full, student, and emeritus members are invited to cast votes. The electronic ballot was introduced in 2004, but paper ballots, if preferred, may be requested from the CIES Secretariat. Tellers appointed by the President ultimately tally the votes and report results.

"The most important thing about the evolution of this committee over many years," recalled Vandra Masemann, "is the attempt to create a fair, representative, and rational process, as well as a clear and fair voting process that captures both U.S. and non-U.S. votes" (e-mail message to authors, October 15, 2015). Over the past several years, reports from the Secretariat (CIES 2015b) have documented voter participation as consistently between 25 to 30 percent of the membership. Yet with such large membership, it can be assumed that voting is most common among the members who attend the annual conference and are/or involved with the activities of standing committees and Special Interest Groups (SIGs).

Nevertheless, respondents to the 2010 post-conference survey reported being either very satisfied (50%, n=120) or satisfied (41.7%, n=100) when asked about "Voting in CIES elections" (CIES 2015b).

Learning from Complications

Whereas the founders of the Society sought to put into place a leadership that was representative, international, evolving, and fairly-elected, a contested election in 1990 exposed that this might not always have been achieved. At that time, air-mail ballots were sent overseas and understandably did not always reach the voters. Matters came to a head when Vice Presidential candidate Stephen Heyneman (World Bank) defeated David Wilson (University of Toronto) by a margin of just one vote. Wilson got word that some members had never received their overseas mail ballots and would have voted for him. A similar situation had happened the previous year, when the margin was only three votes and several overseas members likewise declared that they had not received ballots.

In response, Wilson insisted on a review and modernization of the election process by regular mail. Although some members of the Board of Directors questioned the validity of the election result, the Board meeting did not have a quorum and the matter dragged on for a few additional weeks until all of the Directors had been contacted by mail and "voted to let the election results stand, on the argument that no fraud or malice had taken place" (Swing 2007, 109). Regardless, then President Val Rust (UCLA) and Past President Vandra L. Masemann (University of Toronto) wrote Wilson a letter of apology, and he ran again for Vice President successfully the following year.

As a result of the contested election, an ad hoc Elections Committee led by Steven J. Klees (University of Maryland) was created to review and make recommendations for modernizing the election process by regular mail, ensuring ample time for receipt of ballots and submission of votes. Just a few years later, the Nominations Committee was formally written into the Society's 1998 Constitution. Special precautions were taken in preparation of voting envelopes, and formal rules for counting ballots were established. When electronic voting was introduced in 2004, the voting process became further "tamper-proof" (Swing 2007, 110) and decidedly more accessible.

Yet as the membership of CIES grew rapidly in the 1990s and 2000s, Nominations Committees began to report that it was sometimes difficult to get individuals to agree to stand for the position of Vice President (e.g. CIES 2015b) largely due to the financial and institutional resources required to take on organization of the Society's annual conference (as President-Elect). Even with contractual delegation of tasks to a professional conference planner as well as an abstract submission and review company, the President-Elect was informally expected to secure support – such as reception funds, course release, and/or work-study students – from his or her host institution. Compounded by dwindling institutional budgets in the early 2000s, the burden of Society management was perceived as so great that it persuaded the CIES Board of Directors to establish an Executive Director position to free up leadership from management responsibilities and permit focus on more substantive Society development. As such, it was hoped that taking on the leadership opportunity of Vice President (who would consequently serve as President-Elect, President, and Past-President) would now also appeal to a more diverse slate of candidates.

Echoing such sentiment, introduction of online voting in the 2000s had granted space to CIES members to share comments on the electronic ballot itself. Although Secretariat reports revealed high satisfaction with technical facilitation of the voting process, some Society members criticized what they considered to be a lack of diversity in the slates of candidates put forward for election – in both regional representation and fields of research expertise. One member even protested the lacking representation of practitioners within CIES leadership by abstaining from voting altogether (CIES 2015b).

The Nominations Committee has been affected only by minor complications in the past few years. One exception came in 2008-09, when the Nominations Committee consisted entirely of members who had not served on it before. Their lack of institutional memory led to a recommendation to better formalize the guidelines and procedures for committee work – i.e., a tentative timeline and the specific criteria in the Call for Nominations, which contained guidelines for identifying nominees (CIES 2015b). Another complication occurred in advance of the 2011 annual meeting, which was scheduled to take place in May rather than in March. This meant that the elections process needed to be implemented on a delayed timeline; it also made evident that the articles outlining selection and terms of executive officers and board members needed clarification in regards to start and end points (CIES 2015b).

Looking Forward

Nominations Committee reports (CIES2015b) describe proposals on the vetting process for issuing a slate of candidates for election. One such proposal, in 2008-09, would increase the number of student positions on the board. Although students make up a very significant proportion of Society membership, they are represented by only one seat on the Board of Directors. Because the student representative serves a three-year term, this means that the Nominations Committee is tasked with restricting nominations of several excellent candidates to just two, who then compete for only one position triennially. The non-student Board member positions are much less competitive by comparison, as two to three spots are available each year. The Board has yet to deal with this issue.

In the sixty years that the CIES has evolved, it has become increasingly inclusive with a diverse membership that is reflected in its leadership – not only in terms of regional representation, but also in gender and ethnicity and in areas of research and methods. Further, technological advances have enabled Society members to express their viewpoints more clearly and to make informed choices in selecting their leaders.

In 2014, the CIES Vice President candidates engaged in a live debate in two formats: as a webinar on January 26 and Twitter chat on February 8 (Intl Ed Dev @PennGSE 2015). This was the first time that the Society membership could take into consideration more than the brief biographies assembled by the Nominations Committee. Expressing their visions for the CIES, candidates Gustavo E. Fischman (Arizona State University) and Noah W. Sobe (Loyola University Chicago) responded to questions about strengthening connections in the Global South, expanding publishing opportunities, job market concerns, relevance of the *CIES Newsletter* and regional conferences, and the role of the CIES in influencing education policy. Similar opportunities for engaging with members through social media should continue in future election cycles.

Notes

[1] With approval of the membership, additional executive officers could be elected—such as the soon-added President-Elect (Brickman 1966, 11).

[2] The office of Historian was an appointed position established in 1998. The first Society historian was Elizabeth Sherman Swing, whose PhD dissertation advisor had been William W. Brickman, the first President of the Society.

References

Arnove, Robert F. 2001. "Comparative and International Education Society (CIES) Facing the Twenty-First Century: Challenges and Contributions. *Comparative Education Review 45* (4): 477-503.

Brickman, William W. 1966. "Ten Years of the Comparative Education Society." *Comparative Education Review 10* (1): 4-15.

Brickman, William W. 1977. "Comparative and International Education Society: An Historical Analysis." *Comparative Education Review 21* (2-3): 396-404.

Comparative and International Education Society (CIES). 2015a. CIES Constitution and Bylaws. Mount Royal, NJ: CIES. http://www.cies.us/?page=ConstitutionBylaws

Comparative and International Education Society (CIES). 2015b. Historian's Corner. Mount Royal, NJ: CIES https://www.cies.us/?page=Historian&hhSearchTerms=%22nominations%22&#rescol_2353919

International Educational Development Program at the University of Pennsylvania (Intl Ed Dev @PennGSE), Storify post. "First Ever #CIESChat with VP Candidates." February 9, 2015, https://storify.com/IEDP_PennGSE/first-ever-cieschat-with-vp-candidates.

Johnson, William H.E. 1957. "The Comparative Education Society." *Comparative Education Review 1* (2): 16.

Read, Gerald H. 1959. "Constitution of the Comparative Education Society." *Comparative Education Review 3* (3): 37-40.

Swing, Elizabeth Sherman. 2007. "The Comparative and International Education Society (CIES)." In Vandra Masemann, Mark Bray, & Maria Manzon (eds.), *Common Interests, Uncommon Goals: Histories of the World Council of Comparative Education Societies and its Members*, CERC Studies in Comparative Education 21, Hong Kong: Comparative Education Research Centre, The University of Hong Kong, and Dordrecht: Springer, pp.94-125.

Wilson, David N. 1994. "Comparative and International Education: Fraternal or Siamese Twins? A Preliminary Genealogy of Our Twin Fields." *Comparative Education Review 38* (4): 449-486.

13
Early Leaders:
Isaac L. Kandel, William W. Brickman, and C. Arnold Anderson

Erwin H. EPSTEIN

... our national security depends upon our technological supremacy. Further, with our whole economy dependent upon technical advances, any lag is endangering our entire way of life.

Does this quotation from the *New York Times* sound familiar? It should. Reports that the U.S. is falling behind many countries in technological fields have become commonplace. In response to such claims, U.S. President Barack Obama, on June 13, 2011, announced a program to train 10,000 new American engineers every year and generally promote education in science, technology, engineering, and mathematics, the so-called "STEM" disciplines. The emphasis here is clear that although armaments and soldiers are in the front line of national defense, a modern nation ultimately depends for its security on the intellectual preparation of its citizens.

Yet the view expressed in the *New York Times* quotation is not recent; it appeared over 60 years ago, specifically on June 19, 1955. Throughout the decades since then, U.S. policy makers, like President Obama, have often despaired of the failure of American education to keep pace in science and math in view of the seeming superiority of other nations in these areas. In doing so, these policy makers not infrequently have

Erwin H. Epstein (ed.) (2016): *Crafting a Global Field: Six Decades of the Comparative and International Education Society*. Hong Kong: Comparative Education Research Centre (CERC), The University of Hong Kong, and Dordrecht: Springer. © CERC

glossed over the fact that the body of evidence indicating shortages of scientists and engineers has been inconclusive.

Consider the consequences of extrapolating beyond the evidence. The *New York Times* article claims that the condition and focus of education are matters of national security and economic wellbeing. If it is true that the U.S. falls short in preparing scientists and engineers, national security and economic wellbeing would indeed be at risk. If it is not true, however, then precious national resources will be wasted in trying to fill a gap that does not exist.

Where is the reliable evidence to answer such issues of vital concern? The area of research that most focuses on how schooling affects national security, economic development, wars, revolutions, and peace is **comparative education**, a field that applies the theories and methods of history and the social sciences to understand issues of education that are of international concern. Though having strong roots in the 19th century, comparative education matured in the 20th, guided in good measure by three of the field's giants: Isaac L. Kandel (1881-1965), William W. Brickman (1913-1986), and C. Arnold Anderson (1907-1990).

These illuminati of our field mirror the split between the STEM disciplines and the liberal arts, between universalism and particularism, and between positivism and relativism. Kandel and Brickman were historians but steeped also in philosophy; Anderson was a sociologist with a strong interest in economics. Among the early founders of the Comparative Education Society (now CIES, the Comparative and International Education Society), they set the stage for a running tension between polarities, a divide that has existed in academia at large since ancient Greece, when Plato used the dialectic mode of reasoning and discourse to arrive at "truth", and Isocrates stressed practical knowledge of everyday life.[2] That tension remains in place today, with one or the other side gaining the upper hand in a continuing cycle. In the history of CIES, such a divide played out most visibly in the 1950s and 1960s, with Kandel and Brickman representing one side and Anderson, along with notables such as Harold Noah and Max Eckstein, representing the other side.

Although all three of these leaders knew each other, Kandel belonged to an earlier generation of comparativists, whereas Anderson and Brickman were close contemporaries. However, Kandel and Brickman had much more in common. Both were historians, identified strongly as Jews, and generated ideas on education that were shaped by first-hand experiences with international conflict, revolution and discrimination. As prolific scholars, they advanced many of comparative education's most important topics: how schools indoctrinate children; build national identities, strengthen or weaken democracy; and reduce or exacerbate ethnic and racial cleavages. Anderson's writings reflect epistemological differences with Kandel and Brickman, yet they all shared some common interests, especially a concern over social class inequalities.

The three scholars were raised in different circumstances. Kandel was born in Romania and migrated with his parents to Britain when he was five years old. He was raised in a comfortable but not affluent home, was educated in English schools, and lived and worked in several countries. Brickman, by contrast, was born in the U.S. to poor immigrant parents, but like Kandel lived and worked in various countries. Both were multilingual, lecturing and writing in several languages as well as English, and both were editors of the highly regarded scholarly periodical, *School and Society*, with Brickman, as the younger of the two, following Kandel in that position. Anderson's roots were rural, having been born in Platte, South Dakota in a family that had come from central Nebraska.

No one gave shape to early 20th century scholarship in comparative education more than Kandel, and no one gave rise to comparative education as a professional field more than Brickman and Anderson. Kandel wrote the book *Comparative Education*, published in 1933, that set the stage in Europe and North America for the field's scholarly development in the years and decades that followed. Brickman, together with Gerald Read of Kent State University, organized the meetings that saw the birth in 1956 of the field's first professional association, the Comparative Education Society (CES). As mentioned above, the CES was later renamed the Comparative and International Education Society (CIES), the largest among more than 40 sub-national, national, regional, and language-based comparative education associations that are members of the World Council of Comparative Education Societies. Brickman became the organization's first president. Anderson was the co-founder of the highly influential International Project for the Evaluation of Educational Achievement (IEA) and in 1962 became the Comparative Education Society's fourth president.[3]

Differences in Style and Background

Although Kandel and Brickman shared common philosophical perspectives, their personalities and life styles were notably different. Kandel had a rather aristocratic air and kept a neat and tidy office at Columbia University, as reflected in the impeccably arranged files found in the collection of nine boxes of his papers in the Hoover Institution archives. By contrast, Brickman's files in the Hoover archives are loosely and somewhat chaotically organized in 128 boxes, much like the organization of his office at the University of Pennsylvania. Anderson's office at the University of Chicago, however, resembled that of Brickman's, though unlike Brickman, his lectures tended to be like his office, rather haphazard.[4]

Arguably, their differences in style grew out of their very different upbringings. As a child, Kandel attended an English primary school and then, upon winning a scholarship in a competitive examination, entered the Manchester Grammar School, the largest and one of the oldest (chartered in 1515) independent day schools for boys ages 7-18 in the UK. The Manchester Grammar School enforced strict discipline, emphasized the classics, and taught students mainly by rote. Kandel studied Latin, Greek, French, and German for six years before entering the University of Manchester to take a degree in classics. At one point in his career he spent a year in Latin America, learned Spanish, and gave a series of lectures in that language in Mexico. He also mastered Portuguese, Dutch, and Norwegian. Though not from an aristocratic family, Kandel's education followed classic British upper-class lines.

Brickman's childhood was spent in the impoverished lower east side of New York City. His command of languages was an outgrowth of his home environment, where he absorbed Yiddish, Hebrew, Aramaic, Polish, German, and Russian, and his education was molded by the give and take of the Jewish *cheder*. He eventually learned several other languages – so many, indeed, that in an instruction sheet he handed his students at the University of Pennsylvania, he wrote, "A foreign student may present his paper in his native language, but he should first ascertain if the instructor can read it. (As of this date, the instructor does not read Chinese, Japanese, Arabic, Farsi, and the South Asian languages, among others.)." Few American instructors would allow students to write in any language other than English, and if such allowance were made, it would be for no more than one or possibly two foreign languages. How many instructors would specify the languages in which students would *not* be permitted to write? Whereas Kandel's early international demeanor was influenced by the travels of his parents (his father was an exporter), Brickman's was formed by the stories told by his parents about the old country. His father was born in Germany while his mother grew up in the town of Jedwabne, Poland, and it was there that his parents were married and most of his family lived.

Anderson's rural roots exerted a powerful influence on both his core values and research interests, and he was skeptical about the pretensions of government. Anderson came from largely Scottish (not Scandinavian) pioneer stock, and unlike Kandel and Brickman did not grow up in a household steeped with parental international experience and in a multi-lingual environment. When Anderson came to the University of Chicago to launch the Comparative Education Center in 1958, he was already a prominent figure in American sociology. His main interest was in, to use Philip Foster's (1991) term, the "demographics of education" at a time when few American sociologists paid attention to education. Serving as the Editor of the *American Journal of Sociology* concurrently as the Director of the Comparative Education Center helped to give currency in the social sciences to the upstart field of comparative education. Kandel and Brickman did much to give prominence to comparative education in history and philosophy circles; Anderson did much the same in sociology and economics.

Education under Conflict and Dictatorship

How dictatorship and conflict influenced children was a topic that pre-occupied all three of these early leaders. Much of Kandel's and Brickman's scholarship focused on the ways children were indoctrinated to engage in evil. Kandel wrote what is likely the first book in English on Nazi education, titled *The Making of Nazis*, which appeared in 1935, not long after Hitler came to power. Similarly, Brickman, especially in his final years, wrote on Nazi indoctrination of children, most notably in a trenchant analysis that appeared in *Western European Education*, a journal of which he was Editor. That article deeply probed documents written by the Nazis as they took control of German schools. It was entitled "Ideological Indoctrination toward Immolation: The Inauguration of National Socialist Education in Germany in 1933."

Kandel and Brickman wrote extensively on education in war and its aftermath, as well as on education in general under totalitarianism.

Articles that Kandel authored include such titles as "The Messianic Complex" (coauthored with W.M. Kotschnig), "Reorienting Japanese Education," "We Move toward Centralization," "Education for Enduring Peace," "Conflicts of Power in Modern Culture," "The Vichy Government and Education in France," "Education in an Era of Transition" (referring to educational reconstruction), "Education and Human Rights," and "Approaches to World Peace." Brickman's works include such titles as "Education in the Occupied Countries," "Education under Totalitarianism and Reconstruction," "Communism and American Education," and the "The New Assault on Academic Freedom."

However different were their backgrounds, as Jews Kandel and Brickman were both deeply affected by the rise of Nazism and the holocaust. Kandel was already 60 years old and had lived in New York City for many years when the U.S. entered World War II in 1941, so he did not have a direct role in the war effort, though his book on Nazi education introduced readers to the educational depredations of dictatorship. Brickman, by contrast, was drafted into the U.S. Army in 1943 when he was 30 years old. In view of his command of German, he was recruited by the Office of Strategic Services (the forerunner of the Central Intelligence Agency). His fluency was such that he mastered the dialects of Bavaria, Austria, Silesia, Rhineland, Berlin, and Leipzig. As a spy, Brickman's main task was to infiltrate the German army to locate high-ranking Nazi officers who were attempting to flee the Allied forces as the war was ending. He and several others would enter the Eastern border of Germany where high-ranking German officers were attempting to escape out of the country as the Allies closed in. Brickman would sit at the rear of a shop dressed in a Nazi SS uniform as his co-conspirators visited local taverns where they would let it be known that there was an SS officer capable of arranging escapes to South America. Through this means, Brickman would learn the identity of German officers who wished to escape, and before each would come to the shop for help he would place an insignia on his lapel that was one rank higher than that of the visiting officer. Brickman would then instruct the officer to meet him in the local woods at a specific night and time, when Brickman's co-conspirators would sequester the officer and bring him to Nuremberg for interrogation.

Being a Jew who fought the Nazis from behind front lines and using their own language to defeat them was as frightful as it was heroic. That his ancestral town of Jedwabne was the scene of a horrendous massacre of Jews in 1941 was plausibly an unusually strong incentive for Brickman to engage the enemy. This episode is noteworthy not only because almost all of the town's Jewish population, estimated as high as 1,600 men, women, and children, was cruelly murdered, but also because the slaughter came mainly at the hands of the Jews' own Polish neighbors as Nazi SS officers looked on. Some of Brickman's relatives would almost certainly have been among the victims.

Unlike Kandel and Brickman, Anderson was not Jewish and was not as directly affected by the ravages of Nazism. Kandel and Brickman were fluent in German among other languages and had a profound knowledge of most of the European countries involved in the war. Anderson, by contrast, saw the war from an American perspective, though he too took part in the war effort, producing such titles as "The Iowa Community Faces War," "Wartime Farm Survey," and "Food Rationing and Morale."

Nazi education was thus an abiding interest of both Kandel and Brickman. All three leaders, however, were highly attentive to Soviet education and possessed an antipathy to the Soviet Union. Still, their aversion took opposing forms. Kandel and Anderson declined to travel to the Soviet Union, preferring to study it from afar, whereas Brickman jumped at the chance to go and observe that country first-hand. To some extent, Kandel's and Anderson's reaction may have stemmed from not having a command of Russian, whereas Brickman had mastered that language among the many that he knew.

Essentialism vs. Progressivism and Soviet Education

More than lacking a facility in Russian, Kandel's reluctance to go to the Soviet Union arose from his opposition to the *progressive movement*, several members of which were touting the values of the Soviet system of education in the 1920s and 1930s. Progressivism emerged initially from the ideas of John Dewey, but according to both Dewey and Kandel, those ideas were distorted by some of their colleagues, especially William Kilpatrick and George Counts, at Teachers College, Columbia University. Progressive education stood for "self-realization", "solving the problems of life", spontaneous learning, and catering to the immediate needs of most students. It advocated physical, practical and social activity as against an emphasis on the classics, history, the arts, and mathematics.

Progressive education, abetted by the prominence of the Teachers College faculty who led the movement, began in the 1920s and became a national phenomenon in the 1930s, embraced by many schools throughout the country. Kandel, joined by the equally prominent William Bagley, also at Teachers College, vigorously opposed *progressivism*. They referred to themselves and their allies as *essentialists*, proponents of a traditional curriculum, with a heavy emphasis on traditional subjects in the humanities and the natural and mathematical sciences. As Kandel wrote in *The Parents' Magazine*, "Growth cannot be self-directed; it needs direction through a carefully chosen environment to a pattern or patterns in the minds of those who have charge of the child's education." The battle between these two movements, with their varying vocabularies, has echoed throughout the years, with the popularity of each side ebbing and flowing as the mood in the U.S. changes.

Kandel was particularly alarmed at a direction that Kirkpatrick, at least initially, and Counts had taken. Kilpatrick and Counts had traveled to the Soviet Union to observe the new Russian socialist educational system. They were ecstatic to find that the new Soviet education followed a progressive path in which children worked on solving practical problems relating to agriculture and the work place. Kilpatrick went so far as to invite a Soviet professor to lecture at Teachers College on the benefits of the Soviet educational system. Kandel, however, observed a profound contradiction in the progressives' adoration of the Soviet system: the progressives advocated spontaneity and self-realization in students, yet every detail in the curriculum was planned in advance by the Soviet authorities to conform to the political ideology of the state. Eventually, Kilpatrick recognized the contradiction and, like Kandel, disavowed the system of indoctrinating children and preventing them from thinking for themselves. Counts, however, was not bothered by this contradiction and continued to visit the Soviet Union, extolling the virtues of having schools that molded children for the benefit of society. By contrast, Kandel vigorously criticized the use of schools for indoctrinating children to further the aims of the state's ideology. He often focused on the effects of extreme nationalism in schools, a topic emanating from his concerns over Nazi and Soviet education.

Brickman, like Kandel, was an essentialist. His observations of Soviet education led to a highly influential book, written with George Bereday and Gerald Read, titled *The Changing Soviet School*. He also contributed to understanding Soviet education as a bibliographer. He drew on his vast knowledge of the literature to produce, along with John T. Zepper, a book titled *Russian and Soviet Education, 1731-1989: A Multilingual Annotated Bibliography*. Anderson, as noted below, was much more a positivist than an essentialist. Yet, his work on the Soviet Union was, of all things, on human nature –"Soviet Russia and the Nature of Society"– an abrupt departure from his positivist bent.

Contextualism (Relativism) vs. Positivism (Empiricism)

Brickman fought a different battle, especially in the 1950s and 1960s. He too was an essentialist, but his struggle was not as fierce or as much in conflict with the progressives. Rather, his concern was more with epistemology than ideology. Specifically, he was apprehensive about the growing strength of positivism in comparative education. Brickman and Kandel, who valued the use of history and philosophy and a strong grasp of social and national context in comparative studies of education, stood together on one side of the debate. They insisted that only with a deep probing of a society's history, philosophy and culture, requiring a command of that system's language, can one fully understand a system of education. Kandel, in a paper titled "The Study of Foreign Languages in the Present Crisis," maintained that foreign languages were essential for a sound education, and Brickman, in an article titled "Foreign Languages and the American Educator," claimed that expertise in education required a command of languages.

By contrast, the positivists, whose strength was growing in the 1950s through the early 1970s, advocated studies that isolated and identified universal factors that influenced schooling, and that showed how school-society relationships functioned cross-culturally. Anderson, as a dedicated positivist, de-emphasized context and a fixation on foreign languages in favor of a "science" of comparative education, in which cross-national statistical analyses of education would rank supreme. Anderson went even further than other positivists in comparative education, such as Harold Noah and Max Eckstein, to propose the use of multivariate typologies to discern universal relationships between school and society. These polarities, defined by Kandel and Brickman on one side, and Anderson on the other side, have fashioned an underlying epistemological structure of comparative education (Epstein 2008).

Just as there have been ebbs and flows in the popularity of progressivism and essentialism, so too have there been ups and downs in the embrace of the positivism of Anderson and the contextualism of Kandel and Brickman. Positivists require the tools of statistics; contextualists urge a command of languages. Most comparativists can read and use statistics in their work, but few have the skill or inclination to establish cross-national typologies. Similarly, most comparativists have a command of one or two languages beyond their maternal tongue, but very few have a mastery of languages approaching the command possessed by Kandel and Brickman. Consequently, most comparativists work in the middle ground, using simple statistical analysis for limited purposes, analysis of original documents in a foreign language, or both. Clearly, commonalities and differences in outward style reflected little about these leaders' engagement in epic philosophical contests that were aligned with the different intellectual currents and somewhat different periods of time in which they wrote and lectured.

Setting the Future Course

As Americans gauge the quality, reach and impact of their nation's education as weighed against education abroad, they increasingly turn to comparative education to guide educational policy. Kandel, Brickman and Anderson played a crucial role in making educators and policy makers aware of the ways by which knowledge about education in the United States and abroad is gained, and in doing so, helped to set directions for comparative education.

Too few scholars take into account the monumental contributions of these leaders in setting the platforms for this field. What Brickman (1951) wrote of Kandel in an article entitled "I.L. Kandel – International Scholar and Educator" could just as easily have applied to Brickman himself as well as to Anderson:

> One would have to roam far and wide in educational literature in many languages to escape the name of Kandel.... Prolific author of monographic studies, textbooks, articles, editorials, and reviews; editor of yearbooks, encyclopedias, and journals, teacher and research mentor to advanced students in many universities; active consultant to governments, school boards, and educational bodies of five continents – this is but a bare outline of his achievements.

Besides giving Americans an insight into the educational philosophies and administrations of foreign nations, Dr. Kandel also acted as an interpreter of American education to educators in Europe, Latin America, Asia, Australia, and Africa... It is scarcely an exaggeration to characterize Kandel as an inter-national teacher of teachers.

It should appear plain that his signal achievements earn him a permanent niche, not only in the several branches of education in which he excels, but also in the general pattern of American and international education.... His originality and thoroughness in scholarship ... his penetrative insight into the pressing problems of the world and American education have won the [admiration] of educationists and scholars in academic specialties the world over.

Kandel lived a generation apart from Brickman and Anderson, and all had very different upbringings. Yet all of them witnessed the ravages of Hitler's depravity and were bound by common ideals of democracy and a dedication to comparative education, and, despite their episte-mological differences, embraced that field as a tool for confronting the problems and celebrating the successes of education internationally.

Notes

[1] Much of this chapter is based on Epstein (2013). The research for that article was mainly from the William W. Brickman and Isaac L. Kandel collections at the Hoover Institution at Stanford University. The author gratefully acknowledges the Hoover Institution for permission to reproduce material from that article. Portions of this chapter relating to C. Arnold Anderson are based largely on research on the contents from the five boxes containing the C. Arnold Anderson Papers, 1937-1990, Special Collections Research Center, the University of Chicago Library.

[2] See Kimball, pp. 16-17.

[3] On Isaac L. Kandel, see Brickman (1951) & Cremin (1966). On William W. Brickman, see the special issue devoted to him of the journal, *European Educa-tion*, especially Silova & Brehm (2010). On C. Arnold Anderson, see Epstein (1987) & Foster (1991).

[4] In the interest of transparency, Anderson was my mentor at the University of Chicago. On Brickman, see Silova and Brehm (2010).

References

Brickman, William W. 1951. "I.L. Kandel: International Scholar and Educator." *The Educational Forum 15*: 389–412.

Cremin, Lawrence A. 1966. *Isaac Leon Kandel (1881–1965): A Biographical Memoir.* Chicago: National Academy of Education.

Epstein, Erwin H. 1987. "On Wings of the Gadfly: C. Arnold Anderson, Honorary Fellow." *CIES Newsletter* 85 (October): 2-3.

Epstein, Erwin H. 2008. "Setting the Normative Boundaries: Crucial Epistemological Benchmarks in Comparative Education." *Comparative Education 44*(4): 373-386.

Epstein, Erwin H. 2013. "Taught to Be Evil." *Hoover Digest: Research and Opinion on Public Policy 1*(Winter): 184-196.

Foster, Philip. 1991. "C. Arnold Anderson: A Personal Memoir." *Comparative Education Review 35*(2): 215-221.

Kimball, Bruce. 1886. *Orators and Philosophers: A History of the Idea of Liberal Education*. New York: Teachers College Press.

Silova, Iveta, & William C. Brehm. 2010. "For the Love of Knowledge: William W. Brickman and his Comparative Education." *European Education 42*(2): 17-36.

14
Early Leaders:
Gerald H. Read and George Z.F. Bereday

Linda F. ROBERTSON and Kenneth CUSHNER

John Quincy Adams, the sixth president of the U.S., is often credited with saying the following on the topic of leadership: "If your actions inspire others to dream more, learn more, do more and become more, you are a leader." As shown in the previous chapter on Kandel, Brickman and Anderson, the founders of CIES helped others dream and form a sustainable, thriving and learned society devoted to understanding education across cultural contexts.

The founding of the Society occurred during a time when world headlines were focused on issues as the Cold War, highlighting such events as containment, the Korean War, the Warsaw Pact, the Berlin Blockade, the formation of the North American Treaty Organization, and Radio Free Europe. Set in these various conflicts and reactions, national leaders in the United States saw the need for increased awareness of and involvement in world affairs, and set forth series of legislative actions, including the Fulbright Act (1946), the Information and Educational Act of Smith and Mundt (1948), The National Defense Act for Area Studies (1958), and the Fulbright-Hayes Act (1961) – all forerunners to the establishment of the Peace Corps in 1961. In a conversation with Gerald Read, John Ohles, Kent State University Professor of Education, recorded Read as saying (Ohles 1980),

> After World War II there was a feeling that we were much too isolated and ignorant of other people and educators of the world. There was an interest in things international during that period.

Erwin H. Epstein (ed.) (2016): *Crafting a Global Field: Six Decades of the Comparative and International Education Society*. Hong Kong: Comparative Education Research Centre (CERC), The University of Hong Kong, and Dordrecht: Springer. © CERC

Large numbers of foreign students came to the United States for the first time. They were well received and they contributed to this interest in comparative education. Many of our young people joined the Peace Corps and returned to further this international dimension of American education.

It was in these times, and joining with the other visionary leaders as Kandel, Brickman and Anderson, that Gerald Read and George Bereday, two more of the founding members of CIES, came forth as leaders at the right time to help educators around the world to dream, learn, and become more aware of global issues. These two men are, indeed, a study of contrasts, yet Read's leadership, as the founding Treasurer and first editor of the *CES Newsletter*, and Bereday's leadership, as the founding Editor of the *Comparative Education Review* (*CER*), were critical to the rise in influence of the new Society and for its long sustainability and growth.

George Z.F. Bereday

Born in Poland in 1920, Bereday's worldview was shaped by the combination of his early years in the Polish cavalry and the British paratroops, where he was awarded the Cross Virtuli Militari of Poland in 1944, and by the formal education that he obtained on two continents. Bereday, who served as the first Editor of the *Comparative Education Review,* was the consummate scholar, having been schooled in several disciplines, obtaining degrees in history (Oxford, B.A. and M.A.), economics, and sociology (University of London, B.S.), comparative education and sociology (Harvard, PhD), and law (Columbia). Taking advantage of the increasing opportunity and funding from the U.S. government and private foundations, he was a Fulbright Scholar to Tokyo University in 1961; a Ford Fellow to Poland and a Carnegie Fellow to Singapore in 1963; served on various commissions and CIES delegations to the USSR, Finland, Japan and Western Europe; and served as a professor of education, sociology and juvenile law at Teachers College, Columbia University from 1955 until his death in 1983. He was a productive and proficient scholar whose works were published in eight languages. His ability to relate his extensive awareness of world issues to others helped to make the *Comparative Education Review* (*CER*) a publication admired worldwide.

At the time of Bereday's appointment as Editor of the *CER*, William Brickman, first president of CIES, had this to say of Bereday: "The Comparative Educational Society is very fortunate in having as the editor of this new journal a man who has demonstrated his scholarly, literary and teaching abilities in the field of comparative education, as well as his professional leadership ... [and] who is probably the only full time professor of comparative education in the country" (Brickman 1957).

Gerald H. Read

In contrast to the early geographic influences and broad international experiences of his colleague, Gerald H. Read came from a relatively homogenous and parochial background (David and Spearman 2012). Born in 1913 in Akron, Ohio and educated in the American mid-west, Read played football and studied history and Spanish at Kent State University, from where he received his Bachelor's degree, magna cum laude, in 1936. His interest in Cuba might have been influenced by his father, who spent time in Cuba during the Spanish-American War. His studies took him to The Ohio State University, where he earned his master's degree (1938), writing his thesis on *The History of Cuban Education*; to the University of Havana in 1941, where he improved his Spanish. He returned to The Ohio State University, where he completed his doctoral degree in comparative education in 1950, writing a dissertation titled, *Civic-Military Rural Education in Cuba: Eleven Eventful Years, 1936-1946*. Read served as a Spanish and history teacher and principal at local public schools in Ohio and later as a teacher at the Kent State University Laboratory School before becoming a professor of comparative education at Kent State University in 1948, a position from which he retired in 1975. And, like Bereday, Read, was a Fulbright Scholar, having his experience in Quito, Ecuador.

While Bereday was a life-long student, Read seemed to be an administrative activist. As early as his senior year in college, he organized a study tour for 10 university students to Cuba. He believed that educators must learn from firsthand experience, which led him to organize seminars and visits to schools in Europe, Africa, Australia, South America, Asia, and the Soviet Union. Read served the Society for 15 years as the Secretary-Treasurer, Editor for three years of the *CES Newsletter* from 1963 to 1965, and as Associate Editor of the *Comparative Education Review*. As Treasurer, Read ensured that the newly formed

Society was fiscally sound, connected with educators at all levels, and sustainable for the future. Read was active in numerous professional and honorary organizations, serving as President of *Kappa Delta Pi*, Chairman of the Selection Committee of Fulbright Scholars, a Charter Fellow of the College of Preceptors in the United Kingdom, an Academician in the Russian Academy of Education, and a CIES Honorary Fellow. Although Read retired from his faculty role in 1975, he remained active as a comparative educator until his death in 2005.

Service to the Society

Bereday and Read seemed to be the right people for the right jobs at the right time. World events of the mid-twentieth century created a favorable environment for educators, sociologists, historians and governmental policy makers to come together and establish the newly formed Comparative Education Society as well as to contribute to and benefit from the *CER*. Wallis and Dollery (2005) identify six distinctive tasks that characterize leaders, stating that they: 1) develop a vision for the organization, 2) develop strategies for decision making, 3) serve as advocates and spokespeople for the organization, 4) establish sustainable revenues, 5) inspire others to continue the work, and 6) take steps for the organization to endure in the future. The beliefs and actions of both Bereday and Read demonstrate their understanding and concern for developing new capacities and strategies, establishing new resources, and focusing on what the Society could do to maintain itself. We can examine how Read and Bereday provided these six leadership tasks within the first years of the Society, and how their actions and subsequent decisions provided the Society with a firm foundation to be a thriving and ever-growing organization that has survived for 60 years.

Both Bereday and Read were task-oriented or situational leaders, people who, in McCleskey's words (2014), "define the roles for followers ... create organizational patterns, and establish formal communication channels" (118). Although dramatically different in their backgrounds and prior experiences, their leadership styles support Bass's (2008) premise that there needs to be a "correct fit" between leader and follower in effective situational leadership.

Nanus and Dobbs (1999) emphasize the important role that leaders play in establishing a sustainable vision during the formation of new non-profit organizations. Minutes from the meeting of young professors from around the country who convened during the establishment of the Society at New York University in 1957 reflect the vision developed for the new organization, providing focus for Bereday's and Read's service to the Society. The minutes state that the purposes which the Comparative Education Society set for itself were:

1. to promote and improve the teaching of comparative education in colleges and universities;
2. to encourage scholarly research in comparative and international studies in education;
3. to interest professors of all disciplines in comparative and international dimensions of their specialties;
4. to facilitate the publication of studies and up-to-date information on comparative education;
5. to encourage cooperation among specialists in comparative education throughout the world in joint studies, exchange of documents, and first hand descriptions of education;
6. to facilitate the studies and up-to-date information on comparative education;
7. to cooperate whenever possible with such organizations as UNESCO, the International Institute of Education, Pan-American Union, etc.; and
8. to promote inter-visitation of educators and on-the-spot study of school systems for a better understanding of the theory and practice of education throughout the world.

Consistent with these last two purposes, Read later partnered with many agencies worldwide to lead scores of educational study tours and seminars for the Society.

Bereday's vision for the Comparative Education Society was outlined in a July 1957 correspondence to the U.S. Department of State, from which he sought startup funds for the newly established journal. He stated (Bereday to Walter F. Cronin, July 29, 1957):

> At present, the demand for comparative education has by far outrun the supply, and many who teach the subject, from the point of view of training they received, have no business teaching it. Most specialists in Comparative Education feel no person that who has not himself had a course in the Fundamentals of Comparative Education ought not to teach it. And certainly no person without languages and residence in foreign areas ought

to write about them. Alas, this is not the case at the present time. And my and the *Review's* method of treating the problem has been to start where we are and to upgrade where we can.

Conversations John Ohles had with Gerald Read reflect early discussion of the establishment of the *Comparative Education Review,* first published in June of 1957 (Ohles 1980). Read is quoted as saying, "At one of the meetings we had at New York University, it was suggested that the Society should sponsor a journal. Harold Benjamin contributed $500 to initiate the publication. George Bereday was named editor and I [Read] accepted the business editorship." Bereday later wrote to Chief Walter Cronin at the Office of Intelligence Research at the U.S. Department of State appealing for some funds for the second year, stating, "I do not know what our subscription figures are (Gerald Read handles that side at Kent State University) but my final ambition is that the *Review* should be self-supporting" (Bereday 1957).

Bereday and Read may have had differing ideas of what was needed in the comparative education field, but again their efforts ultimately complemented one another. Bereday saw the *CER* as a resource written primarily for teachers of comparative education or for those able to combine this with the teaching of other subjects and who themselves were not able to devote their fulltime resources to the discipline. As stated in the preface of the inaugural issue, the *CER* was "conceived as a service organ of the discipline and of the profession" (Bereday 1957). Features Bereday saw as important included a resource section on textbooks and classroom teaching methodologies, articles of geographic-specific interest, and discussion of methodologies of research in the field. Bereday defended this position for the *CER* in a letter to Robert Templeton dated January 13, 1958, where he stated, "The Review as a service organ is also to serve readers as a quick reference source in the fields in which they do not have a chance to do much reading. We will continue with bibliographical and area interests as well as with truly comparative interest."

Read's more practical priorities for the Society are reflected in the last two of the initial goals of the Society: to cooperate whenever possible with such organizations as UNESCO, International Institute of Education, Pan-American Union, etc., and to promote inter-visitation of educators and on-the-spot study of school systems for a better understanding of the theory and practice of education throughout the world. Evident in the organizational meetings was an expressed interest by many professors who had been to Europe during the war to return, but this time to meet their counterpart European educators. Brickman had the most extensive contacts and was asked to develop a seminar program. In conversations with Professor John Ohles, Read claimed that Brickman was not enthusiastic about taking on the role by himself, as he did not like the administrative and organizational aspect of such a task, and that Read would work with him. Brickman thus became the academic director and Read the administrative director. Read reportedly also said, "Actually, the Comparative Education Society was formed as an organization to sponsor seminars and study tours" (Ohles 1980).

When Brickman contacted professors in Europe about the feasibility of assisting with the development of the programs, they asked who was sponsoring the seminars. Brickman's reply that this was a group of American educators was not received well – an informal group was not sufficient for the recognition of the Soviet officials, for instance. This response furnished the motivation to organize formal travel seminars, which were consistent with Read's vision and also were a means to provide income for the Society. In the first five years, seminars were held each September in Western Europe (1956), Japan (1957), the Soviet Union (1958), South America, (1959), and again the Soviet Union (1960). Beginning in 1961, CIES partnered with Kappa Delta Pi to sponsor over 17 study tours, and from 1967-1970 with Phi Delta Kappa to sponsor three study tours a year.

During the Cold War, the work of getting into the Soviet Union was ground breaking. Read was asked by the "Ford Foundation to establish contact with various Soviet educators through the cultural attaché at the Soviet Embassy in Washington" (Ohles 1980). Through the assistance of Llewellyn Thompson, the U.S. Ambassador to the Soviet Union (1957-1962), study tours were organized with support from the Ford Foundation. Nevertheless, these tours had to overcome several obstacles. For one thing, Read's arrangement for tours to the Soviet Union conflicted with U.S. State Department exchange agreement efforts. For another thing, William G. Carr of the National Education Association (NEA) voiced concern over Read's Soviet tour arrangement, because that arrangement was with the Communist (Soviet) trade union of teachers, an organization that opposed the free labor principle for which the NEA stood.

The relationship between Read and Bereday was not without tension. To be sure, Read relished the association with the *Review*. As he wrote, "The Review brought us into contact with many educators throughout the world. Soon we visited all the continents." Yet, Bereday warned Read in a letter dated July 24, 1959, that, "we are still a young society and have still to be careful not to appear to have too many enthusiastic contacts with the Russians" (Bereday 1959). The interaction between Read and Bereday over financing shows both the respect and the disagreement of these two very strong leaders as they worked collaboratively toward ensuring the financial future for both CIES and *CER*. In a July 1957 correspondence to the U.S. Department of State addressing the issue of funding, Bereday reflects the disagreement he had with Read's desire to sponsor travel seminars, saying, "The one source of unsettledness in the society so far has been the subject for foreign tours. Last year's European and this year's Latin American tour took some forty educators around each continent on a 'three days in each country' basis. There are some of us who feel that this is shear [sic] nonsense" (Bereday 1957). The written publications from the study tours, however, provided profits, as did book sales from some of the members and founders of the Society.

To assure sustainability and growth of the CES and *CER*, and to view ways to empower others and involve others, discussions occurred in 1959 and 1960 between Bereday and Read to consider the addition of new supportive positions. An Editorial Board with members from Europe and the United States was formed. When Bereday and Read left their respective positions, the structure they had created was sufficient to sustain a vital organization.

Long before social scientists studied such fields as organizational development and management, and before people could take structured courses on leadership development, those who sought to create new organizations either drew on their own skills, drive and personality to carry them, or the organization struggled to even get off the ground. CIES was fortunate, indeed, that George Bereday and Gerald Read had the requisite passion, skill and vision to forge a new organization and advance knowledge and understanding of education around the world.

Correspondence and Documents Cited

Bereday, George Z.F. (January 13, 1958). Letter to Dr. Robert G. Templeton, Cambridge MA. Comparative Education Review Papers, Series 1, Box 1 (Bereday) CIES records. Kent State University Special Collection Archives. Kent, OH.

Bereday, George Z.F. (July 29, 1957). Letter to Walter F. Cronin, chief, Private Branch, External Research Staff, Office of Intelligence Research, Department of State, Washington DC. Comparative Education Review Papers, Series 1, Papers, Box 1 (Bereday), CIES records, Kent State University Special Collection Archives, Kent, OH.

Bereday, George Z.F. (July 24, 1959). Letter to Gerald Read. Comparative Education Review Papers, Series 1, Box 1, Editor's Files (Bereday), The CIES records, Kent State University Special Collection Archives, Kent, OH.

Ohles, John. (December 3, 1980). A Conversation with Gerald H. Read Comparative Education Review Papers, Series 4, Box 2, Founding Members Gerald H. Read Papers, CIES records, Kent State University Special Collection Archives, Kent, OH.

References

Bass, B.M. 2008. *The Bass Handbook of Leadership: Theory, Research and Managerial Applications (4th edition)*. New York, NY: Free Press.

Bereday, George Z.F. 1957. "Preface". *Comparative Education Review* 1(1): 3-4.

Brickman, William W. 1957. "A New Journal in Comparative Education" *Comparative Education Review* 1(1): 1.

David Jr., O.L. & Mindy Spearman. 2012. *A Century of Leadership, Biographies of Kappa Delta Pi Presidents*. Charlotte, North Carolina: Information Age Publishing.

McCleskey, J.A. 2014. "Situational, Transformational and Transactional Leadership and Leadership Development." *Journal of Business Studies Quarterly* 5(4): 117-130.

Nanus, B., & S.M. Dobbs. 1999. *Leaders who make a difference: Essential strategies for meeting the nonprofit challenge*. San Francisco: Jossey Bass.

Wallis, J., & B. Dollery. 2005. "Leadership and Economic Theories of Nonprofit Organizations." *Review of Policy Research* 22(4): 483-499.

15
The Oral History Project: Comparatively Speaking I and II

Gita STEINER-KHAMSI

Just in time for the 50th anniversary of the Comparative and International Education Society (CIES), the video *Comparatively Speaking: An Oral History of the First 50 Years of the Comparative and International Education Society* was released. Victor Kobayashi scheduled the premiere screening for the annual conference that he, as CIES President-Elect, had organized in Honolulu. A few weeks later, he sent a letter to the past presidents of the CIES (dated 24 April 2006) that succinctly summarized the content of the video:

> It features interviews with 25 past presidents of the Society conducted by faculty and doctoral students in the field. Starting with R. Freeman Butts (1964) and ending with Steven Klees (2007), the video traces the history and scholarly debates from its fragile inception to its current strength and growth.

In effect, *Comparatively Speaking* was the oral history project of the Society in that it gathered historical accounts on the debates and developments in comparative and international education, as told by elected leaders in the field. The video was sponsored by CIES and Teachers College (TC), Columbia University. Two individuals were instrumental in assisting me with production. Eric M. Johnson, at the time a doctoral student in International and Comparative Education, spent many hours with me, including his winter semester break 2005/06, brainstorming how to reduce over 33 hours of video-recorded interviews into a meaningful,

Erwin H. Epstein (ed.) (2016): *Crafting a Global Field: Six Decades of the Comparative and International Education Society*. Hong Kong: Comparative Education Research Centre (CERC), The University of Hong Kong, and Dordrecht: Springer. © CERC

coherent and interesting 73-minute video. At every step of the process we had the guidance of a professional video-producer. Wairimu Kiambuthi had already completed her dissertation and later became a successful film director and video producer. She was able to masterfully bridge the two worlds of academia and the media community: capturing the debate culture of academics and producing a video that satisfies professional and technical standards.

Context

Teachers College, Columbia University is generally acknowledged as being the birthplace for the formal academic study of comparative education. The first comparative education course was taught by James Earl Russell in 1899 (Bereday 1963). Russell was not only the first faculty member to teach a course entitled "Comparative Education" but he was also the first dean (later president) of the College. Even better for the stature of comparative education at TC, James Earl Russell was succeeded by his son William Fletcher Russell, who upon his retirement as President of TC in 1954, assumed a high post in the International Cooperation Administration. That agency eventually merged into the newly established U.S. Agency for International Development (USAID), which was engaged in international education activity. For this reason, the history of comparative education and the history of TC are inextricably linked.

There is a long and illustrious history of faculty and alumni who helped professionalize teaching and research in comparative education, both in the United States and internationally: Paul Monroe established the International Institute of Education in 1923, Isaac L. Kandel launched the series *International Yearbook of Education* in 1924 and served as its editor for 20 years, and George Z.F. Bereday was the founding editor of the flagship journal *Comparative Education Review* and, together with Joseph Lauwerys, the founding editor of the book series *World Yearbook of Education* (Routledge) in 1965. Finally, several faculty members (David G. Scanlon, R. Freeman Butts, Harold J. Noah, Henry M. Levin, Gita Steiner-Khamsi) and distinguished alumni of TC (Max A. Eckstein, Rolland Paulston, Noah Sobe) have served as CIES presidents and helped to grow the membership, visibility, and professional credibility of the Society. Given Teachers College's legacy in the field, it took little persuasion to enlist the support of the administration for co-sponsoring the CIES oral history project.

Several elements help professionalize a field, including structures that allow professionals to be trained, meet, publish, and exchange professional knowledge (see the chapter by Wiseman and Matherly in this volume). Professional associations are then charged by their members to organize such venues, bearing in mind the interests of members. Relevant structures are, for example, courses or degree programs in comparative and international education, book series or journals such as *Comparative Education Review, Current Issues in Comparative Education, Compare, Comparative Education,* and *Research in Comparative and International Education,* as well as networks and meetings such as the annual CIES conferences. My generation of comparative and international education scholars in the United States experienced over the past 20 years a boom in degree programs, publications, and initiatives. Attendance at the annual CIES conferences grew from a handful of professors in 1956 to a few hundred in the 1990s to almost 3,000 professors, practitioners, and graduate students in 2015. In view of this growth, it is relevant to ask what constitutes professional knowledge, what knowledge is essential for comparative and international education research, or to put it more bluntly: what binds us?

Comparatively Speaking I

The issue of canon, or perhaps more broadly, the question of a common intellectual ground, motivated me to dig deeper and embark on the oral history project. Is there a "canon" of comparative and international education knowledge? That is, is there a body of literature that *every* student of comparative and international education *must* learn regardless of theoretical-methodological orientation or geographical location of the degree program in which the student is studying? Erwin H. Epstein brought up the canon question periodically and prominently in CIES (see especially Epstein 2008). One of the goals that I pursued with the video project was to bring to life the Society's common past and document the contemporary debates, that is, both agreements *and* disagreements.

The canon question has become an empirical question. In the era of digital technologies (e.g., Google Scholar) and social network analyses (e.g., bibliographical network analyses), the perennial canon question of what *should* be read may at long last be resolved by examining what *is* read. If one were to carry out a bibliographical network analysis of publications written by comparativists and investigate who is reading or who is citing, one would most likely find that there are quite a few clusters within the comparativist networks. Each of these clusters, at times coinciding with the Special Interest Groups (SIGs) of CIES and at other times cutting across several SIGs, constitutes its own epistemological community. In other words, there is not *one* body of Great Books and articles in comparative and international education but several shelves or clusters. The combination of these diverse clusters could then be loosely labeled "professional knowledge" or "comparative and international education knowledge".

Keeping in mind the broader canon question, we were hoping that agreements and disagreements among the CIES presidents would come to light by asking them the same set of so-called "sample questions." Eric Johnson and I saw it then as our task to edit the video in ways that reflected the areas of agreement and disagreement among the CIES presidents. We wanted the video to span across three generations of scholars: the past CIES presidents, their younger-generation peers or colleagues, and their students. We therefore asked the CIES presidents to select interviewers at their own universities that were either peers or students (three of the interviewers – Gita Steiner-Khamsi, Karen Mundy, and Noah Sobe – were later elected as presidents of CIES).

The following is a list of the sample questions:

1. Were there any specific external events (political, social, economic) that have shaped the field of comparative and international education during your presidency?
2. In which direction did you want to see the CIES develop? Did you, as a president, pursue a specific mission or vision for the Society?
3. In retrospect, do you think that CIES neglected (or was insensitive to) important developments in the field, and in academe?
4. In your opinion, what should be the relation between comparative education and international educational development or development studies in education?
5. In your opinion, what should be the role of government organizations (e.g., USAID), non-governmental organizations (e.g., Save the Children, Soros Foundation), multi-

laterals (UNICEF, UNESCO, etc.) and international financial institutions (World Bank, Inter-American Bank, etc.) in CIES?

6. Is there a body of academic literature that you would consider "comparative and international education literature"? Is there, and should there be a canon in comparative and international education. Are there "great" books in comparative education? If yes, which books should everyone in comparative and international education read?

7. In which direction did the field of comparative and international education develop over the past 50 years (with regards to methods, theories, practice fields, and people)? What was positive, what was negative about this development?

8. What advice would you give new scholars in comparative and international education?

9. If you were a CIES president *today*, in which direction would you want to see CIES develop?

10. What was the highlight during your presidency? What event is memorable to you?

The next two sections present first a few textual excerpts from the video, Comparatively Speaking I, on agreements, labeled "the common past," and then highlight a few issues where CIES presidents expressed diverse views, reflecting the different trajectories that exist in the present.

The Common Past

When asked about important historical events that had shaped the field (question 1) and about issues that CIES had neglected in the past (question 3), the presidents agreed on two facts: (i) the emergence of development studies at the height of the Cold War in the late 1950s and the 1960s, and (ii) the underrepresentation of women and ethnic/racial minorities in the early days of the CIES leadership. Indeed, the first 20 presidents of the Society (1957-1976) were men, and it took another 12 years for a person of color (Beverly Lindsay) to stand for, and be elected, President of CIES in 1988. Over the past 10 years, that is, the period 2006-2016, five of the 10 presidents have been female.

The following provides a glimpse into the first point of assertion: the development and area studies turn in comparative education. In the United States, the shift from comparing educational systems in "industrialized nations" to working in developing countries coincided with, and more accurately was a response to, the period of de-colonization and the Cold War. Situated at one pole was the USA and its allied countries of the First World and at the other pole the Soviet Union and its Second World allies. Both superpowers entered into an international race over winning the hearts and minds of the people in the non-aligned former colonies, at the time sometimes referred to as the "Third World".[1] By the end of the 1960s, the turn was also reflected in the name change of the Society in 1968 from the Comparative Education Society (CES) to the Comparative and International Education Society (CIES).

Two past presidents, R. Freeman Butts (1911-2010) and Rolland Paulston (1930-2006), were in fragile health at the time of the video project, but we managed to locate earlier recordings in which they had spoken about the developments of the field. A graduate of Teachers College, an out-of-the box thinker, a dear friend and informal mentor to me, Rolland Paulston, passed away a few weeks before the 2006 CIES conference, unable to commemorate with us the 50th CIES anniversary. The oldest interviewed president was R. Freeman Butts (President, 1964) who in 2010 passed away at the age of 99. This is how Butts recalled the early days of international education:

> I was on the faculty of Teachers College from 1935 to 1975. First, I was mainly teaching the history of education until 1955. This was just about the time when Teachers College began to get both feet into the international education field, called "technical assistance" at the time. A contract was signed with Afghanistan in 1965.... The project went on from 1955 until the Communists took over in 1979. In the late 60s, the Government began to cut down on technical assistance, especially in education. The international exchange and the education side of the operations began to decline. But we at Teachers College were determined to keep it alive.

Several presidents commented on the period of the National Defense Act (1958) that brought an influx of U.S. federal funding to universities for area and development studies as well as for education exchange programs with developing countries. Given the larger political agenda of "technical assistance," notably re-entry into the decolonized world and winning the Cold War in developing countries, funding for establishing international education programs in the United States was attacked as "academic colonialism" and criticized as "CIA money." In fact, John Weidman (University of Pittsburgh) bluntly asked President Donald K.

Adams (1965) the question: "I am wondering whether it was in the 60s when academics started to serve as spies, or did that come a bit later?" Adams replied: "There was an inkling of that at the time. But that came a bit later." Adams continued:

> In many regards we profited from the Cold War ... The Russians put up Sputnik and money came flowing in for a lot of international education programs. I directed two programs that were at the time directly funded from the government: first at the Peabody College at Vanderbilt and then at Syracuse.

During the 1960s, a great number of international education programs were established. Harold J. Noah (President, 1973) explained how at Teachers College the established field of comparative education rapidly went out of fashion and was ridiculed as bookish and Euro-centric. He furthermore observed that comparative education increasingly became impoverished compared to its younger sibling, international educational development, which received all the funds, and as a corollary, all the students and all new faculty lines. Reflecting on the same period, two of the past presidents, Joseph P. Farrell (President, 1977) and Rolland Paulston (President, 1975), provided accounts of how they were able to fund their studies with the help of these government scholarships.

> We both joined hands and went to Peru to be part of the Teachers College team in the Ministry of Education. We didn't know much about Peru. We had to go to the library and read books about Peru. But yet we were sent as instant experts to reform the Peruvian educational system. The assumption was that we use the model of the American educational system. Actually, you take the *ideal*, not just the model but the ideal, and then you subtract the Peruvian practices. The difference is then the "aid project." You know, we could play that game too! (Rolland G. Paulston)

The same generation as Paulston, Joseph P. Farrell also studied at a time when scholarships were readily available for studies in international education. He explained how graduates of international education or development studies in education revamped the field of comparative education in the 1960s:

> The field at the time was history-oriented and Euro-centric ... At the same time ... there emerged a whole new generation of

young scholars that was trained under Ford Foundation money or had National Defense Education Act scholarships in the 60s. They were development specialists and all of them did field work or Peace Corps.... They were the new "Young Turks" of the field. (Joseph P. Farrell)

Many other presidents also made noteworthy statements about important historical events that shaped their year of the presidency (sample question 1). Only a few are mentioned here: the end of Apartheid in South Africa (Masemann, President, 1989), the fall of the Berlin Wall (Heyneman, President, 1992), "the fact that Asia [China and India] was rising" (Hayhoe, President, 1999), the bombing of the World Trade Center (Ross, President, 2001), and the War on Terror (Freeman, President, 2003).

The Trajectories of the Present

The oral history project also brought back to the surface several contested themes and intellectual debates. For reasons of length, I mention only two here: (i) What should count as comparison? (ii) What is the qualification framework for degree programs in comparative and international education?

First-generation CIES presidents Harold J. Noah and Max Eckstein observed that comparative education scholars ceased to produce foundational studies that would allow them to advance theory or make generalizations across a vast array of contexts or countries. To their dismay, the majority of articles to this day published in journals of the field have been one-country studies with little explanatory power for other contexts or countries. Perhaps one of the most articulate in the group of past CIES presidents, who was 80 at the time of the interview, Harold J. Noah (President, 1973), summarized his call for more cross-national studies as follows:

Obviously, the 35 years since 1970 has seen tremendous organizational growth [in U.S. comparative and international education]. Now, I will not speak at all; my lips are sealed on whether there has been qualitative improvement. There certainly are differences.... It is just very different in one way, but very much the same in another way. There are still, as there were before, lots and lots of single-country studies. And the big question always is: Is that comparative education? Couldn't these studies just as well have been published in a society of education journal in *that* country, a political science journal in *that* country, or in an educational journal in *that* country? Why is this comparative education? That question still worries me.

Surprisingly, with the exception of Steven Klees (President, 2007), who critically observed the advance of quasi-experimental design, no other CIES president commented on comparison as a method. It is noticeable how, with a few exceptions, methodological questions are neglected in the journals and at professional conferences.[2] Many of those discussions center more narrowly on issues related to indicator research. Based on the publications and presentations of CIES members, it appears fair to state that there is, to use a term coined by Rolland Paulston, "heterodoxy" in terms of comparative method and theories (Paulston 1993), ranging from one-country studies that have little ambition to generalize to cross-national comparison that minimally attempt to understand context.

Another point of contestation has to do with the scope of knowledge and skills, that is, the qualification standard, of future scholars and practitioners in comparative and international education: how special-ized should their qualifications be? What knowledge and skills are essential for the profession? Should one advocate for a stand-alone specialist degree in comparative and international education or should the comparative study of education, or development work, only be part of a larger degree program in education, development studies, or policy studies?

The following two views on this issue that were diametrically opposed: Martin Carnoy advised the next generation of scholars to acquire discipline-based knowledge, do field work, and become an area specialist. Martin Carnoy (President, 2005) opined:

> One advice that I tell new scholars is that they are coming into an important and growing field. A second piece of advice is that they should devote some time in their study, perhaps as a minor, in a social science discipline.... A third one, listen carefully to what people with different methodological approaches have to say. And a final one: spend a lot of time in the field, observe and interpret what is going on. Do not do things from a distance.

In stark contrast are the statements made by Stephen Heyneman (President, 1992), who warned the next generation of scholars of becoming too "ghettoized" and "pigeon-holed" as "development specialists only" and suggested that they instead do analytical work on educational problems regardless of whether it is "in Minnesota or in Malawi," or "in China or Chicago."

As mentioned in the beginning of this chapter, the question of "what binds us?" has been intriguing. Having a distinct ancestry and a common past, which the oral history project helped to (re-)construct, and at the same time promoting a climate of agreeing to disagree, is what the debate culture in CIES stands for. Steven Klees (President, 2007) elegantly wrapped up his advice to new scholars in ways that takes into account the various viewpoints, theoretical positions, and diverse methods of inquiry in the CIES community: "Understand the debates in our field. Recognize that there are no right or wrong positions."

Outlook of Comparatively Speaking II

In 2014, CIES President Karen Mundy approached me to produce a sequel to the first oral history project, tentatively entitled *Comparatively Speaking II*. The second video covers the next 10 years of the Society, 2006-2016. As before, I have worked with a team of experts from Teachers College, Columbia University, notably with Whitney Warner and Sheila Matsuda (M.A. students in the program International and Comparative Education) and Hua-Chu Yen, media specialist and professional video-producer. Different from the first oral history project, however, I expanded the range of voices reflecting the current trends and composition in the Society.

The main cast of characters still consists of CIES presidents, namely ones that were elected over the period 2006-2016, starting with Victor Kobayashi (President in 2006) and ending with Noah Sobe (due to become President in 2017). We also included other important voices that comment on developments in the profession of the past 10 years, such as representatives from agencies, think tanks, and philanthropy. In addition, we were able to record during the CIES 2015 conference and capture some of the diverse networks, and also the lively debates in our Society and profession.

Notes

[1] William deJong-Lambert and I guest-edited two special issues (2006/07) of the journal *European Education* devoted to an analysis of the 1960s development turn in comparative education. The two special issues 38(3) and 38(4), entitled Post-Cold War Studies in Education, provided a historical account of the growth of "Third World" and development studies in education against the backdrop of the Cold War. We released the publication for the 50th anniversary of CIES, because we believed that this connection was not sufficiently told.

[2] More recently, there has been heated debate on the inflationary use of quasi-experimental designs or randomized control trials in comparative education (See Burde 2012). However, most panels during CIES conferences that address methodological issues deal with international learning assessments or cross-national comparisons. Many of those discussions center more narrowly on issues related to indicator research.

References

Bereday, George Z.F. 1963. "James Russell's Syllabus of the First Academic Course in Comparative Education." *Comparative Education Review* 7(2): 189-196.

Burde, Dana. 2012. "Assessing Impact and Bridging Methodological Divides: Randomized Trials in Countries Affected by Conflict." *Comparative Education Review* 56(3): 448-473.

Epstein, Erwin H. 2008. "Setting the Normative Boundaries: Crucial Epistemological Benchmarks in Comparative Education." *Comparative Education* 44(4): 373-386.

Paulston, Rolland G. 1993. "Mapping discourse in comparative education." *Compare* 23(2): 101-114.

16
CIEclopedia:
Profiling Distinguished Society Leaders

Maria MANZON

CIEclopedia is a who's who website database for comparative and international education. It was established in 2006 as an initiative of Teachers College, Columbia University. The project was supported by the Comparative and International Education Society (CIES) and was launched on the occasion of the Society's 50th anniversary celebrations. This chapter explores the nexus between *CIEclopedia* and CIES leadership. It commences with a brief introduction on the nature and role of who's who publications. It then gives a history of *CIEclopedia*, explores developments over time, and takes stock of achievements after a decade of existence. Finally, it focuses on profiles of CIES leaders featured in *CIEclopedia* and analyzes variations in the way these biographees have viewed themselves to be an integral part of the Society. The chapter draws on oral histories, the author's experience as a participant in the project since its early stages, and the actual database. It argues that *CIEclopedia* is not only a medium to portray the distinguished leaders of CIES and others but also one more testimony of CIES' leadership in pioneering meaningful initiatives to professionalize the global field of comparative education.

'Who's who' refers to a list or directory of facts about notable people (see www.oxforddicctionaries.com). The oldest known publication of this genre is the annual British publication *Who's Who*, which describes itself as "the essential directory of the noteworthy and influential in all walks of life, in the UK and worldwide, published annually since 1849" (see www.ukwhoswho.com). Another significant and longstanding publica-

Erwin H. Epstein (ed.) (2016): *Crafting a Global Field: Six Decades of the Comparative and International Education Society*. Hong Kong: Comparative Education Research Centre (CERC), The University of Hong Kong, and Dordrecht: Springer. © CERC

tion is the *Canadian Who's Who*, which dates from 1910. While these two examples have a national scope, others focus on academic disciplines (e.g., Blaug & Vane 2003 on economics) or institutions (e.g., UK Parliament; see "MPs, Lords and the Monarch – who's who?" http://www.parliament.uk/education/about-your-parliament/mps-lords-monarch/). Biographies are invited by the publisher, a selection committee, and/or are nominated. Selection of candidates is based on merit, because of the positions they hold in society or in the profession, or the contributions they have made in a particular domain. Some publishers require auto-biographical accounts to be regularly updated by the biographee, while others are written by a third person based on questionnaires or other data collection methods. Most who's who publications are in hard copy, but some have also gone online in recent years, and some have never been in hard copy – *CIEclopedia* itself being an example. With this basic understanding of the literary genre to which *CIEclopedia* belongs, the following section explores the origin of this project.

Brief History

The idea of developing a who's who website database for comparative and international education originated from Sina Mossayeb, *CIEclopedia*'s founding editor, in 2006. At that time, he was a PhD student in the International and Comparative Education Program of the Department of International and Transcultural Studies, Teachers College, Columbia University. Mossayeb was a technology-savvy person. He was convinced that it was time for comparative education to be more visible in and through the world of technology. Taking inspiration from *Wikipedia*, a popular on-line interactive encyclopedia, Mossayeb sought to develop an online who's who in the field of Comparative and International Education. Thus the name *CIEclopedia* was coined.[1]

In a proposal dated March 10, 2006, Mossayeb outlined the main ideas of the project (Mossayeb 2006a). The *CIEclopedia* website would serve as a systematic repository of biographical profiles of individuals associated with the field of comparative and international education. Profiles would contain:

- personal particulars (i.e. name, vitae dates),
- short biography and significant contribution,
- academic and professional background,

- institutional affiliations, and
- publication history.

Gita Steiner-Khamsi, who was Mossayeb's PhD advisor and Program Coordinator, supported his idea and gave seed funding. In an interview on *CIEclopedia* in 2015, she elaborated on the goals of the project. She described *CIEclopedia* as a strategic endeavor in a higher goal of professionalizing the field of comparative and international education: "*CIEclopedia*, by making visible who is in the field, helps to establish comparative education as a profession rather than as a perspective" (Steiner-Khamsi 2015). Subsumed under this main goal, she added, were three integral objectives: "to democratize the 'canon' [making it widely accessible] in comparative education, to have geographic diversity, and to increase visibility to the field by using technology."

The proposal was presented by Steiner-Khamsi to the CIES Board of Directors during the Society's 50th anniversary conference in Honolulu, Hawai'i under the leadership of President Victor Kobayashi. The CIES Board endorsed *CIEclopedia* as a CIES project, extending moral support. This enabled Teachers College as *CIEclopedia*'s founding sponsor to invite universities from around the world to become co-sponsors in order to ensure that the database reflected international scholarship and was not limited to or dominated by U.S. and Anglophone scholars (Mossayeb 2006b; Steiner-Khamsi 2015). By November 2006, the project had four co-sponsor universities: Kobe University in Japan, Loyola University Chicago in the USA, the University of Hong Kong in China, and the University of London in the UK.

In 2009, Maria Manzon succeeded Sina Mossayeb as the second editor of *CIEclopedia*, representing the Comparative Education Research Centre at the University of Hong Kong. Her transfer to Singapore's National Institute of Education (NIE) in 2013 led to NIE becoming a co-sponsor and current institutional website host. The website appears prominently on NIE's research publications webpage (see http://www.nie.edu.sg/research-publications/cieclopediaorg). One change is in the mode of submission. Originally there were two options: either by online submission using an HTML editable form or by email to the editor. With the migration of the site to NIE, the first option is no longer available.

Project Aims and Scope

The project sought and still seeks to achieve three outcomes. First, it aims to provide an agent-centric knowledge repository that traces an idea, movement, or field through the life and works of its innovators, participants, and members. Second, it seeks to offer a resource for network analysis as well as a nexus of academic and international organization networking. Lastly, it is a medium to promote awareness of comparative and international education to participants and individuals outside the field.

CIEclopedia's agent-centric approach and its objective to democratize the "canon" reflected the struggles of actors in the intellectual field who compete for distinction and for symbolic capital to define the field's boundaries (Bourdieu 1977). In this respect, an intellectual product such as a who's who database that is seemingly a disinterested contribution to knowledge can also be viewed as a "political" strategy to establish or even reverse a specific structure of relations of symbolic domination in the field (Manzon 2011), by democratizing who can act as the field's gatekeepers and allowing diverse voices to be heard.

The project was designed to begin by profiling key historical figures in the field and go onto current researchers. The website included the ability for self-entry of profile (but overseen by an editor for quality control), and supplemental resources (links, etc.). While being a relatively open source repository that allows anyone to submit a profile entry, *CIEclopedia* established the following criteria for eligibility of profile candidates. They must have:

- At least five article/chapter publications or at least three books (edited or authored);
- At least five years of professional activity at an academic institution or organization related to comparative and international education.

Except for self-entries, bio-sketch submissions required the approval of the profile by the nominated individual (by email or print). Profiles of deceased individuals who meet the two criteria above were (and will be) given the title "historic figure".

Building the Database

In March 2008, on the occasion of the 52nd CIES annual conference in New York City, Gita Steiner-Khamsi organized a meeting of the *CIEclopedia* project sponsors. The organization of work was divided between the editor and regional or area coordinators. The editor was to have a three-year term, after which a new editor would be selected from another sponsoring institution. The editor was responsible for reviewing new profile submissions, contributing profile entries, encouraging coordinators in their work, and maintaining the website. The coordinators were the designated persons (either faculty members or graduate students) from each co-sponsoring institution, whose task was to oversee the contributions of profiles from their respective geographic remits. The responsibilities of the co-sponsors were to contribute content (profiles), coordination and funding (which could take the form of covering the expenses of the designated coordinator).

Figure 16.1: Number of Profiles Submitted

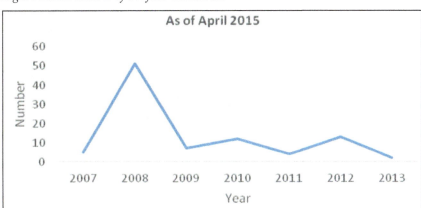

The 2008 meeting had a notable impact on the growth of the database, particularly in that year. As shown in Figure 16.1, the project started with only five profiles in 2007 but increased tenfold after the New York meeting. These profiles were contributed mainly by Teachers College, Loyola University Chicago, and the University of Hong Kong, with a few by the Institute of Education (London) and the University of Sydney. The momentum slowed in 2009, but slightly picked up in 2010 with significant contributions from Loyola University Chicago, and again in 2012 notably from Lehigh University.

The institutional contributors exhibited some patterns in the *nature of their profile submissions*. Loyola University Chicago, then under the leadership of Erwin H. Epstein, featured prominent historic figures in the field, including founding fathers like Michael Sadler and Marc-Antoine Jullien de Paris. Teachers College worked on both historical figures (e.g., Isaac Kandel, Isa Sadiq) and current researchers in the field. The University of Hong Kong capitalized on the linguistic skill and social networks of its graduate students and targeted speakers of Chinese, Spanish and Russian with the main purpose of giving voice and visibility to non-Anglophone actors.

In terms of the *types of contributors*, as of April 2015 there were: scholars who self-contributed (14 autobiographical profiles or 15 percent of the total); professors who wrote about colleagues and/or their mentors; and the majority who were graduate students of comparative and international education. In this respect, while institutional support is important, personal agency played a valuable role. As Steiner-Khamsi (2015) remarked, "you need a designated person who really does the work (e.g., a doctoral student or a research assistant) and not only a name that endorses it." Professors convinced about *CIEclopedia* have asked their graduate students to work on profile submissions either as a class assignment or as part of their service to the department. This benefits not only the project, but also the students who gain research and publication experience, which they can include in their resumes (Epstein 2015). This has been the strategy adopted by institutions such as the University of Hong Kong, Teachers College, Lehigh University and Loyola University Chicago.

The database originally adopted a semi Web 2.0 philosophical approach, meaning that contribution to the database, its expansion and content, were dependent on interaction with its users, leaving entries always a work-in-progress and open to change. While the concept of *Wikipedia* specifically included a multiplayer feature with no central organization controlling editing, *CIEclopedia* allowed for self-entry of profile, but the process was overseen by the editor for quality control. Mossayeb envisioned decentralizing the online entry of profiles to the different institutions and eventually to individuals, as in *Wikipedia*. Steiner-Khamsi (2015), however, anticipated two barriers. First, a technological barrier inhibited some potential contributors from fully engaging with a technology-based medium of publication. A second barrier was psychological: some consider it rather impolite to write about themselves.

As of April 2015, the database contained 94 biographic profiles. Among them were 10 historical figures born between the end of the 19th century and the first two decades of the 20th century. In terms of geographic diversity, the major regions represented[2] were North America (44 percent), Europe (33 percent), and Asia (16 percent), while Africa, Latin America and Oceania were hardly visible (see Figure 16.2). Moreover, *CIEclopedia* is dominated by Anglophone scholars from North America, the UK, Australia, and South Africa with 65 entries (69 percent of total). This reflects the dominance of English as a language of scholarly communication, which is convenient for some yet marginalizes others (see e.g., Tietze & Dick 2013). It signals the need to reach out to institutional partners in the under-represented geographic regions and linguistic groupings to address the imbalance.

Figure 16.2: Geographic Diversity of CIEclopedia Profiles

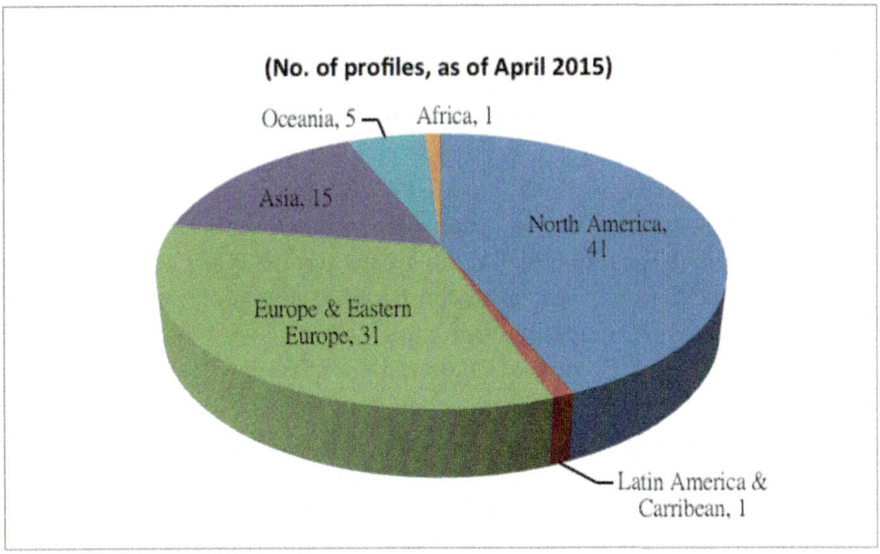

(No. of profiles, as of April 2015)

Oceania, 5 — Africa, 1

Asia, 15

North America, 41

Europe & Eastern Europe, 31

Latin America & Carribean, 1

CIEclopedia and CIES leadership

This section explores the ways in which *CIEclopedia* mirrors the leadership roles of individuals in the CIES through the discourses employed in their profiles. It also comments on the leadership that the CIES exercises in the global field of comparative education by examining how other individuals represented on *CIEclopedia* view their relationship with the CIES.

Out of the 94 profiles in *CIEclopedia*, half have explicitly stated their affiliation with the CIES. These include 24 CIES (past-) presidents and 23 members. Among the CIES presidents featured in the database, the 24 individuals represent only 41 percent of the total of 58 presidents of the Society to date. This indicates another gap in the database, aside from its lack of geographic diversity.

An analysis of the profiles of the 24 CIES presidents featured in the database reveals some interesting patterns. While most entries briefly mentioned the candidate's role as a CIES leader (either in the short bio-graphy or under institutional affiliations), several entries offered a more detailed description of the individual's significant contributions to the Society and to the field, some of which were recognized publicly by the Society (see chapter by Landorf in this book). The first three profiles pertain to the protagonists in the foundational era of the Society: William Brickman (founding president), Joseph Katz (third president), and Arnold Anderson (fourth president).

Brickman's important roles as co-founder of CIES, then called the Comparative Education Society (CES) in 1956, and as the Society's only two-time president, were highlighted in his profile by Hardacker and Brehm (2010). Another organizational giant was Joseph Katz. Roungchai (2008) described the huge role that this Canadian scholar portrayed in the institutionalization of the field of comparative education, not only in the U.S., but also in Canada, Europe, and globally, with his initiative to establish the World Council of Comparative Education Societies (WCCES) in 1970. Katz proposed the name change of the CES to incorporate the word "international", thereby becoming CIES (see also the chapter by Berends & Trakas in this book). The profile on C. Arnold Anderson, written by his former student, Erwin H. Epstein (2008), cites his significant contributions to CIES, thereby earning him the honor of being "inducted as one of the earliest Honorary Fellows of that organization." It further describes the methodological debates initiated by Anderson during the CIES meetings as "among the most memorable" in the development of the field.

The next three detailed profiles pertain to presidents who served the Society during the 1980s. These were: Erwin H. Epstein (1982-83); Beverly Lindsay (1988-89); and Vandra L. Masemann (1989-90). Beverly Lindsay's profile is worth highlighting, since she "made international history in 1988 when she was elected as the first African American president of CIES" (Cruz & Jaar 2008). The profiles of Epstein and Masemann also deserve further comment. Both Epstein and Masemann exemplify a lifelong dedication to the Society and to the global field. Epstein marked 1962 as the beginning of his involvement in CIES (then called CES) when he was a graduate student, and the 60th anniversary of the Society marked nearly 55 years of his unflagging commitment in various capacities. These include as CIES president, as the *Comparative Education Review*'s editor for 10 years, and as CIES Historian. Masemann's first CIES conference was in 1975, and her distinguished service was recognized in 2008 when she was inducted as CIES Honorary Fellow. Like Katz, both Epstein and Masemann have assumed senior leadership roles in the WCCES. Both Epstein and Masemann were Presidents, and Masemann was also Secretary-General and the first Historian of the World Council.[3]

In the succeeding decades, two CIES leaders who made significant contributions to the field as reflected in their *CIEclopedia* profiles[4] were Robert Arnove and Gita Steiner-Khamsi. Arnove was named a CIES Honorary Fellow in 2003 "for lifelong contributions to scholarship in this field of study" (Arnove 2008). The profile of Steiner-Khamsi exhibits her important initiatives, in close collaboration with her graduate students, to professionalize the field by institutionalizing the online journal *Current Issues in Comparative Education*, and "her dedication to preserving our [CIES] past and fostering our future" (Silova, Johnson & Magno 2008) through such innovative projects as the video production (with Eric Johnson) *Comparatively Speaking: An Oral History of the First 50 Years of CIES* (see Steiner-Khamsi's chapter in this volume) and *CIEclopedia* (developed by Sina Mossayeb).

As for the 23 CIES members who cited their affiliation with CIES in their bio-sketches, half were based outside the USA. Some cited their involvement in the Society's Board of Directors (e.g., Edmund King from 1961-65). Others even specified the year they joined the Society. This demonstrates the significance of the Society, being the largest and oldest among the professional societies in the field of comparative education. It also reflects its international membership and the sense of loyalty that members feel towards CIES.

Conclusion

This chapter has traced the evolution of the *CIEclopedia*. The project was definitely a step forward in visibly positioning the field of comparative education in a digital era. The aims of the project to contribute to the professionalization of the field and to democratize the canon of comparative education are noteworthy. Through its open source and inclusive philosophy, this database offers the potential to make visible a diverse range of scholars, theories and approaches in this global area of study.

An analysis of the *CIEclopedia* database reveals that while the original vision was to ensure a global outreach, and attempts have been made to achieve this by involving partner universities to cover different regions and linguistic groups, the outcomes have been modest. Substantially under-represented regions include Latin America and Africa. Moreover, parts of Asia with long histories in comparative education (e.g., Japan, Korea) are absent. This may be due to the limiting factor of language, with English as the dominant medium of scholarly communication. Going forward, imbalances may be addressed by forging strategic institutional partnerships worldwide, possibly through the professional societies of comparative education, with the specific condition that graduate students be involved under the supervision of a faculty member to ensure quality of submissions while providing these students the experience and recognition for their work.

With respect to the nexus between *CIEclopedia* and CIES leadership, this chapter has noted that profiles of some distinguished CIES presidents have prominently described their contributions to the Society and to the field. By contrast, some other biographies have only listed their role as CIES president as one item without elaboration. Moreover, while some individuals have provided detailed information as to the quality and length of their involvement with CIES, others have only listed the Society as one – and not necessarily the first – among a set of discipline-based societies. While this may be a reflection of varying degrees of dedication and loyalty to CIES, this conclusion cannot be definitive since most profiles have been written by third parties, albeit with the biographee's consent.

Lastly, viewing the theme of CIES leadership through the lenses of *CIEclopedia*, this CIES project evidences the Society's role as a pioneer and protagonist in the field of comparative education. It represents a strategic move to assert the "academic territory" occupied by the field as distinct from other fields of educational studies by portraying the features of the "academic tribe" and its diverse members (see Becher & Trowler 2001). This quest for distinction in the intellectual field (Bourdieu 1977) occurs not only between comparative education and other neighboring fields. It also takes place within the new "intellectual field" of *CIEclopedia* as a non-hierarchical arena for actors to shape the contours of comparative education with their life and works.

Notes

[1] The early documents on the project spelled it as *Cieclopedia*. Eventually, the first three letters were capitalized, to connote that it was the acronym for Comparative and International Education (CIE), and thus the name *CIEclopedia*. It is possible that the proponents of the project from Teachers College may have been inspired or influenced by the 1911 volume entitled "Cyclopedia of Education" edited by Paul Monroe, assisted by Isaac Kandel (see Mossayeb 2008), both of whom were famous scholars in Teachers College, Columbia University.

[2] Geographic origin was defined by the institutional affiliation of the biographee at the time of writing.

[3] Other CIES presidents who either later became or previously served as WCCES presidents were David Wilson, Mark Bray, and Carlos Alberto Torres.

[4] This qualification *"as reflected in their CIEclopedia profile"* is important. Many other CIES presidents who could have been featured in this commentary but they were not because they were either not profiled on *CIEclopedia* or the description of their relationship to CIES was not detailed.

[5] As of July 2015, 44 sub-national, national, regional, and language-based comparative education societies were members of the World Council of Comparative Education Societies (WCCES). In addition, several professional societies in the field were not (yet) members of the WCCES. For more information on the WCCES and its member societies, see Masemann, Bray and Manzon (2007) and visit www.wcces.com.

Communications

Epstein, Erwin. 2015. Personal communication, 24 March.
Steiner-Khamsi, Gita. 2015. Interview by Maria Manzon, 28 March.

References

Arnove, Robert. 2008. "Robert Arnove." *CIEclopedia*. http://www.nie.edu.sg/research-publications/cieclopediaorg/cieclopediaorg-a-to-z-listing/Robert-Arnove.

Becher, Tony, & Paul R. Trowler. 2001. *Academic Tribes and Territories: Intellectual Enquiry and the Culture of Disciplines.* 2nd ed. Buckingham: The Society for Research into Higher Education & Open University Press.

Blaug, Mark, & Howard Vane, eds. 2003. *Who's Who in Economics,* 4th ed. Massachusetts: Edward Elgar Publishing, Inc.

Bourdieu, Pierre. 1977. *Outline of a Theory of Practice* (Trans. R. Nice). Cambridge: Cambridge University Press.

Cruz, Jessica, & Alcira Jaar. 2008. "Beverly Lindsay." *CIEclopedia*.

Epstein, Erwin H. 2008. "C. Arnold Anderson." *CIEclopedia*.

Hardacker, Erin, & William Brehm. 2010. "William W. Brickman." *CIEclopedia*.
Manzon, Maria. 2011. Comparative Education: The Construction of a Field. Hong Kong: Comparative Education Research Centre, University of Hong Kong, and Dordrecht: Springer.

Masemann, Vandra, Mark Bray, & Maria Manzon, eds. 2007. *Common Interests, Uncommon Goals: Histories of the World Council of Comparative Education Societies and Its Members.* CERC Studies in Comparative Education 21. Hong Kong: Comparative Education Research Centre, The University of Hong Kong, and Dordrecht: Springer.

Mossayeb, Sina. 2006a. "Who's Who in Comparative and International Education Studies. Proposal 2006, 10 March." Teachers College, Columbia University.

Mossayeb, Sina. 2006b. "Who's Who in Comparative and International Education Studies. Proposal 2006, 4 July." Teachers College, Columbia University.

Mossayeb, Sina. 2008. "Isaac Kandel". *CIEclopedia*.

Roungchai, Chaitut. 2008. "Joseph Katz." *CIEclopedia*.

Silova, Iveta, Eric Johnson, & Cathryn Magno. 2008. "Gita Steiner-Khamsi". *CIEclopedia*.

Tietze, Susanne, & Penny Dick. 2013. "The Victorious English language: Hegemonic Practices in the Management Academy." *Journal of Management Inquiry* 22 (January): 122-134.

17
Honoring Merit

Hilary LANDORF and L. Bahia SIMONS-LANE

Since 1956, the Comparative Education Society (CES), and then Comparative and International Education Society (CIES), has worked to increase "the understanding of educational issues, trends and policies through comparative, cross-cultural and international perspectives."[1] One way CIES promotes excellence in the field is through six awards that reflect the commitment of the Society to honor the achievements of its members. These awards honor multiple forms of scholarship, from the best article in the *Comparative Education Review* (*CER*), to sustained accomplishments of long-standing members of CIES, an outstanding dissertation, and research in any refereed journal or a book.

While there is a comprehensive account of the purpose, structure, and selection process for each award in the CIES Awards Handbook, no document to date puts the awards into the larger context of scholarship in the Society or the academic field as a whole. Nor does any article relate the purpose of the awards to the contributions of the individuals for whom the awards are named. This chapter draws on foundational documents, CIES records, and recollections of prominent members of the Society to describe the purpose of each award, the significance of the individuals for whom the awards are named, and their scholarly context. Then, we offer recommendations pertaining to raising the visibility of the awards and further differentiating the awards through various forms of public recognition.

Erwin H. Epstein (ed.) (2016): *Crafting a Global Field: Six Decades of the Comparative and International Education Society*. Hong Kong: Comparative Education Research Centre (CERC), The University of Hong Kong, and Dordrecht: Springer. © CERC

Methods

This chapter focuses on merit honored by CIES through six awards that are given by the Awards Committee. The awards are: Honorary Fellows, George Bereday, Gail P. Kelly, Joyce Cain, Jackie Kirk Memorial Fund, and International Travel Grant. Each of these awards has a subcommittee that recommends winner(s) on an annual basis by adhering to the criteria and assessment procedures created by the Awards Committee. We recognize that there are other ways the Society honors merit. For example, The George P. Kneller Lecture, delivered at the CIES annual conference, each year recognizes a scholar who has made significant contributions to the field. However, since the choice of presenters for these lectures does not include a call for submissions or nominations, they are not included in this chapter. The New Scholars and Under-Represented Racial, Ethnic, and Ability Group (UREAG) committees also honor merit by providing travel grants to increase the representation of new scholars and students from under-represented racial, ethnic, and ability groups at the annual conference. These are given by the afore-mentioned committees and determined outside the Awards Committee. Therefore, we are not addressing these very worthwhile travel grants in this discussion of honoring merit.

To research the six awards we collected documents from the CIES Archives at Kent State University, gathered information from the CIES website, and interviewed members of CIES who, at the time the awards were established, held executive positions or were involved in the award proposals. To obtain records from the CIES archives, we contacted the Kent State Library Special Collections Department. We specifically looked for documents in the years around the date that the awards were established, including the award contracts, award proposals, newsletters mentioning the awards, memos about the awards, and mentions of the awards in business meetings. The CIES website provided historical and current CIES documents and lists of awardees.

Awards

The six CIES awards recognize individuals and research in the field of comparative and international education. Each award focuses on a different type of achievement or area of research. Some awards honor significant contributions to the field and to the Society, while others support young and under-represented scholars or scholarship in specific areas of study. All honor merit in their own way. We will now explain the details of each award, the significance of the concepts or people for whom they are named, and place the awards in a historical context.

George Bereday Award

In 1980, CIES established its first award. It was to be for the best article of the year published in the *CER*. Initially unnamed, in 1989 it became the George Bereday Award in honor of *CER*'s founder and first editor. Overseen by the Outstanding Scholarship Committee, the award is given each year to the author(s) of the article published the previous year in the *CER* that has contributed most to scholarship in the field of comparative education. Awards are evaluated on their theoretical framework, methodology, data collection and analysis, social and policy implications, and uniqueness of contribution, with additional criteria considered if there are several strong contenders (CIES 2014). As of 2015, the authors of 35 articles had received the award.

The renaming of this award was appropriate, not just because Bereday was the first editor of the *CER*, but also due to Bereday's long and distinguished history in the field of comparative and international education. Lawrence Cremin (1984), then President of Teachers College at Columbia University, wrote a tribute to Bereday's achievements upon his death in 1983. It took Cremin an entire page to list Bereday's accomplishments in the fields of law, sociology, and comparative education. Most relevant to the appropriateness of naming the *CER* award after Bereday were his accomplishments in writing and editing. He wrote 34 books, founded the *CER* and edited it for nine years. As Vandra Masemann, President of CIES in 1989 and winner of the Bereday Award in 1990, said: "Bereday exemplified excellence in writing and scholarship."[2]

Honorary Fellows Award

The Honorary Fellows Award recognizes long-term and influential contributors to the Society and the field. To date, 26 individuals have been given this award.[3] The proposal for the Honorary Fellows Award was put forth in 1982 by the Outstanding Scholarship Committee[4] and officially announced in 1983.[5] This award honors members with a career lasting more than 30 years for their scholarship, teaching/mentoring, active participation, and contribution to CIES.[6] In addition to being an honor, Honorary Fellow is a membership category in which fellows receive free registration to CIES meetings for life.

Honoring the achievements of senior members of CIES was introduced as early as 1970 with a proposal for an honorary membership category for "Elder Statesmen" that would be limited to 10 individuals, but it was not approved that year.[7] In one of the earliest references to the award, a memo from then President Erwin H. Epstein[8] suggested renaming the Outstanding Scholarship Committee the Awards Committee to include honoring, thus providing for honoring "Elder Statesmen" who were retired or nearing retirement. At that time this committee was only overseeing the Outstanding Scholarship Award (now the Bereday Award). In 1983, the President's Report of the April/June 1983 *Newsletter* announced the approval of an additional award by the Board of Directors, referring to it as "Fellows of CIES".[9]

While the Honorary Fellows Award was not the first award officially established, discussion of this award was the first recorded instance of talk of honoring overall merit within CIES. Elizabeth Sherman Swing (2007) identified the establishment of the Honorary Fellows Award as a societal identity marker of CIES. The proposal put forth by the Outstanding Scholarship Committee[10] provided two main rationales for the award: CIES should emulate other academic societies by honoring the achievements of their senior members; and now that the Society was 25 years old and its founders were nearing retirement, the time to create such an award was appropriate.

Gail P. Kelly Award

Proposed in 1992 and first awarded in 1994, the Gail P. Kelly award is given annually for an outstanding doctoral dissertation on topics related to social justice and equity in an international context (CIES 2014). The award has been given 22 times as of 2015. It was originally awarded every two years, but since 2000 it has been awarded annually.[11] Shortly after Kelly's death in 1991, the Awards Sub-committee discussed the idea of an award recognizing her and encouraged others to submit proposals to that effect.[12] Carlos Torres, then chair of the Awards Sub-committee, proposed the award in 1992, and it was first awarded in 1994 (CIES 2014). The Board unanimously accepted the proposal for this award.[13]

Gail Kelly's scholarly achievements, which were particularly focused on social justice and equity, make the naming of an award of this nature highly appropriate. Kelly was a professor of the State University of New

York at Buffalo for 16 years and wrote or edited 13 books, including several on comparative education.[14] The respect that members of the Society had for Kelly is noted in the Annual Business Meeting Minutes[15]: "The Board formally recognizes the supreme contribution of Gail Kelly to humankind and the Society and regrets her untimely death" (p. 7).

Joyce Cain Award

The Joyce Cain award was established in 2000 to honor the memory of Joyce Lynn Cain, a scholar-practitioner at Michigan State University whose work on Africa and African descendants was a reflection of her commitment to expanding the understanding of Africans and African culture. The award is given annually for an outstanding scholarly article that explores themes related to people of African descent, demonstrates originality and methodological, theoretical, and empirical rigor, and contributes to the increase in the understanding of the experiences of African descendants.[16] The Joyce Cain award has been given 14 times since it was first awarded in 2001.

The idea for this award originated with discussions in the UREAG committee after Joyce Cain's passing at a young age in 1996. According to Kassie Freeman, who along with Susan Peters proposed the award, "Africa seemed a lost part of the comparative and international education field at the time."[17] Since Joyce Cain's scholarship and practice focused on Africa, Freeman said that the UREAG committee thought that an award in her honor would be a powerful symbol for recognizing scholarship in and about Africa and the African Diaspora.[18] Once the award was proposed, the CIES Board fully supported its establishment.

The Joyce Cain Award carries no remuneration but, in the viewpoints of Kassie Freeman and Ruth Hayhoe, should be given more attention than has been the case in the last several years.[19] In 2014 no one received the Joyce Cain Award due to a lack of nominations. Instead, the chair of this award sub-committee, José Cossa, created a video illustrating the significance of the award that was shown at the 2014 awards ceremony. In 2015, the award was given to three recipients for three separate articles on education in different areas of Africa.

Jackie Kirk Memorial Award

Like the Gail Kelly and Joyce Cain awards, the Jackie Kirk Memorial Fund honors the memory of a dynamic and vibrant scholar-practitioner who died at a young age. Kirk was working for the International Rescue

Committee in Afghanistan when she was killed in 2008. A well-published scholar and an advocate for education in fragile states and education for girls, Jackie Kirk was well known and much respected in the CIES and broader international development communities.

Gita Steiner-Khamsi, President of the Society at the time, established an ad-hoc committee in 2009 to explore the possibilities of setting up a fund to enable the Society to "regularly carry out an activity at CIES annual meetings"[20] in honor of Kirk's work. The ad-hoc committee, chaired by CIES vice-president Ratna Ghosh, secured a donation of $20,000 from Kirk's husband, Andrew Kirk, and $10,000 from the International Rescue Agency, to establish the Jackie Kirk Memorial Fund. After extensive dialogue among these parties, in 2010 the ad-hoc committee proposed that CIES match these funds and create a restricted endowment fund called the Jackie Kirk Memorial Fund, to annually recognize a published book that "reflects one or some of the varied areas of expertise represented in Jackie Kirk's areas of commitment, primarily gender and education and/or education in conflict."[21] The Board approved this proposal in its 2010 meeting at the CIES annual conference in Chicago. The first Jackie Kirk Award was given in 2011, and one such award has been given each year since then.

International Travel Grant

In May 2008, CIES president-elect Gita Steiner-Khamsi secured $80,000 from the Open Society Institute (OSI) to be distributed in the following ways: $51,000 for the 2009 CIES annual conference activities, including travel and accommodation costs for 27 OSI affiliated participants; $9,000 for three individual travel grants, each in the amount of $1000, to be given to eligible applicants for travel to the CIES annual conferences in 2009, 2010, and 2011; and $20,000 for a non-restricted endowment fund called the International Travel Grant for Distinguished Service in Educational Reform.[22] This endowment fund was approved at the 2009 annual conference held in Charleston, South Carolina.

The International Travel Grant for Distinguished Service in Educational Reform was established to "encourage distinguished scholars, researchers and practitioners working in development contexts to present their work at the CIES annual meetings" (CIES 2014). Gita Steiner-Khamsi[23] cited several reasons for why she sought to secure this award. In addition to wanting to increase the presence of scholars and practitioners at the CIES annual conferences who serve in post-communist countries in Central and Eastern Europe, Central Asia, and Mongolia, she thought that the establishment of this award would motivate other non-governmental organizations and international non-governmental organizations to contribute funds to CIES, and that it would encourage greater attendance in the annual conferences by OSI and other organizations.

Beginning in 2012, each president-elect has secured Board approval to use CIES funds, in addition to the International Travel Grant funds, to support several International Travel Grant awardees' travel to present papers at the annual conferences. As of 2015, the International Travel Grant has been awarded to 65 individuals.

Discussion

Each of the six awards has unique purposes and represents specific issues in our field. Looked at as a group, these awards reflect the evolution of the Society and its intellectual strands. What follows is a short discussion of the awards as seen within these larger contexts.

The George Bereday and Honorary Fellows, the first two awards that the Society established, legitimated scholarship in the field and raised the status of the Society. The Bereday award was created at a time when CIES was concerned with strengthening the *CER* and supporting the field, which faced challenges enumerated in a *CER* editorial by Philip Altbach (1980). Altbach highlighted the position of comparative education as an add-on in education departments, scarcity of funding, and declining interest in international activities by funding organizations. Altbach's view in 1980 (152) remains valid: "Comparative education is often seen as a 'frill' in undergraduate education programs and as an unnecessary part of professional graduate training. Its relevance to American education must continually be argued."

The overall purpose of the next three CIES awards turned from legitimizing the field to honoring achievement in specific areas. The Gail Kelly Award recognizes the superior research of new scholars in social justice and equity issues in an international context. The Joyce Cain Award is for distinguished research on African descendants, while the Jackie Kirk Award is for an outstanding book on the empowerment of women and girls or the improvement of education in conflict and post-conflict settings.

Regarding the Gail Kelly award, Mark Ginsburg[24] explained that there was a clear "line to the award" from Kelly's accomplishments in her work on gender studies and the representation of minorities. He also commented that the Kelly Award related to the growth of committees like UREAG and the Gender and Education Committee within CIES. These were established in 1989 and 1990, respectively (Swing 2007). Much content at the time in the *Comparative Education Review* related well to discussions in comparative and international education in the early 1990s and to the aims of the Gail Kelly Award. In particular, the presidential address published in *CER* in 1992 (Ginsburg et al.) discussed the political implications of educators and issues of power in education, while a guest editorial by Wirt and Shorish (1993) addressed comparative ethnicity research. Such subject matter from the early 1990s, along with the establishment of committees dealing with gender equity and marginalized groups, aligned well with topics of the dissertations considered for the award and their focus on social justice and equity. The Under-represented Racial, Ethnic, and Ability Groups (UREAG) Committee was was formed to address issues of equity in both ethnic and disability contexts, and this committee established the Joyce Cain Award (Swing 2007).

The Jackie Kirk Award was also timely given the long-term conflicts in Iraq and Afghanistan during the 2000s. The destabilization of the region had great impact on access to education, particularly for girls, and this was Jackie Kirk's area of focus. As Ratna Ghosh explained, terrorists were targeting education and attention was being paid to the significance of girls' education. The violence of Jackie Kirk's death made it an appropriate award to highlight access to education during conflict as an important issue in the field.

The Jackie Kirk Award was also timely given the conflicts in Iraq and Afghanistan during the 2000s. The destabilization of the region had great impact on access to education, particularly for girls, Jackie Kirk's area of focus. As Ratna Ghosh[25] explained, terrorists were targeting education and attention was being paid to the significance of girls' education. The violence of Jackie Kirk's death made it an appropriate award to highlight access to education during conflict as an important issue in the field.

The International Travel Grant for Distinguished Service in Educational Reform is similar to the others in that its significance is tied to the historical context in which it was created. Education in post-communist states was of interest to many CIES scholars and practitioners alike when the award was created, attracting more academics from post-communist areas to participate in the annual conference. The obvious differences between this award and the previous three discussed are that the International Travel Grant is not conferred on the basis of a published piece and that it is technically a "grant" rather than an award. Beyond these differences, the criteria for winning the International Travel Grant focus on practice while the others are conferred on the basis of scholarship.

Recommendations

Based on our research for this chapter, and on one of the authors' experience in CIES as its Treasurer (2004-2010) and Awards Committee Chair (2011-2014), we have several recommendations regarding the maintenance and expansion of recognition of the CIES awards and their recipients within the Society and the greater comparative and international education community of scholars and practitioners.

Our first recommendation is to increase the visibility of the awards and the awardees on the CIES website and in the online and printed versions of the annual conference program. Most of these awards represent a significant achievement for the scholar(s) who receive them. However, during our research we found that while lists of past awardees are available on the website, they are quite difficult to find, incomplete, and could be displayed more prominently. With regard to the conference program, along with the name of the awardee and article or book, we recommend adding lists of past awardees, similar to the list of past presidents that is presently included in the annual program.

Our second recommendation is to differentiate the awards at the annual conference more than is currently the case. Looking into conference programs for the past 10 years, we found that the awards have been publically conferred during an awards ceremony that has lasted between 60 and 90 minutes. This allows very little time for the award winners to thank their colleagues, let alone give a scholar who has made major contributions to the Society over a 30-year span the time to make a short speech. If each award is given equal recognition on the website, and in the online and printed conference programs, then public recognition at the conferences can be differentiated and, in the words of Mark Ginsburg, "Different ways can be found for the public recognition for different kinds of awards."[2]

Our third recommendation is for the Society to more prominently display the significance of each of the individuals for whom awards are named. While very short descriptions of the legacies of Gail Kelly, Joyce Cain, and Jackie Kirk are included in the Awards Handbook (CIES 2014), no such description of George Bereday exists in the Handbook. Each of these scholars' biographies can be easily displayed on the CIES website and in the conference program.

The honoring of merit at CIES is a tangible recognition of accomplishment and an encouragement to all members to take pride in their professional and scholarly contributions to the Society and to the field of international and comparative education. As our Society continues to grow, we hope that the awards, their recipients, and the individuals for whom the awards are named are given the public prominence that they so richly deserve.

Acknowledgements

Many individuals generously gave of their time to speak with us about the awards and the Society. We thank Erwin Epstein, Philip Altbach, Kassie Freeman, Ratna Ghosh, Mark Ginsburg, Ruth Hayhoe, Vandra Masemann, and Gita Steiner-Khamsi. Beyond the valuable information and historical memory that these individuals provided, their dedication to the Society and its continuing development was palpable in our conversations. We also thank Cara Gilgenbach, the Head of Special Collections and Archives at Kent State University, for her assistance in locating critical information regarding the awards.

Notes

[1] "About CIES," CIES, accessed April 10, 2015, http://www.cies.us/?page=About.

[2] Vandra Masemann (former president, CIES), in discussion with the authors, March 25, 2015.

[3] "Honorary Fellows," CIES, last modified October 13, 2014. www.cies.us/resource/collection/4057538F-26FE-4448-9644-F43B3E15D06E/fellows1.pdf

[4] Outstanding Scholarship Committee, "Rationale and Proposed Set of Procedures for the Nomination and Selection of Honorary Fellows of the C.I.E.S," 9 October 1982, CIES Archives, Secretariat Records, Kent State University Library.

[5] CIES, "Newsletter Nos. 67-68 April/June 1983" (newsletter, CIES), 1-20.

[6] "Honorary Fellows," CIES, accessed February 26, 2015, https://cies.site-ym.com/?HonoraryFellows.

[7] Annual Business Meeting Minutes, March 23, 1970, CIES Archives, Secretariat Records, Kent State University Library.

[8] Erwin Epstein, Memo to Executive Board, July 7, 1981, CIES Archives, Secretariat Records, Kent State University Library.

[9] CIES, "CIES Newsletter Nos. 67-68 April/June 1983" (newsletter, CIES), 1-20.

[10] Outstanding Scholarship Committee, "Rationale and Proposed Set of Procedures for the Nomination and Selection of Honorary Fellows of the C.I.E.S," 9 October 1982, CIES Archives, Secretariat Records, Kent State University Library.

[11] Board of Directors Meeting Minutes, March 7, 2000, CIES Archives, Secretariat Records, Kent State University Library.

[12] Awards Committee, Interim Report, 1991, CIES Archives, Secretariat Records, Kent State University Library.

[13] Annual Business Meeting Minutes, March 14, 1992, CIES Archives, Secretariat Records, Kent State University Library.

[14] New York Times, "Gail P. Kelly, 51, dies; professor of education," January 29, 199, accessed April 18, 2015, http://www.nytimes.com/1991/01/29/obituaries/gail-p-kelly-51-dies-professor-of-education.html.

[15] Annual Business Meeting Minutes, 1991, CIES Archives, Secretariat Records, Kent State University Library.

[16] CIES, "CIES Newsletter No. 124 May 2000" (newsletter, CIES).

[17] Kassie Freeman (former president, CIES), in discussion with the authors, March 23, 2015.

[18] Ibid.

[19] Ibid.; Ruth Hayhoe, (former president, CIES), in discussion with the authors, March 21, 2015.

[20] Gita Steiner-Khamsi, CIES President's Report, 2009-10.

[21] "Jackie Kirk," CIES, accessed March 20, 2015, http://cies.site-ym.com/?page=JackieKirkAward

[22] Gita Steiner-Khamsi, CIES President's Report, 2009-10.

[23] Gita Steiner-Khamsi, (former president, CIES), in discussion with the authors, March 30, 2015.

[24] Mark Ginsburg, (former president, CIES), in discussion with the authors, April 7, 2015.

[25] Ratna Ghosh, (former president, CIES), in discussion with the authors, March 20, 2015.

[26] Mark Ginsburg, (former president, CIES), in discussion with the authors, April 7, 2015.

Unpublished Documents

Secretariat Records. Comparative and International Education Society Records. Kent State University Library.

Comparative and International Education Society. 2014. Awards Committee Handbook. Mt. Royal: Comparative and International Education Society.

References

Altbach, Philip 1980. "Whither Comparative Education?" *Comparative Education Review* 24(2): 151-154.

Cremin, Lawrence. 1984. "Professor George Bereday." *Comparative Education* 20(1): 5.

Ginsburg, Mark B., Sangeeta Kamat, Rajeshwari Raghu, & John Weaver. 1992. "Educators/Politics." *Comparative Education Review* 36(4): 417-445.

Swing, Elizabeth Sherman. 2007. "The Comparative and International Education Society (CIES)." In Vandra Masemann, Mark Bray, & Maria Manzon, eds. *Common Interests, Uncommon Goals: Histories of the World Council of Comparative Education Societies*. CERC Studies in Comparative Education 21. Hong Kong: Comparative Education Research Centre, The University of Hong Kong, and Dordrecht: Springer, pp. 94-115.

Wirt, Frederick M., & M. Mobin Shorish. 1993. "The Uses of Comparative Ethnicity Research." *Comparative Education Review* 37(1): 1-8.

Prime Resources

18
Developing the Archive

Erwin H. Epstein

The establishment and development of the official Comparative and International Education Society (CIES) Archive three and a half decades ago is a crucial part of CIES history and a cause for celebration. The existence of an official archive is a mark of distinction for a professional organization. It signifies that the organization has been properly and solidly institutionalized, and, more importantly, that the field and people it represents have a sense of institutional memory.

Constructing the Archive

The Archive stands as a monument to the creativity and wide-ranging professional interests of the Society's members. However, until recently it was not much more than a large deposit box and a big stuffed space filled with correspondence, drafts of articles by the Society's founders and early leaders, and miscellaneous other materials. It needed to be organized by people tending to its growth and development and used by others who would draw wisdom from its contents. These individuals needed to nurture each other. The work of those assigned to put the collection in order was largely lost without scholars willing to utilize the information and knowledge it contained. Conversely, those few scholars who sought to draw knowledge from the collection were thwarted in their efforts, because resources were insufficient to ensure the Archive's management and expansion. The establishment and development of the

Erwin H. Epstein (ed.) (2016): *Crafting a Global Field: Six Decades of the Comparative and International Education Society*. Hong Kong: Comparative Education Research Centre (CERC), The University of Hong Kong, and Dordrecht: Springer. © CERC

records collection – and the assignment of people to tend it – marked the Archive's early years.

The Archive's development has been focused mostly on building – as opposed to using – the collection. The idea of having an official collection was first proposed by Beatrice Szekely, Editor of the journal *Soviet Education*, in 1978. CIES President George Male appointed an Archive Committee composed of Franklin Parker, Claude Eggertsen, and William Brickman. In 1980, the CIES Board of Directors established the Archive, to be housed in the Special Collections section at Kent State University, and the Board voted a two-year grant of US$1,200 for the project (see the chapter by Swing in this volume).

People at Kent State, especially Gerald Read, a founding member of CIES, and his colleague Vilma Seeberg, contributed their time and guidance. That university has been a reliable repository for the Society's records. In 1980, James W. Geary, Director of Library Administration at Kent State, wrote the following to Phil Altbach in his proposal to house the Archives:

> Before closing, Dr. Altbach, let me add that I believe that the records of the Comparative and International Education Society will be a welcome addition to our holdings. Let me also apologize sincerely for the necessary formality of this letter, but part of Kent State's success in this area stems from honoring commitments made. Rest assured that should these institutional records be transferred here, they will have a good home (Geary 1980).

Kent State has indeed been true to its promise.

The first donation to the collection was made in January 1981 by George Z.F. Bereday, the first Editor of the *Comparative Education Review* (Kim & Sebaly 1986). By the beginning of 1986, the Archive contained largely the records of the Secretariats at the University of California-Los Angeles (1973-76), Pennsylvania State (1976-79), and Southern California (1979-83); of the *Comparative Education Review* from 1957-62 and 1979-85; and a hard-copy set of the *Review* (including one of the only two official sets in existence); and copies of the Society's *Newsletter* (1965-83), which replaced earlier *Newsnotes*. Philip Altbach, when he was Editor of the *Review*, did much to facilitate the Archive's establishment.

Growing the Archive

After the early years, much of the work at the Archive aimed at systematizing the deposit of current records and files of Society officials, inventorying them, and seeking donations of materials to fill in gaps of the older records. By 1995, the Archive contained substantial (though by no means complete) files of the Society's presidents; complete files of the *Review* editorships of George Bereday, Philip Altbach (1979-88), and Erwin H. Epstein (1989-94; subsequent collection through 1998); business files (only) of the editorships of Harold J. Noah (1966-71) and Andreas Kazamias (1972-78); and a variety of miscellaneous formal reports and conference planning documents (CIES inventory nd, 1-2).

During the mid-1990s the Archive became the official depository of records for the World Council of Comparative Education Societies,[1] a role that the Society's Board of Directors had declined to take on some years earlier. The new posture of the Board reflected its recognition of the importance of the World Council to the field of comparative education generally and to the part the American Society was now playing in the Council's welfare and development.[2] Nevertheless, about a decade later the World Council decided to keep its records separate from the CIES Archive at Kent State, and in 2015 moved its collection from Kent State to the University of Pittsburgh.

By the late 1990s, the Archive had become a substantial collection ready to be properly mined. I attribute this maturation in good part to the sustained efforts of Kim Sebaly and the archivists at Kent State, who have been stalwarts in developing the collection, even during times that the Society displayed little interest in the enterprise.

Appointing the Historians

It took almost three decades to establish a firm platform for the Archive. Yet even now the Archive is underused. A few critical steps have been taken to make the Archive a living collection. The Society only recently has begun to breathe real life into the Archive, to make it truly useful for the field and its practitioners, and not just a preserve of passive records. The Board of Directors took a critical step in this direction in 1999 by appointing the first Historian, Elizabeth Sherman Swing, with tangible responsibility for over-sight of the Archive. Swing spent considerable time in examining the collection and identifying topics of importance to the field for which key sources reside in the Archive (see Swing 2000).

Such measures have been important to avoid having scholars discouraged by the large investment in time and resources required to make use of the collection.

In March 2008, I succeeded Elizabeth Sherman Swing as CIES Historian (Epstein 2013). During my six years (two terms) in that position, I introduced amendments to the CIES Constitution and Bylaws that formalized the place of the Archive in the Society's organizational structure and described the responsibilities of the Historian and the Immediate Past President for ensuring that the records would be properly monitored and kept up-to-date. I went on to establish a link to the Archive on the CIES website that contains guidelines for contributing to the collection and shows linkages to collections of potential importance to comparativists at the Hoover Institution in Stanford University and at the Special Collections Research Center at the University of Chicago. I also arranged CIES support for a two-year project with Cara Gilgenbach, Director of Special Collections at Kent State University, to appraise and process the Archive's records, which had lain largely dormant for many years, and to update the Archive's Finding Aid (see this book's Appendix: *Finding Aid for the Comparative and International Education Society Records*), providing a gateway for using the collection.

To stimulate use of the Archive, I received approval from the Board of Directors in 2012 for my proposal to fund grants to encourage research using the collection. That project drew five fine proposals, showing how keen the interest in doing research in the Archive had become, and I was able to fund two of them: one by José Cossa and the other by Martha Merrill. Both of these scholars are authors of chapters in this book ("Shaping the Intellectual Landscape" by José Cossa, and "Developing the *Newsletter*" by Martha Merrill). In view of the evident value, strong interest in, and success of this grant initiative, I proposed in the following year a grant renewal to fund additional research in the Archive, but my proposal was tabled and renewal was rendered inactive.

Certainly more needs to be done to make the Archive a living, breathing part of the profession. However important may be the measures taken thus far, the collection is still largely untapped, though now much less opaque to members of the Society. Still, as a testament to how far use of the Archive has advanced, consider that eight of the chapters in this book – those by Swing, Cossa, Berends and Trakas, Masemann, Robertson and Cushner, Landorf, Merrill, and me – relied extensively on the collection.

Proposed Next Steps

What then are to be the next steps? How is the Archive to move from passive preserve to an actively used facility? The keys are to give the Archive the recognition it deserves and to make the records readily accessible. I propose three actions that I believe would advance these purposes.

First, as a long-term project the records should be converted to electronic form and made accessible on the World Wide Web. Such an undertaking would require considerable time and resources, but it can be done gradually, starting with the inventory listings and a records catalogue. Such a project would have value from the very beginning. However incomplete may be the records to be accessed early on, accessibility is immediate as soon as even partial records come on line, giving the collection a vastly magnified exposure. Some years ago I had explored the prospect of digitizing the records, but, at the time, such a task proved to be too expensive. As the technology for digitization advances and becomes less costly, the Society should reconsider funding a long-term digitization project. Indeed, digitization is now being done on the World Council of Comparative Education Societies records at the University of Pittsburgh, though, to be sure, these records are far less extensive than those in the CIES Archive.

Second, a network with other relevant archival collections should be established. More than two decades ago, Gerald Dorfman, Curator of the Paul and Jean Hanna Archival Collection in the Hoover Institution at Stanford University, wrote me regarding his interest in such collaboration. The Hanna Collection contains extensive personal papers of such illuminati as I.L. Kandel, William W. Brickman, R. Freeman Butts, and Paul Hanna, as well as important documents of interest to the field, such as original IEA papers from the University of Stockholm. As mentioned earlier, I had already posted a link to the Hoover and University of Chicago collections, but the Society should explore expanding linkages with important records of comparativist interest at such institutions as the University of London Institute of Education, the University of Hong Kong Comparative Education Research Centre (CERC), the Institute for International Studies in Education at the University of Pittsburgh (IISE), the Ontario Institute for Studies in Education (OISE) of the University of Toronto (OISE), and the UNESCO International Bureau of Education (IBE) Documentation Centre.

Finally, the Society should release funds to continue the work of encouraging the use of the Archive for research on the field's development. Inviting scholars to submit proposals for funding support would foster activity to advance institutional memory and knowledge of important events and figures in our field, vital elements in stimulating interest and securing an enduring identity for our profession.

In conclusion, we have a legacy to pass on to new scholars, but the legacy is still mostly hidden in the collection boxes at Kent State. Those boxes contain valuable secrets that will remain locked without devices for unlocking them. It is only a question of our having the will to put those devices in place.

Notes

[1] See the chapter by Vandra Masemann in this volume.
[2] During the early years of the World Council, many members of the American-based Society regarded the Council as a largely European organization, having little to do with the issues of interest to American comparativists. That attitude began to change in the 1980s and changed further in the 1990s.

Unpublished Documents

CIES Inventory. nd. *Comparative and International Education Society, Records, 1956-1994*, pp. 1-2.

Dorfman, Gerald A. to Erwin H. Epstein, October 31, 1991. Personal papers of Erwin H. Epstein.

Epstein, Erwin H. 2013. *Annual Report of the CIES Historian for 2013*, December 30, 2013. Personal papers of Erwin H. Epstein.

Geary, James E. to Philip Altbach, September 10, 1980. Personal papers of Erwin H. Epstein.

Kim, Yongchu, & Kim P. Sebaly. 1986. *Comparative and International Education Society, Records, 1954-84, Inventory*. January.

Swing, Elizabeth Sherman. 2000. *Comparative and International Education Society Historian's First Annual Report*, March 2000.

19
Developing the CIES Newsletter

Martha C. MERRILL

The CIES *Newsletter* has changed since the organization was founded in 1956, for four reasons. First, the organization itself grew, matured, and adopted more formal structures. Gerald Read's purple mimeographed notes, distributed whenever he had news to transmit, gave way to quarterly printed documents, numbered in sequence. Second, the Internet happened. Many of the original functions of the *Newsletter* – announcing where the next conference would be, providing a form for membership renewal, introducing candidates for office and distributing ballots – now are handled electronically, via the website, rather than on paper. Similarly, the syllabus summaries that appeared periodically in the *Newsletter* have been replaced by the Comparative and International Education Course Archive Project (CIECAP) – See Kathleen M. Stone's chapter in this volume – and news of members is posted by members themselves on Facebook and Linked-in. Third, *Newsletter* editors appear to have had a remarkable degree of flexibility in choosing what to include and what to focus on. Finally, the shift from a university-based Secretariat to a professional Secretariat has caused a cessation – perhaps temporary – in the publication of the *Newsletter*. Table 20.1 features a list of all CES/CIES *Newsletter* editors and their years of editorship, from the beginning of the *Newsletters* until its recent controversial suspension.

Erwin H. Epstein (ed.) (2016): *Crafting a Global Field: Six Decades of the Comparative and International Education Society*. Hong Kong: Comparative Education Research Centre (CERC), The University of Hong Kong, and Dordrecht: Springer. © CERC

Table 19.1 List of all CES/CIES Newsletter editors*

##	Dates	Names of Editors
1	August 1963-January 1965	Gerald H. Read
2	May 1965-January 1968	Franklin Parker
3	March 1968-June 1971	Barbara A. Yates
4	March 1972, December-January 1973	Edward J. Nemeth
5	May 1973-May 1975	Val D. Rust
6	September 1975-June 1976	John N. Hawkins
7	October 1976-April 1979	Beverly Lindsay
8	June 1979-June 1981	W. Tapscott Steven
9	October 1981-June 1982	Helena Somraty Stone
10	October 1982-April/June 1983	William B. Lee
11	October 1983-May 1989	Abdul A. Al-Rubaiy
12	Sept-Oct. 1989-January 1992	Philip G. Altbach
13	May 1992-January 1995	Michael L. Basile, Joshua A. Muskin, Kim Hughes
14	May 1995-May 1998	Paige Baldwin
15	October 1998	Daniel Heyduk
16	January 1999	Todd Davis
17	May 1999-January 2003	Hey-Kyung Koh, Todd Davis
18	January 2004	Lynn Ilon
19	2005-2010	Editor-in-chief: Hilary Landorf; Editor: Roger Geertz Gonzalez
20	2011-2012	Kevin Kinser

*Prepared by Chynarkul Ryskulova

Information Sources

The primary sources for this chapter are the *Newsletters* themselves, as contained in the CIES Archive at Kent State University. The issues produced when the Secretariat was at Florida International University (2004-2010) were, with eight exceptions, produced only as electronic versions. Most of those issues were retrieved from an archived page of the CIES website. Half a dozen issues of the *Newsletter* are not available in the archives or electronically.

The very earliest mimeographed *Newsletters* also are missing. Although the organization was founded in 1956, the first *Newsletter* on file, written by Gerald Read, is from August 1963. From the content of that *Newsletter*, it does not appear to be the first one published: no announcement is made of "we are beginning a new venture." On the contrary, the publication of the *Comparative Education Review* is mentioned, a couple of the seminars for educators that Read was organizing were promoted, and members were reminded to pay their dues. So it is likely that some issues were published earlier and now are lost.

The process for transferring *Newsletters* to the archives, at least early on, appears to have been informal. A number of the *Newsletters* in the files are personal copies of the person who was the Editor at the time, or of someone who was a Board member or other official in the Society. This, at times, leads to amusing insights. One copy (November 1964), apparently donated by a person who later became a president of CIES, contains his notes on several academic papers, including his evaluation of one speech: "Balderdash!" The notes also include the reminder, "diapers, vitamins, cigarettes, Valentines," and the initials of seven people for whom Valentines are needed.

This informality of donating means that, with rare exceptions, all that is in the file is the *Newsletter* itself. The file for Issue 103, from May 1993, edited by Michael Basile, Joshua Muskin, and Kim Hughes at Florida State, is an exception; it contains correspondence, copies of e-mails, and other back-up materials. Such back-up materials are available only in two or three other files. Thus a researcher seeking to understand the editors' creative processes and choices has little to work with.

The process for donating materials to the archives in an age of electronic publishing appears to need review. When the *Newsletter* was edited by Hilary Landorf, assisted by Fernanda Pineda and Joan Oviawe at Florida International University (2005-2010), it was published only electronically, with the exception of some issues that were published in a limited print run:

> The FIU Secretariat from 2005 until 2010, when Dr. Landorf and I were running the office, produced every issue of the newsletter electronically. We only produced paper versions in mid-2009 and 2010...per petition of an Honorary Fellow who preferred paper version. I only printed about 20 of each (Fernanda Pineda, personal communication, March 12, 2015).

Numbers 136 to 144 and Number 146, issued between 2004 and 2007, are not currently in the archives. Joseph Sapp, the Account Executive for CIES at its current professional Secretariat, Talley Management, was able to retrieve an archived web page with links to those *Newsletters*. Two links did not work, but of those, one was for an issue also published in print and available in the archives. Mr. Sapp was able to find further links that did work. However, for the links that did work, each separate article in the *Newsletter* had to be downloaded individually. Of these links within an issue, all of the article links seemed to work, but some of the more time-sensitive materials, such as calls for papers or announcements of forthcoming conferences, were no longer functioning.

One further issue related to sources is the numbering system of the *Newsletters*. As noted, early on the *Newsletters* and much else about CIES (and CES) was informal, so the *Newsletters* had no established numbering system. In May 1965, Franklin Parker, upon succeeding Gerald Read as Secretary and the Treasurer, initiated a system of numbering. By this point, the organization already was nine years old, and the *Newsletter* had been published for several years. The archive file numbers thus do not correspond to the issue numbers of the *Newsletter* itself, as the first several archive files contain un-numbered *Newsletters*. The archive file numbers are seven numbers higher than the *Newsletter* numbers throughout Box 1. The archive file numbers in Box 2 start again with 1, but the issue number of the *Newsletter* in that first file is #74, from January 1985. After file number 59 in Box 2 (Newsletter 132), the archives no longer use file numbers; the files are labeled just with *Newsletter* numbers.

Functions of the *Newsletter*

Early in the Society's history, the *Newsletter* was a major source of information for members. Announcements of where the next conference would be, hotel locations, and registration forms; dates and locations of regional conferences; membership applications; elections and candidate biographies; reports of the Society's committees; calls for papers; news of members; events in the field; recent dissertations; members looking for new positions; positions available; In Memoriam notices – all were included in various issues of the *Newsletter*. The Fall 1963 issue, edited by Gerald Read, for example, contained information about the forthcoming Society "meeting" (not yet called a conference), a teaching opportunity in Southern Rhodesia, a call for summer school staff, announcements of regional meetings of the Society and a summer seminar, an order blank for *Comparative Education Review,* and a report of the Nominating Committee. The January 1966 issue, edited by Franklin Parker, provided a page and a half of reporting on the Annual Meeting, two pages on the regional meetings, an announcement of a program on Latin American education at the University of Florida, discussion of the creation of a metro New York City group of CES members, notice of a teacher exchange, summaries of current research, a list of recent doctoral graduates in the field (announced as "will soon be ready for positions"), personal news from 12 members, a new comparative education book series in the UK, fellowships at the East West Center in Hawai'i and through the National Defense Education Act, the description of a new German university, a listing of new publications, appreciation for those who supported the *Newsletter*, a member renewal form, and an election ballot. Through the end of the 1980's, the June issue was a list of the names and addresses of all members. Philip Altbach, who became Editor starting with issue #93 (January 1990), announced that he would publish four full quarterly issues, with the membership list as supplemental.

In addition to information items, each Editor had the opportunity to add features he or she wanted. Barbara Yates, in the third issue she edited (December 1968), announced that the previous Editor, Franklin Parker, would be compiling a list of "Recent and Noteworthy Publications" for each issue. Val Rust, in the early 1970s, often included sample comparative education course syllabi. He also published a number of opinion articles, including one by John Lipkin (September 1974, p. 11) called "Breaking down elitism in CIES." Point #6 in that article: "Graduate students should have the opportunity to hear the Presidential Address without paying the banquet fee." W. Tapscott Steven, in the late 1970s and early 1980s, also published content articles. For example, in issue #53, October 1979, Jerrold Burnell and David Adams wrote on "A Rationale for the Ethnic Foundations of Education." By the 1990s, the *Newsletter* often was filled with lively debates. Philip Altbach, who was the Editor in the early 1990s and who asked readers to send articles, reflects:

> ... yes, we were interested in adding content – sort of what I do in our INTERNATIONAL HIGHER EDUCATION publication. We thought that it would be more interesting for readers (Personal communication, April 14, 2015).

Michael Basile, Joshua Muskin, and Kim Hughes, who were Editors from May 1992 until January 1995, similarly tried to spark reader interest. In an editorial titled "Thththththaaaaat's All, Folks!" in their final issue, they explain:

... we have attempted to use the *Newsletter* as a means to foster the sort of stimulating, open debate we enjoy annually at the CIES conference.... Without compromising the announcements functions – books, conferences, members' activities – we have tried to interest and stimulate the Society's members with pieces on provocative topics from a variety of perspectives.

Indeed, in that final issue of their editorship, they included a front-page article on "Increasing Underrepresented Groups in Education;" an editorial by Joshua Muskin about the apparently quite hot issue that the National Science Foundation's Board on International Comparative Studies in Education had published guidelines on the scope and conduct of research in comparative and international education without consulting CIES (and perhaps without being aware that CIES existed); an article by William Cummings on the same debate; a report from CIES President Nelly Stromquist noting that CIES' letter to U.S. President Bill Clinton asking for the embargo on Cuba to be lifted was met with a form letter (reproduced in the *Newsletter*); a substantive piece by David Post, Joe Farrell, and Heidi Ross, titled "Prologue to the Investigation of Comparative and International Education Graduate Programs in North America: Part I"; and an article by Kassie Freeman titled "Marginalization on the Eve of Globalization."

As the announcement function of the *Newsletter* could be fulfilled by e-mails and website postings, the *Newsletter* indeed began to focus more on articles. The online *Newsletters* published under the editorship of Hilary Landorf at Florida International University (2005-2010) contain half a dozen articles in each issue, followed by a section on Conference Reports and the "CIES Bulletin," with the sub-heading "Information about conferences and events, recently-published books, positions available, etc." The issues published at SUNY-Albany in 2011-2012, under the editorship of Kevin Kinser, followed a similar model: articles first, with announcements second. The Albany staff also increased the use of photos and graphics. Kevin Kinser comments:

We regularly debated here at Albany what the purpose of a printed newsletter was, as contrasted with a listserv or a blog or some other ways of distributing information. We ultimately came to look at it as a way of documenting more officially the communications of CIES, as well as being the place for official announcements or public calls for comment and debate within the society (Personal communication, April 15, 2015).

However, the first *Newsletter* that went out by e-mail was something for which the sender felt she needed to apologize. In an undated letter, Paige Baldwin of the Institute for International Education, who was the *Newsletter* Editor from May 1995 to May 1998, wrote:

> Please find enclosed a copy of *CIES Newsletter* issue number 113. This issue was originally sent out electronically to those members ... whose e-mail addresses were on file.... This issue was produced electronically in an effort to balance the Society's budget for 1996-97. We have decided to return to our policy of producing three printed issues ... each year. These issues will have fewer pages and be printed on less expensive paper in an effort to save money....

Yet, less than a decade later, the *Newsletter* was entirely on line. In addition, the issue just preceding 113 – the May 1996 Issue 112 – featured a front-page article presenting the now well-known Bray and Thomas (1995) cube. Despite the looming financial problems, the *Newsletter* appeared to be functioning as an important vehicle of communication about scholarly issues in the field.

The Society's website was announced in the September 2001 *Newsletter* in a two-page spread. Miguel Angel Escotet, the Website Director, and Karan Casey, the Assistant Website Manager, introduce the website:

> In hopes of enhancing the efforts and undertakings of the Comparative and International Education Society, efforts are being made towards constructing an online community to support the Society and its members in their educational and professional endeavors. (p. 4)

The Professional Secretariat and Suspension of the *Newsletter*

As the Society grew and the annual conference became a complex event requiring signing hotel contracts and other arrangements made years in advance, it became clear that a university-based Secretariat staffed by faculty volunteers and perhaps a few paid graduate assistants was no longer a tenable model. The Board asked a committee, chaired by Noah Sobe, to investigate the possibility of shifting to a professional association management company. The committee report, which was issued on November 26, 2012 and accepted at the 2013 Puerto Rico conference, proposed the appointment of the Kasselen Meeting and Events (KME) management company, and the Board voted to give that company a one-year contract to include production of "a quarterly newsletter and coordinate communication with membership" (Request for proposals, 2013).

In May 2014, the Board declined to renew the KME contract and engaged the Talley Management Group (TMG) to manage the Society's affairs. TMG was not assigned responsibility to produce the *Newsletter*. Contrary to the 2013 Request for proposals, Noah Sobe writes:

> In March 2013 the CIES Board decided to hire an Executive Director and excluded newsletter production from the tasks contracted out to an Executive Director, with full awareness that this decision effectively suspended the production of the CIES newsletter. The vision was that production of the newsletter would be studied and that an effective plan or strategy would be arrived at. In what manner – or whether – to resume the production of the CIES newsletter is still an item under consideration by the Board as of Spring 2015 (Noah Sobe, personal communication, April 11, 2015).

Nevertheless, as David Post has noted, producing the *Newsletter* is included in the CIES Constitution (David Post, personal communication, April 7, 2015; CIES Constitution as amended on November 27, 2014, Section V.1.b, "Regular Publications").

Conclusion

The history of the *Newsletter* reflects changes in the Society. In addition to being a topic of research itself, the *Newsletter* also is a source for researchers with other interests. For example, the Society's name change and revisions to the Constitution were debated in the pages of the *Newsletter*. In addition, the published membership lists and Board lists are a source of data for understanding how international the Society's membership and governance has been, as well as for analyzing participation by women. The topical articles published in the *Newsletter* also provide insights into debates that were relevant at particular points in time.

In an era when announcement functions, membership, and conference planning are done via a website and a listserv, is there a role for a

Newsletter? David Post, past Editor of the *Comparative Education Review*, argues that there is:

> First, as an organization – especially one with now many SIGs since their initiation in 2004 – I think that there needs to be something to give a common sense of purpose and identity to members. When the organization only had 800-900 participants come to the annual meeting (as recently as 15 years ago), most people interacted personally and most attended big events there (awards, presidential speech, etc). Now most people gather in their own groups ... there is less sense of mission as an organization ... (Personal communication, April 7, 2015)

The *Newsletter* thus may be the one debate and information vehicle on topics such as girls' education in China, non-formal education in Lesotho, hybridity theories, analyses of the conditions of educational policy transfer, work with huge international data sets, and interviews with small numbers of parents or students. In its renewed form, the Newsletter should excel at engaging the CIES membership in a wide range of interests and activities. [Editor's Note: Since this Chapter was written, the CIES Newsletter resumed publication under the editorship of Marianne Larson, University of Western Ontario.]

Acknowledgement

The author is grateful for information provided by Kevin Kinser, Hilary Landorf, Joan Oviawe, Fernanda Pineda, David Post, and Noah Sobe.

Unpublished Documents

The Constitution of the Comparative and International Education Society. As amended on November 17, 2014. Available: http://www.cies. us/?page=ConstitutionBylaws.
Request for Proposals/Open Position Announcement. January 2013. Albany: CIES Secretariat.

Reference

Bray, Mark, & R. Murray Thomas. 1995. "Levels of Comparison in Educational Studies: Different Insights from Different Literatures and the Value of Multilevel Analyses." *Harvard Educational Review 66*(3): 472-490.

20

The Comparative and International Education Course Archive Project (CIECAP)

Kathleen M. STONE

The field of comparative and international education has experienced an on-going dialogue relating to theoretical frameworks, thematic shifts, and teaching. Open debate regarding the teaching of comparative and international education was especially animated in 1998 at the 10th World Congress of Comparative Education Societies in Cape Town, South Africa. Follow-up discourse continued at Comparative and International Education Society (CIES) conferences beginning in Toronto (1999) and San Antonio (2000), as well as at the 11th World Congress of Comparative Education Societies in the Republic of Korea in 2001. In particular, strong interest was displayed in surveying content boundaries, organizational resources, teaching programs, personnel, literatures used, and themes pursued in the content of university coursework (see Tikly & Crossley 2001, 561). Carlos Alberto Torres discussed the poverty of theory in the field, and the poverty of research and theory that abounds in academic meetings. He reflected that Comparative Education is a field in perpetual transformation and is enduring what could be perceived as an identity crisis. The perpetual questions about identity appear to besiege the field of Comparative Education and many of its practitioners (Torres 2001). Bradley J. Cook, Steven J. Hite, and Erwin H. Epstein also addressed the absence of comprehensive assessments of what the field actually contains

Erwin H. Epstein (ed.) (2016): *Crafting a Global Field: Six Decades of the Comparative and International Education Society*. Hong Kong: Comparative Education Research Centre (CERC), The University of Hong Kong, and Dordrecht: Springer. © CERC

in a study on discerning trends, contours, and boundaries in Comparative Education (Cook, Hite & Epstein 2004).

The evolving interest in examining the course content of comparative and international education emerged into a dynamic international research project and web-based global resource designated as the *Comparative & International Course Archive Project* (CIECAP). The project was initiated when a significant number of course outlines were secured through Erwin H. Epstein, a past President of CIES and a former Editor of the *Comparative Education Review*. By the end of 2001, Epstein had collected course outlines from 30 universities mainly in the United States but elsewhere as well. In 2002, Epstein and doctoral student Bruce Collet at Loyola University Chicago developed a research design that included an extensive database of course outline information. As the richness of the CIECAP course outline data became apparent, the database was expanded by Loyola doctoral alumna Kathleen Stone to include qualitative coding of topics covered in each course outline, as well as bibliographic references with data entry fields for type of publication, title, author, and copyright date.

The original CIECAP project covering 30 universities was completed in 2002, and the complete database files, as well as pivot table analyses, charts and graphs, were integrated into a CIECAP link of the Loyola University Chicago Comparative and International Education website. In March 2003, the CIECAP website was introduced at the CIES conference in New Orleans as part of a symposium, *The Introductory Course in Comparative Education: Commonalities & Variations,* where presenters analyzed the manner in which the introductory course in comparative education was taught at various universities. The symposium chair was Erwin Epstein, and symposium participants included Martin Carnoy of Stanford University, Antoinette Errante of Ohio State University, Jennifer Vega LaSerna of the University of Southern California, and advanced graduate students from Indiana University and Stockholm University.

Following the CIECAP session at the 2003 CIES conference in New Orleans, continued refinements were made to the CIECAP database and website. In March 2004, evaluation of the CIECAP website was the topic of another symposium at the CIES conference in Salt Lake City. There were a number of specific recommendations made by the symposium panel, and those recommendations were integrated into the evolving CIECAP website. During the remainder of 2004, the CIECAP team began a formal plan for acquisition of additional course outlines.

At the 2005 CIES meeting at Stanford University, the CIECAP project was presented to an informal meeting of the executive committee of the World Council of Comparative Education Societies (WCCES), and formal approval came during the summer of that year. The CIECAP website was also presented at the Stanford CIES meeting as part of a symposium on introductory course content in comparative and international education. Through distribution of a CIECAP brochure, a concerted effort was made to increase inclusion of outlines from universities in both the United States and overseas institutions of higher education. A coding system identifying each two-year batch of course outline submissions was integrated into the database to add updated content without eliminating original data. The project design's goal was to facilitate future analyses of course and bibliographic content over time.

Topics and Themes in the Course Content of Comparative & International Education

The methodology of the qualitative process in CIECAP topic documentation began with a spreadsheet database listing fields for each university, each weekly topic, and a topic code word derived as part of the weekly topic title. These topic codes began to develop into repetitive patterns that became the grounded research in developing the final generalized terms to describe groups of specific topic codes. Topics covered in the introductory course in comparative education represent a significant CIECAP component, and it was important that topic codes be taken directly from each course outline. From the CIECAP data analysis of 30 course outlines, Table 20.1 outlines 37 topics included in the CIECAP website frequency distribution data.

Table 20.1: CIECAP Topic Frequency Based (N = 30 Course Outlines)

3	Adult Education	19	Education	9	National	24	Research
7	Assessment	1	Environment	3	Non-Formal Ed.	1	Secondary Ed.
11	Case Study	10	Equity	5	Organization	5	Society
1	Childhood	15	Gender	1	Patterns	14	Systems
1	Classical	24	Globalization	1	Peace	15	Teaching
8	Colonialism	2	Interdependency	1	Planning	55	Theory
13	Cultures	3	International Ed.	13	Policy	3	Trends
1	Debates	3	Linguistics	9	Political		
28	Development	2	Literacy	4	Reform		
8	Economic	1	Multicultural	2	Religion		

It is interesting to compare the CIECAP data on topics used in course outlines with similar data derived from the study by Cook, Hite, and Epstein. That study examined the field's contemporary dimensions through an attitudinal survey of the members of CIES, the largest and oldest constituent organization of the WCCES. The research was based on the premise that a field's contours and boundaries are best discerned through assessing the thoughts and actions of the field's practitioners, and that individuals in the profession determine the field's contours. The targeted sample was the 2000 CIES membership directory, and the final sample was 419 usable responses representing 49 percent of the 853 accessible members (Cook, Hite, & Epstein 2004). Table 20.2 indicates what themes were considered salient to the state of comparative education, and results indicate a high level of similarity between the top 10 topics in the CIECAP database, and the top 10 themes in the survey of comparativists. Also, the Cook, Hite, and Epstein study included a review of literature that noted only two previous studies which compared comparative and international education course outlines. In 1994, there was a worldwide survey of individuals, programs, and centers in comparative and international education, covering 120 institutions. A second study in 1995 reviewed course outlines at all levels in 34 colleges and universities in the United States. The interpretation intuited from the survey reported "striking variability" in course content (Cook, Hite, & Epstein 2004). The review of these studies clearly provides evidence that previous studies contained a level of data analysis not nearly as extensive as either the new 2004 research or the CIECAP database.

Table 20.2: Top 10 Topics and Themes in Comparative Education

Rank	Topics in Course Outlines	CIECAP Course Outline Topics N = 33	Survey Frequency of Themes	Themes Generated from CIES Member Survey N = 419
1	55	Theory	105	Globalization
2	28	Development	101	Gender in Education
3	24	Globalization	62	Education & Development
4	24	Research	54	Equality in Education
5	15	Gender	49	Multiculturalism, Race, Ethnicity
6	15	Teaching	43	Methodology
7	14	Systems	42	Change & Reform
8	13	Cultures	39	Economics, Microcredit, Privatization
9	13	Policy	37	Funding/Development
10	11	Case Study	33	Policy/Politics/Planning

Geographic Areas of Study

The CIECAP database also identifies geographic areas included in course outlines as topics of study. Robert Arnove noted in his 2001 CIES Presidential address that discussions about the history of CIES often contrast the international side with the comparative side of the field. The international side is concerned with the movement of scholars and students between countries and the various accounts of what they observed, and is more oriented toward peace and cultural understanding through international education. That orientation would be found in course outline topics that address comparative education from a geographic perspective. The comparative side is more explanatory and oriented to comparative education as a social science, and concerned with theory building (Arnove 2001, 496). Course outline topics shown in Tables 20.1 and 20.2 would be more in line with those conceptual perspectives. With relation to the geographic perspective, the distribution of geographic areas in topics occurring in the original CIECAP database showed approximately 25 percent Asia and Europe, 16 percent North America, and 10 percent each for Africa, Latin America, and the Middle East. It will be valuable information to track longitudinal distribution in geographic emphasis as future course outlines are added to CIECAP.

Bibliographic References

A significant aspect of the CIECAP database is the analysis of extensive bibliographic references. Each course outline was examined, and every bibliographic reference cited in the outline was entered into the database by author(s), type of reference, title, and copyright date. The types of references and number cited are indicated in Table 20.3. There were a total of 1,031 references. The CIECAP database analysis also includes an

Table 20.3: CIECAP Database – Types of Bibliographic References (N=30 Course Outlines)

Textbooks	41	Readings	120
Textbook Chapter	61	Paper/Report/Stats	23
Books	273	WorldWideWeb	5
Book Chapters	175	VHS	18
Encyclopedia	29	Lecture/Case Stud	3
Journals	248		

analysis of the bibliographic references by decade of copyright date, and over half of the references had copyright dates of 1990 or later, not surprising given the likelihood that course outlines favor recent material.

The CIECAP database also analyzed the bibliographic references according to a journal code. There were a total of 61 journals cited. Many of the journals only had between one and three references; but several were referenced at least 10 times in the database. Rust et al. (1999), after reviewing over 1,800 articles from 1955-1997 in the journals *Comparative Education Review, Comparative Education,* and *International Journal of Educational Development* found that over 70 percent of the research was qualitative and relied mainly on natural settings. Arnove believed that case studies are likely to continue to be the most commonly used approach to studying education-society relationships. According to Charles Ragin, "The comparative method is essentially a case-oriented strategy of comparative research" (Arnove 2001: 496).

A significant CIECAP component relates to data on authors cited in the 1,031 bibliographic references. There were a total of 586 author references, which indicates a wide variance in the authors cited for review in comparative and international course outlines. It was especially interesting to compare the frequency of authors cited in course outlines with the authors who were indicated as influential figures in the study by Cook, Hite, and Epstein referred to in Table 20.1. Table 20.4 shows similarities between the CIECAP data and the Cook, Hite, and

Table 20.4: Most Frequently Cited Authors in Comparative Education

CIECAP – Course Outlines N = 30	CIES Authors & Influential Figures	Survey - Cook, Hite, and Epstein N = 419
20	Philip Altbach	83
25	Martin Carnoy	65
34	Robert Arnove	52
20	Harold Noah	47
3	George Bereday	42
13	Nelly Stromquist	38
4	Paulo Freire	36
12	Erwin Epstein	32
7	Gail Kelly	28
7	Ruth Hayhoe	27
5	Carlos Torres	25

Epstein study (2004, 141). These data provide a valuable resource for scholars that continue to significantly influence the field of Comparative Education. The work of those scholars has a strong influence on the status and developing trends in the field of Comparative Education, and their work becomes a strong component of the texts and readings used in introductory courses.

The content of the CIECAP database is a rich source of information that contributes to the evolving discussion regarding a comparative and international education canon (see the chapter by Steiner-Khamsi in this volume). Leon Tikly and Michael Crossley define the field's canon as "a body of literature that is recognized by teachers and practitioners of comparative and international education as encompassing the major areas of knowledge, issues, axioms, theoretical frameworks, and methodologies that define comparative and international education as a field of study (Tikly and Crossley 2001, 564). In the proposal to recommend CIECAP as an official program of the WCCES, it was emphasized that, "CIECAP operates from this definition of a canon, recognizing, as do the authors, that comparative education is far from being a fixed entity, and that in many cases it comprises a contested terrain. Indeed, it is one of the functions of CIECAP to serve as a window into this very lively aspect of the field" (Erwin H. Epstein and Bruce Collet, Proposal to Adopt the Comparative and International Education Course Archive Project as an Official Program of the World Council of Comparative Education Societies, February 4, 2005).

With further regard for the nature of comparative education, Robert Arnove referred to the requirements of Erwin H. Epstein:

> ... the requirements for establishing comparative education as a legitimate academic discipline have involved developing a body of thought, fashioning "proper methodological tools to test theories about schooling," employing analyses "sufficiently broad to enable proper use of those tools," and establishing a scholarly "infrastructure that would include communication networks and professional associations to bring comparativists together to share their knowledge, and institutional centers to train future scholars" (Arnove 2001, 492).

The original CIECAP proposal to the WCCES provided a rationale that supported such a communication network. Through access to the CIECAP website, instructors involved in teaching comparative education can use the database information to compare their preferred course content to other programs and as a unique tool for designing their course outline. The data found in CIECAP confirm earlier research that reports little consensus in the field related to the various aspects of course outline contents. Rather, CIECAP confirms that the field remains strongly heterogeneous and dynamic.

Since its inception in 2002, CIECAP has continued to evolve in alignment with the tremendous expansion of the internet and web-based resources. What originally began as a project developed from paper copies of acquired course outlines soon began to expand based on a demand for the actual hosting of complete course outlines for direct access on the CIECAP website. All of the CIECAP work had been completed without any financial resources, and the funding for time and labor in maintaining the CIECAP website became challenged by its own success. Collection of course outlines and posting of those outlines on the website continued at Loyola University Chicago under the volunteer facilitation of various members of the Loyola's Comparative and International Education Graduate Student Association (CIEGSA), and facilitation changed hands several times in maturation of the project. Allison Blosser, Yao Chen, Allison Harvey Blosser, Jennifer Schmuhl, and Annmarie Valdes of Loyola all made significant contributions through CIES conference presentations reporting on steady progress in the CIECAP project.

Yao Chen, as part of the Loyola University work, completed a second research analysis of topics covered in 24 of the CIECAP course outlines, and presented results at the 2011 CIES conference in Montreal. The expanded methodology included the content analysis of themes and pedagogy, using earlier CIECAP analysis to help in refinement of the coding system. This research increased statistical content analysis reliability, showing a Cohen's kappa coefficient of 0.643 ($p<0.01$) as evidence of substantial agreement between two raters (Chen 2011). Topic results from that study are included in Table 20.5.

An additional research project related to topics in comparative education was completed by Angelyn Balodimas-Bartolomei and Kathleen Stone and presented at the 2005 CIES conference at Stanford University. Their presentation, *Dichotomies Emerging from Longitudinal Analysis of CIES Conference Presentations*, was a report on collected and analyzed data from five CIES conferences: 2000 San Antonio, 2001 Washington, 2002 Orlando, 2003 New Orleans, and 2004 Salt Lake. The

Table 20.5: Comparative Education Topics Across CIECAP and CIES Samples

Topics and Themes	CIECAP N = 43	CIECAP N = 20	CIECAP N = 24 Chen	CIES N=3289 5 Year	Themes N = 419 Survey
Comparative Education/ Theory	55	19	19	145	-
Development/ Economics	36	13	13	168	138
Research/ Post-Modern/ Case Study	35	12	12	120	43
Education/ Curriculum/ Teaching	34	11	11	380	-
Gender/ Equity/ Multi-Cultural	26	29	29	408	204
Globalization/ Peace/ Conflict Resolution	24	-	2	59	105
Systems/ Organization/ Patterns/Trends	23	6	6	67	-
Culture/ Linguistics/ Language/ Society	21	15	17	347	-
National/Political/ Citizenship/Ideology	18	10	12	128	-
Policy/ School Choice/ Privatization	13	6	6	152	33
Colonialism/ History of Comparative Education	8	25	25	60	-
Assessment	7	10	10	96	-
Reform	4	9	9	229	42
Higher Education/ International Education	3	0	-	294	-

topic results are also included in Table 20.5. Approximately 60 percent of the CIES conference presentations over five years were related to Asia, the Middle East, and Africa. Stone also extended international recognition to the CIECAP website through presentation of a paper related to CIECAP in September 2005 at the Oxford Conference of the United Kingdom Forum on International Education & Training and in an article titled "The Introductory Course in Comparative Education: Course Outline and Bibliographic Database" (Stone 2005).

Table 20.5 compares related topics and triangulates evidence of a general pattern of themes in comparative education, providing a framework for future coding and analyses in defining contours of the field. In merging similar topics, a more concise pattern of themes is shown. The topic list in Table 20.5 is ranked in order based on the original and second CIECAP sample covering 43 course outlines. Where there is variance of topics between course outlines, CIES member surveys, and CIES conference presentations, it would seem to reflect the difference in the examination of introductory courses versus the dynamics of progress and status that might emerge from the survey of comparativists and CIES conference presentations. The comparativists' survey also had a more inclusive response focus on overall themes, showing less distinction by more specific topics.

Conclusion

Since CIECAP's emergence in 2002, this course outline resource has transitioned from its initial website hosting by Loyola University Chicago. In 2011, the website was hosted by the State University of New York at Albany, under the continuing leadership of CIECAP's founder, Erwin Epstein. At the 2013 CIES conference in New Orleans, a formal announcement was released integrating CIECAP as a resource within the website framework of the Comparative Education Instructional Materials Archive (CEIMA) hosted at Bowling Green State University, under the leadership of Patricia Kubow, and with the continued support of Erwin Epstein. As of 2014, the entire CIECAP project is now linked as a "Resource" under CEIMA as a major feature of the Teaching Comparative Education SIG website hosted through the Center for International Education, Development and Research (CIEDR) in the School of Education at Indiana University, under program Director Patricia Kubow (see the chapter by Kubow in this volume).

CEIMA is now the active project for continued contribution of comparative education syllabi, course assignments and evaluation tools, and ethnographic projects. CIECAP continues to play a pragmatic role as a dynamic vehicle for those interested in examining the historical development of the introductory course in comparative education. The enhanced version of the CEIMA website with the CIECAP link was launched at the 2015 CIES meeting in Washington, DC, manifesting a strong campaign to solicit a larger collection of course outlines from universities worldwide, including outlines from over 80 members of the Teaching Comparative Education SIG. CIECAP's ongoing resource of course outlines in the teaching of comparative education can facilitate a pragmatic network for use by scholars of comparative education throughout the world. To encourage ongoing growth and updating, the CEIMA website contains guided instructions to facilitate ease in submission of future course outlines to the dynamic CIECAP resource: http://www.ciestcesig.org/submit-materials/.

References

Arnove, Robert F. 2001. Presidential Address: Comparative and International Education Society (CIES) Facing the Twenty-First Century: Challenges and Contributions. *Comparative Education Review* 45(4): 488-489.

Balodimas-Bartolomei, Angelyn, & Kathleen Stone. 2005. "Dichotomies Emerging From Longitudinal Analysis of CIES Conference Presentations." Paper Presented at the 49th Annual Conference of the Comparative International Education Society, Stanford University, March 22-26.

Chen, Yao. 2011. "Comparative & International Education Course Archive Project (CIECAP)." Paper Presented at the 55th Annual Conference of the Comparative International Education Society, Montreal, May 1-5.

Cook, Bradley J., Steven J. Hite, & Erwin H. Epstein. 2004. "Discerning Trends, Contours, and Boundaries in Comparative Education: A Survey of Comparativists and Their Literature." *Comparative Education Review 48*(2): 123-149.

Rust, Val, Soumaré, Aminata, Pescador, Octavio, & Shibuya, Megumi. 1999. "Research Strategies in Comparative Education." *Comparative Education Review 43*(1): 86-109.

Stone, Kathleen M. 2005. "The Introductory Course in Comparative Education: Course Outline and Bibliographic Database." *International Review of Education 51*(5-6): 1-14.

Tikly, Leon, & Michael Crossley. 2001. "Teaching Comparative and International Education: A Framework for Analysis." *Comparative Education Review 45*(4): 561.

Torres, Carlos Alberto. 2001. "Globalization and Comparative Education in the World System." *Comparative Education Review 45*(4): vi-viii.

21

The Comparative Education Instructional Materials Archive (CEIMA)

Patricia K. KUBOW

The Comparative Education Instructional Materials Archive (CEIMA) is an electronic, publically accessible website for the gathering and sharing of teaching resources among comparative educators worldwide. The Teaching Comparative Education Special Interest Group of the Comparative and International Education Society (CIES) is now the home of CEIMA (http://www.ciestcesig.org/ceimahome/), an ongoing web-based archive, partially funded by CIES, which collects and shares comparative and international materials to enhance instructional practice, extend inter-university dialogue, and document the dynamic and evolving nature of the comparative and international education field. CEIMA provides access to course syllabi, assignments, research projects, and other innovative resources from comparativists around the globe. The materials sought as part of CEIMA include syllabi for comparative and international education courses, descriptions and explanations of in-class activities, paper and presentation assignments, small-scale ethnographic research projects, or other innovative instructional materials used in comparative and international education courses. Materials can be submitted for graduate and undergraduate courses in one or more of the following areas: *Comparative Education, International Development Education, Cultural Studies, Cross-Cultural Education, Cross-Cultural Psychology, Social Foundations of Education, Comparative Methodology,*

Erwin H. Epstein (ed.) (2016): *Crafting a Global Field: Six Decades of the Comparative and International Education Society*. Hong Kong: Comparative Education Research Centre (CERC), The University of Hong Kong, and Dordrecht: Springer. © CERC

Research-oriented Courses, and *Globalization of Education.* All materials submitted to CEIMA must be the original work of the submitter.

CEIMA Development

Patricia Kubow and Bruce Collet are the founding creators of the Comparative Education Instructional Materials Archive (CEIMA), and graduate students at Bowling Green State University at the time, namely Meghan Burley, Leilani Kupo, and Christina Wright Fields, contributed to its initial electronic development between 2008-2013. CEIMA was then transferred to Indiana University (IU) when Patricia Kubow assumed a professor appointment and position as Director of the Center for Social Studies and International Education, now called the Center for International Education, Development and Research (CIEDR), in the IU School of Education. CEIMA's development continued during 2013-2014 with the help of IU graduate students James Brown and Evan Mickey, who placed CEIMA on CIEDR's website.

With the advent of the newly created website for the CIES Teaching Comparative Education Special Interest Group (SIG) by Patricia Kubow and Evan Mickey in 2014-2015, it was deemed beneficial to locate CEIMA on the SIG website, as CEIMA is an ongoing major activity of the SIG and provides greater visibility for the CIES membership and the World Council of Comparative Education Societies (WCCES). The Teaching Comparative Education (TCE) SIG Co-Chairs, Allison Blosser (Loyola University Chicago) and Patricia Kubow (Indiana University), obtained funding from CIES for CEIMA to be housed on the SIG website. To bolster CEIMA's resources, several steps were undertaken by Evan Mickey with supervision by Patricia Kubow. First, CEIMA has been announced in the CIES on-line weekly announcements informing the CIES membership of CEIMA's new location on the TCE SIG. Second, all TCE SIG members have been invited to contribute materials to CEIMA with instructions for doing so. Third, CEIMA has been announced to the presidents of all of the comparative education societies that compose the WCCES to encourage resource submissions.

Structure of CEIMA and the Submission Process

CEIMA is structured for easy navigation. To access CEIMA, its resources, or submission of materials, one goes to the TCE SIG website (http://www.

ciestcesig.org/) and clicks on "CEIMA" in the upper menu bar. Once on the CEIMA page, a navigation bar on the left-hand side of the screen displays the following categories: Home, Courses, Authors, Materials, Benefits, FAQ (Frequently Asked Questions), Terms of Use, and Submit Materials. The Home page describes CEIMA as an online repository for the collection and posting of comparative and international education instructional materials from universities worldwide. The Courses section lists the course name, instructor, and institution. The Authors section provides the author's name, email address, and institutional affiliation. The Materials section makes available the material item through a live link for easy access, identifies the category of the material (i.e., syllabus, rubric, presentation, class discussion, or writing assignment), and states the author of the material.

The Benefits section discusses how submitting to CEIMA helps comparative educators learn about current practices and approaches to comparative and international course content by fellow colleagues. Moreover, CEIMA resources assist instructors in planning courses, modifying courses, tracing trends and innovations in the field, and making connections with peers worldwide. In the FAQ section, frequently asked questions are posed and answered, including how one can update and replace documents already on the CEIMA site. The Terms of Use section speaks of the terms and conditions of fair use of materials. And, finally, the Submit Materials section provides a simple submission form for authors to input the following information: their name, title of course, email address, category (i.e., a pull down menu from which the author selects the category that best represents their submitted item, namely syllabus, rubric, presentation, class discussion, or writing assignment), institution, the opportunity to select their file for upload, a check box to acknowledge that the author has read and agrees with CEIMA's terms of use, and then a click on the submit button to submit the item. Each contributor receives a message indicating that the material was received and that it will be reviewed immediately for likely placement on the CEIMA site.

Initial Contributors

CEIMA, like the CIES Teaching Comparative Education Special Interest Group (SIG), is designed to bring together instructors of comparative and international education from around the world for purposes of understanding and enhancing the contours of course work in the field and promoting the teaching of comparative and international education in higher education. Teaching materials and assignments are collected from courses in comparative and international education, cultural studies, and globalization and education. An examination of the materials by the initial contributors to CEIMA provide insight as to the *what* (concepts) and *how* (pedagogical processes) within comparative education courses (Kubow and Collet 2015).

Aaron Benavot's (State University of New York-Albany) syllabus in *Comparative Education* focused on issues such as educational achievement and finance, curriculum, and learning outcomes, with attention to gender, equality, governance and privatization. Four course assignments were required: 1) a biography and presentation on a key figure in the field of comparative education; 2) a critical review of a past CIES presidential address; 3) a book review essay from a predetermined list of books in the field with oral report to the class; and 4) a critical literature review on an educational topic within the context of a world region. The issues-oriented approach by Mark Bray (University of Hong Kong) in his course, *Comparative Education: Approaches, Methods, and Themes,* engaged students in the examination of educational similarities and differences in Hong Kong and elsewhere. Bray's pedagogical approach included posing questions such as: "Who should compare? Why should they compare? What should they compare? and, How should they compare?" (Bray 2010/11, 1).

Erwin Epstein (Loyola University Chicago) in his course, *Comparative Theory*, sought to give students a sound understanding of the field's major epistemological directions. Students examined historical function-alist, positivist, and relativist theoretical perspectives and applied those perspectives to educational practice. In a small group assignment, students posed a particular question, wrote a history of comparative education theory, and associated the field's theoretical development with its professional development. For Antoinette Errante (The Ohio State University), the course *Globalization Processes and Education* afforded students the opportunity to investigate the comparative sociocultural, anthropological, and historical perspectives of education processes in light of neoliberal economic expansion, geopolitical shifts, and rapid movement of peoples and knowledge. Students used ethnographic methodology to complete an individual final paper in which they integrated course content with a topic/interest/book of their own choosing. Errante's course on *Children, Families, and Communities in Conflict Transformation* explored the meaning of conflict transformation in situations of prolonged or escalating conflict. Attention was given to the African continent with comparisons made to the U.S. Students learned that transformation is a cultural practice and of the role that socialization plays in shaping children's attitudes, dispositions, and behaviors.

Steven Klees (University of Maryland), in his *Political Economy of Education in a Global Context* course, had students inquire about the relation of education to development, globalization, and inequality. Theoretical perspectives such as human capital and modernization were drawn upon to better understand educational policy and practice. Students debated education and development (e.g., Education for All) and considered alternative directions for the various regions studied. In *Modes of Inquiry in Education Research*, Klees had his students explore the relationship of research to practice. Students examined quantitative/positivist paradigms, ethnographies and case studies, and correlational and survey research. Of particular note, students were also exposed to critical/feminist/transformational paradigms, including phenomenology and grounded theory as well as qualitative versus quantitative debates. Personal reflection on their paradigm journeys was also integrated into the course. Roozbeh Shirazi (University of Minnesota) used the film *Syriana* to teach about *Globalization, Education, and Politics.* Students examined structures of power, representations of culture, and the role of media and political observers in framing causes of terrorism. Through film critique, students questioned whether education reform can foster democracy in non-democratic regimes while also reflecting on what they learned about youth and education in the Middle East.

In Noah Sobe's (Loyola University Chicago) *Seminar on Globalization and Education,* students problematized "globalization" in relation to schooling specifically and education issues more broadly. Theoretical perspectives such as world-system, world polity, and world culture were examined, and students explored ethnographies of globalization in different countries with attention to how race, ethnicity, and socioeconomic status influence educational opportunity and achievement. For Qiang Zha (York University, Canada), students in *Issues in Globalization and Education* explored historical and theoretical debates to analyze interpretations of globalization, its influences on world education, and the role of global organizations and agendas in education. Students give weekly presentations on globalization that integrated scholarship, reviewed literature, and summarized current issues within the globalization-education debate.

The teaching content and pedagogies used by these comparative educators reveal the ways in which students are encouraged to engage deeply in comparative inquiry. The collection of more instructional materials from TCE SIG members, the CIES membership overall, and those globally from comparative societies that compose the WCCES will add to the learning that can be gained, and the courses developed, as a result of CEIMA.

Conclusion

Arguably, the purpose of comparative and international education is to engage students in the comparative study and critique of the role of education in national and global development. Courses in comparative and international education acquaint students with knowledge of the field, theories guiding comparative study, and perennial issues impacting teaching and learning worldwide. Comparative education, therefore, is useful for all individuals engaged in the task of educating learners through policy and practice. As such, it is desirable for comparative educators everywhere to contribute to CEIMA for purposes of making apparent the concepts, processes, themes, theories, cultures, and regions to which students and, presumably, future comparative educators are exposed. CEIMA plays a role in helping academics and practitioners to offer, plan, and modify courses in the areas of comparative and international education, cultural studies, and globalization and education. Through such courses, students examine what is meant by "comparison" or "comparative" as related to the study of education, examine factors (cultural, social, political, and economic) to be considered in drawing comparisons, and become acquainted with theoretical perspectives and analytical frameworks to guide systematic study of education in diverse countries and contexts.

References

Bray, Mark. 2010/11. *Master of Education (MEDD7013): Comparative Education: Approaches, Methods, and Themes.* Hong Kong, China: Faculty of Education, University of Hong Kong.

Kubow, Patricia K., & Bruce Collet. 2015. "Themen und Ressourcen der Internationalen und Vergleichenden Erziehungswissenschaft: Ein Beispiel aus dem universitären Kontext in den USA [Topics and Resources of the International and Comparative Education: An Example from the Context of a University in the United States]." In *Internationale und Vergleichende Erziehungswissenschaft. Geschichte, Theorie, Methode und Forschungsfelder [International and Comparative Education. History, Theory, Method, and Research Fields],* ed. Marcelo Parreira do Amaral and S. Karin Amos. Münster, Germany: Waxmann Verlag GmbH.

Conclusion: Lighting the Society

Erwin H. EPSTEIN

Throw the windows widely open:
Light! more light! before I go.
-Frances Ellen Watkins Harper (from "Let the Light Enter")

A home cannot function without light, and so it is for a professional association that has taken 60 years to build. I began this volume by saying in the introductory chapter that the Comparative and International Education Society has been my professional home for most of those years. Over the decades, the light of knowledge has made the Society a dynamic place. How is this light reflected in the contents of this book? What are the sources of the light?

We have viewed the Society as a home having several floors (sections) and many rooms (topics/chapters), with staircases and passageways connecting them. Yet this home also has many windows that let the light of knowledge shine in. The light shining through windows is natural. As natural light emanates from the sun, and as the earth rotates and orbits the sun, the light's exposure is first from the east and later from the west, so that the afternoon light differs from the light in the morning. Here, the morning and afternoon exposures are metaphors for two overriding themes that have brought energy to the Comparative and International Society since its very beginning: the interplay between comparative education and international education, and the tension between empiricism (positivism) and contextualism (relativism). As reported by Iveta Silova, Robyn Read, and Karen Mundy in their chapter on "The Mobilization of Knowledge", the Society has known many tensions.

Erwin H. Epstein (ed.) (2016): *Crafting a Global Field: Six Decades of the Comparative and International Education Society*. Hong Kong: Comparative Education Research Centre (CERC), The University of Hong Kong, and Dordrecht: Springer. © CERC

There are those between idealism and pragmatism, researchers and practitioners, scholars pursuing research interests and individuals seeking employment, viewpoints of older and younger generations, and single nation studies versus cross-national studies, to name but a few. Yet none of the other tensions has characterized the orientations and activities of the Society's members more than the stresses between comparative education and international education, and between empiricism and contextualism.

Although tensions of competing orientations are pervasive throughout the book, the Society and the field it embraces are also driven by many other topics, and these, which we may view as light from "lamps", are addressed in particular chapters, that is, in the "rooms" in which they are placed. A home, after all, needs light not only from the sun; when the sun goes down and there is no longer exposure from the east or the west, a home relies on lamplight to continue to function. Such is the way this book approaches the knowledge – the light, natural and lamp-lit, that is comparative and international education – embodied by the Society.

The Interplay between Comparative Education and International Education

The Comparative Education Society came into being in 1956. The word "International" was not inserted into the Society's name until 1968. From most accounts, it appears that this insertion did not represent a change in direction, but rather an acknowledgment of something that had been an integral component all along yet had somehow been omitted.

The controversy surrounding this change is described in several of this book's chapters. Elizabeth Sherman Swing in her chapter, "Setting the Foundation," tells us that in organizing the group that was to become the Society, William Brickman set as a primary goal to rescue the field from "junketlike tours abroad and the resultant courses run by amateurs," and in this way disassociate international education from what was to become the Comparative Education Society. Yet, conversely, international education played such a crucial role in the Society's creation that the very impetus for forming an association was "the discovery that group rates for study tours required a pre-existing group." Indeed, Louis Berends and Maria Trakas, in their chapter, "Inserting International Education into the Comparative Education Society," report that "Study tours were central to the establishment of the Comparative

Education Society in its formative years, and the tours continued to be an integral part of the Society's activities." As the field grew and diversified, Berends and Trakas add, the membership of the Society felt a need to change its name to one more representative of a focus that increasingly included international educational activities of government and non-government agencies.

Alexander Wiseman and Cheryl Matherly, in their chapter, "Professionalizing the Society," cite David Wilson's description of "a new breed of academic-practitioner" as an amalgamation of comparative education and international education to serve "as a benchmark for investigating and evaluating the degree to which the field of comparative and international education has been professionalized." Iveta Silova, Robyn Read, and Karen Mundy, in "The Mobilization of Knowledge," observe that the binding of comparativists and internationalists of education "signaled an institutional attempt to identify the ways in which research could inform policy and practice and vice versa." Gita Steiner-Khamsi, writing on the Oral History Projects, found that several Society presidents were keenly aware of the importance to CIES of the 1958 National Defense Act that brought an influx of U.S. federal funding to universities for area and development studies as well as for international education exchange programs with developing countries.

Despite these many observations of the two fields becoming linked, there has always been a tension between them. Linda Robertson and Kenneth Cushner, in their chapter on Gerald Read and George Bereday, uncover an interesting anomaly in the Minutes of the organizational meeting to establish the Society: two of the eight purposes for which the Society was formed included *comparative* **and** *international* "studies" or "dimensions" but four included the words *comparative education* alone, i.e., without *international*. Even so, one could argue that the final two of the eight purposes favored international education – one of these emphasized cooperation with international education organizations (e.g., UNESCO, International Institute of Education, Pan-American Union), and the other sought "to promote inter-visitation of educators and on-the-spot study of school systems" – thereby bringing the two fields into a kind of equilibrium. Several chapters – those by Swing, Wiseman and Matherly, and Berends and Trakas – cite my 1968 "Letter" in the *Comparative Education Review* that observes the discontinuity, on the one hand, in using "International" in the newly renamed Comparative *and* **International** Education Society, but the decision to forego insertion of that word in the name of the *Comparative Education Review,* on the other hand.

The Tension between Empiricism and Contextualism

Permeating the theoretical foundation of comparative education is the tension between empiricism, or positivism, and contextualism, also known as interpretivism or relativism (see Epstein 2008). Empiricism and contextualism are rival approaches of academic research. This is not at all the same as the interplay between Comparative Education and International Education, since comparative education is oriented toward research, and international education is focused largely on policy implementation. Positivism and contextualism are in this respect domains within the comparative education side of the Comparative and International Education Society. It therefore follows that of the Society's two fields, the tension between empiricism and contextualism is found mainly in comparative education, as reflected most notably in the Society's flagship journal, the *Comparative Education Review.*

The tension between empiricism and contextualism is reminiscent of C.P. Snow's *The Two Cultures and the Scientific Revolution* (1959) in which Snow famously lamented the split between scientists and humanists. In comparative education, the split is epistemological: though CIES meetings and the *Comparative Education Review* feature research by both humanists and empirically oriented social scientists, within these forums the tension between humanists and social scientists is palpable. Hence, as seen in comparative education, the two cultures are divided by those who follow the scientific method (empiricists) and those who insist on the importance of focusing on historical and cultural context (contextualists) to understand the nature of education. Snow first proclaimed his two-culture lament not in his famous lecture and book that gave it prominence, but in an article published three years before the book – in the October 1956 issue of *New Statesman* magazine (Snow 1956) – in the very same year the Society was founded.

Alexander Wiseman and Cheryl Matherly, in their chapter on "Professionalizing the Field," note that a key factor in developing a legitimate knowledge base in comparative education was the shift towards social science disciplines in the early years of the Society, which encouraged a methodological and theoretical fragmentation, because some scholars closely identified with their primary social science disciplines (e.g., economics, sociology, political science). This inclination toward "science" came to a head in the 1969 book by Harold Noah and Max Eckstein, *Toward a Science of Comparative Education*. Yet, others, such as Isaac Kandel, Nicholas Hans, and William Brickman, just as closely associated themselves with the contextual field of history. In this way we can understand the shift observed by José Cossa in his chapter, "Shaping the Intellectual Landscape," in the orientation of the *Comparative Education Review* from strong emphasis on the scientific approach under the editorships of Bereday and Noah to a more balanced trajectory under succeeding editorships, although Bjørn Nordtveit in his chapter on the *Review* argues that "Bereday himself was open-minded, even curious, about new approaches."

This fragmentation is further interpreted by Allison Blosser in her chapter, "Program Development." She observes a lack of consensus on what to teach in courses and how to orient programs in the field. Indeed, as reported by Louis Berends and Maria Trakas in their chapter, "Inserting International Education into the Comparative Education Society," "[s]hifts between qualitative and quantitative emphasis, distinct ideologies of purpose, and variation in style of research have been part of the comparative education field since its inception. Naturally, as a result, there has been much discourse among scholars in the field about what constitutes 'comparative education'." According to these authors, so pervasive were these shifts and variations that they influenced the 1968 change in the name of the Society, suggesting a connection between the two great tensions – comparative education and international education, and empiricism and contextualism – I am describing in this chapter.

The tension between empiricism and contextualism in the Society can be viewed in many ways. One can see it in the Special Interest Groups (SIGs) described by Oren Pizmony-Levy, with, for example, the emphasis on empiricism in the Large Scale Cross National Studies SIG, and the contextualism represented most clearly in the Cultural Contexts of Education and Human Potential SIG. Nowhere do we see this tension manifested more clearly than in Erwin Epstein's chapter on "Early Leaders", which features the debates between Isaac Kandel and William Brickman on the one side, and C. Arnold Anderson on the other side. Kandel and Brickman "insisted that only with a deep probing of a society's history, philosophy and culture, requiring a command of that system's language," can one truly grasp education. Anderson, by contrast, urged "the use of multivariate typologies to discern universal relationships between school and society."

Still, year after year for 60 years the Society has remained whole, displaying a unity despite its tensions and fragmenting issues. And, as Maria Manzon observes in her chapter, scholars on all sides of these debates are included in the CIES' broad umbrella as shown in *CIEclopedia*, the who's who of comparative and international education.

How, then, has the Society been able to sustain this unity? Perhaps Gita Steiner-Khamsi sums it up best when she observes in her chapter on the Oral History Projects: "Having a distinct ancestry and a common past, which the oral history project helped to (re-) construct, and at the same time agreeing to disagree is what the debate culture in CIES stands for."

The Lamps of Unity

We turn at this point to the time when the afternoon light moves to nightfall. Now the lamps unifying the Society turn on brightly. These "lamps" are the Society's prime resources: key among these are its Archive at Kent State University, the *Newsletter*, the course archive project, and the instructional materials archive, all discussed in the final chapters of this book. There are, of course, other lamps lighting the Society, such as the website, CIES meetings, the Constitution and Bylaws, the officers, the Secretariat, the Board of Directors, members' publications and courses taught, but limited space allows for only a few prime resources to be addressed in this volume.

So germane is the CIES Archive, as described by Erwin Epstein's chapter on the topic, that it sheds direct light on no fewer than seven of the rooms/chapters in this book – those by Elizabeth Sherman Swing, Louis Berends and Maria Trakas, José Cossa, Linda Robertson and Kenneth Cushner, Hilary Landorf and Bahia Simons-Lane, Erwin Epstein, and Martha Merrill. Further, it gives indirect light to several other chapters that rely on secondary sources that in turn drew upon the Archive at Kent State University. As such, the CIES Archive has lit many of the Society's "rooms", and has thereby been a prime resource for understanding the Society and its development. Such broad reliance on the Archive makes it a critical unifying resource for the Society.

As described in Martha Merrill's chapter, the *CIES Newsletter* has been at times a major source of information on CIES activities and events, a forum for rigorous debate, and a resource for teaching when it made available sample comparative education course syllabi. As is the case with the CIES Archive, several of the rooms/chapters in this book are lit by accessing information from issues of the *Newsletter*. Unfortunately, the *Newsletter*, despite being mandated by the CIES Bylaws, as Merrill informs us, had been discontinued a few years ago when the Secretariat was shifted to a professional management company. As David Post, quoted by Merrill, says, the *Newsletter* served "to give a common sense of purpose and identity to members." Currently, the Secretariat puts out a "weekly announcement" via the Internet that is/was hardly a substitute for the lively forum that the *Newsletter* had been for so many years. The light of unity represented by the *Newsletter* had been dimmed, though only temporarily as it fortunately turns out.

The two final chapters on Prime Resources are on course archival projects: the Comparative and International Education Course Archive Project (CIECAP) by Kathleen Stone, and the Comparative Education Instructional Materials Archive by Patricia Kubow. These chapters are a fitting reminder that comparative and international education course-work is crucial for the preparation of upcoming generations of comparativists and internationalists of education, and thereby, for the perpetuation and development of the field. As described by Stone, CIECAP relies on a research design that includes an extensive database of course outline information, a qualitative coding of topics in the database, and bibliographic references with data entry fields for type of publication, title, author, and copyright date. Two of this book's chapters highlight CIECAP's contribution to the unity of the field: the chapter by Wiseman and Matherly and the chapter by Merrill. Wiseman and Matherly rely extensively on CIECAP for their analysis of author and course content information in comparative and international education introductory courses, and Merrill shows that CIECAP made available information on course outlines in the field when the *CIES Newsletter* no longer furnished that information.

CEIMA is CIECAP's fraternal twin. As described by Kubow, CEIMA "collects and shares comparative and international materials to enhance instructional practice, extend inter-university dialogue, and document the dynamic and evolving nature of ... comparative and international education...." Both CEIMA and CIECAP are currently managed by the Center for International Education, Development and Research at Indiana University under Kubow's direction, and both are featured in the newly created website of the Society's Teaching Comparative Education

Special Interest Group. As prime resources for the teaching of comparative and international education, they have become indispensable "lamps" that light the field.

Light Radiating from the Home

To be sure, the "rooms" of the home that is the Society contain ample light. Indeed, so bright is this light of knowledge that it shines well beyond the Society itself. As described especially in the chapter by Vandra Masemann, the Comparative and International Education Society, as the first and largest of its kind, has inspired the creation and development of many other such associations – indeed the majority of the 40 plus constituent societies of the World Council of Comparative Education Societies. As Masemann remarks, "The World Council ... is bound up almost inextricably in the history of the Comparative and International Education Society ... because some of the same central figures were involved in their founding and development."

Thus, what had begun as a handful of scholars meeting as a group initially in New York City six decades ago has mushroomed into an organization of more than 2,500 members, with its home base in the U.S. Ironically, the founders of the Comparative Education Society viewed their new enterprise, tiny as it was, as a world organization, and therefore gave no thought to attaching the appellation "USA" to its name. As Ratna Ghosh and Mariusz Galczynski show in their chapter on "Shaping Leadership", the Society's founders were prescient in casting their leadership recruitment net over many countries. Indeed, several of the Society's presidents have been Canadians, notwithstanding that these presidents have also belonged to their own Canadian Society. Moreover, the annual conference has been held not infrequently outside of the U.S., including once in Jamaica, once in the U.S. commonwealth of Puerto Rico, twice in Mexico, and several times in Canada. As time goes on, the Society is becoming ever more worldly as it inaugurates a President from outside the North American continent – Mark Bray from Hong Kong – meeting in its celebratory 60th year in Vancouver, BC, Canada. Even more ironic, because the Society has spawned or inspired so many national, sub-national, regional, and language-oriented comparative and international education associations, the expansion in the number of those societies has enhanced the Comparative and International Education Society's global reach. We members of the Comparative and International Education Society, who value the bright light shining the world over from the wide open windows of our professional home, have much to celebrate.

References

Epstein, Erwin H. 2008. "Setting the Normative Boundaries: Crucial Epistemological Benchmarks in Comparative Education." *Comparative Education* 44(4): 373-386.

Noah, Harold J., & Max A. Eckstein. 1969. *Toward a Science of Comparative Education*. New York: Macmillan.

Snow, Charles Percy. 1956. "The Two Cultures." *The New Statesman* October: 6.

Snow, Charles Percy. 2001 [1959]. *The Two Cultures and the Scientific Revolution*. London: Cambridge University Press.

Appendix A
Finding Aid for the Comparative and International Education Society Records: the CIES Archive

Author: Prepared by Youngchu Kim and Kim P. Sebaly, January 1986
Revisions: April 1995, Revised by Kim P. Sebaly and Nancy Birk; 2013-2015, Extensively revised by Philip C. Shackelford, Cara Gilgenbach, and Elizabeth Campion
Descriptive Rules: *DACS*

Origination: Comparative and International Education Society

Inclusive Dates: 1956-2014
Bulk Dates: 1980-1994

Extent: 57.16 cubic feet
Physical Location: 10th floor, Kent State University Libraries, Special Collections and Archives
Language of Materials: English

Abstract: The collection contains the official records and publications of the Comparative and International Education Society (CIES), an organization founded in 1956 as the Comparative Education Society. The Society promotes the study and teaching of comparative education and international studies in education.

Scope and Content: The CIES records are comprised of documents and audio-visual materials representing the history, activities, and interests of CIES since its creation in 1956. These files include materials from the CIES Secretariat, volumes of *Comparative Education Review* and associated records, files of the various presidents of CIES, records of the CIES annual conference, and CIES study tours undertaken during the organization's earlier years.

Statement of Arrangement: The collection is currently organized into six series.

Series 1:   *Comparative Education Review* records *(currently under revision)*

Series 2:   Secretariat records (Note: includes annual conference files, newsletters, membership directories, committee files, and much more)

Series 3:   Presidential files

Series 4:   Founding Members
                 William W. Brickman papers
                 Gerald H. Read papers

Series 5:   Subject files

Series 6:   Regional Organizations files

Preferred Citation: Comparative and International Society records. Kent State University Libraries. Special Collections and Archives.

Separated Material: The *Comparative Education Review* is cataloged separately in KentLINK and shelved on the 10th floor.

Related Material: Researchers may also wish to consult the records of the World Council of Comparative Education Societies (WCCES) located at the University of Pittsburgh's Institute for International Studies in Education.

Restrictions on Access: Unpublished manuscripts and correspondence in the *CER* records series are restricted for 10 years after the date on which they were created.

Restrictions on Use: Kent State University does not own the copyright to materials in this collection. Copyright resides with CIES or individual authors of manuscripts, when applicable.

Acquisition Information: The Kent State University Archives became the official depository of the records of the Comparative and International Education Society by action of the Society's Board of Directors in October, 1980. Professor George Z. F. Bereday, Editor of the *Comparative Education Review* (1957-1966), made the first donation to the collection in January,

1981. Since then, records from the Secretariat, various Presidents of the Society, and the *Review* have been placed in the collection.

Accruals: Materials are added to the collection on a regular basis.

Processing Information: The CIES records at Kent State University are currently undergoing extensive revision and further processing, and thus the organization of the collection and structure and content of this finding aid will change until project completion. As of January 2015, the Secretariat series and Presidential files have been extensively revised and updated, and the Founding Members series including the papers of William Brickman and Gerald Read as well as a Subject Files series have been added to the collection. Processing work on the *CER* records is continuing at this time.

Web URL for the finding aid: http://www.library.kent.edu/cies

Appendix B
*CIES Presidents**

William W. Brickman, New York University (1956, 1957, 1958)
William H.E. Johnson, University of Pittsburgh (1959, 1960)
Joseph Katz, University of British Columbia (1961)
C. Arnold Anderson, University of Chicago (1962)
Claude Eggertsen, University of Michigan (1963)
R. Freeman Butts, Columbia University (1964)
Donald K. Adams, Syracuse University (1965)
David G. Scanlon, Columbia University (1966)
William W. Brickman, University of Pennsylvania (1967)
Stewart E. Fraser, Vanderbilt University (1968)
Reginald Edwards, McGill University (1969)
Philip J. Foster, University of Chicago (1970)
Andreas Kazamias, University of Wisconsin (1971)
Cole S. Brembeck, Michigan State University (1972)
Harold J. Noah, Columbia University (1973)
Robert F. Lawson, University of Calgary (1974)
Rolland G. Paulston, University of Pittsburgh (1975)
Susanne M. Shafer, Arizona State University (1976)
Joseph P. Farrell, University of Toronto (1977)
Mathew Zachariah, University of Calgary (1978)
George A. Male, University of Maryland (1979)
Thomas J. LaBelle, UCLA (1980)
Erwin H. Epstein, University of Missouri-Rolla (1981)
Max A. Eckstein, Queens College, CUNY (1982)
Barbara A. Yates, University of Illinois-Champaign/Urbana (1983)
John N. Hawkins, UCLA (1984)
R. Murray Thomas, University of California-Santa Barbara (1985)
Gail P. Kelly, State University of New York at Buffalo (1986)
Peter Hackett, University of Virginia (1987)
Beverly Lindsay, University of Georgia (1988)
Vandra L. Masemann, University of Toronto (1989)
Val P. Rust, University of California-Los Angeles (1990)
Mark B. Ginsburg, University of Pittsburgh (1991)

Stephen Heyneman, World Bank (1992)
David Wilson, University of Toronto (1993)
Nelly P. Stromquist, University of Southern California (1994)
Noel McGinn, Harvard University (1995)
Gary L. Theisen, Academy of Educational Development (1996)
Carlos Alberto Torres, University of California-Los Angeles (1997)
William K. Cummings, State University of New York at Buffalo (1998)
Ruth Hayhoe, University of Toronto (1999)
Robert Arnove, Indiana University (2000)
Heidi Ross, Colgate University (2001)
Karen Biraimah, University of Central Florida (2002)
Kassie Freeman, Vanderbilt University (2003)
Donald B. Holsinger, Brigham Young University (2004)
Martin Carnoy, Stanford University (2005)
Victor Kobayashi, University of Hawaii (2006)
Steven J. Klees, University of Maryland (2007)
Henry Levin, Columbia University (2008)
Gita Steiner-Khamsi, Columbia University (2009)
María Teresa Tatto, Michigan State University (2010)
Ratna Ghosh, McGill University (2011)
David Baker, Penn State University (2012)
Gilbert Valverde, University at Albany (2013)
Karen Mundy, University of Toronto (2014)
N'Dri T. Assié-Lumumba, Cornell University (2015)
Mark Bray, University of Hong Kong (2016)
Noah W. Sobe, Loyola University Chicago**

*Date in parentheses represents the year in which the individual assumed the presidency. Institutions shown were those in which the individuals were located at the time of their presidency.

**To assume the office of President in 2017.

Notes on the Authors

Louis Berends (louis.berends@gmail.com) has worked extensively in international and comparative education at U.S. colleges, universities and non-profits since 2000. He holds a PhD (Loyola University Chicago) in cultural and educational policy studies with a concentration in comparative and international education. He studied at Brunel University and at the University of Oxford (St. Catherine's College). Dr. Berends has presented many papers in various settings including Harvard's Graduate School of Education, the Comparative and International Education Society, the Forum on Education Abroad, and NAFSA: Association of International Educators. He teaches part-time at Walden University in Global and Comparative Education as a Contributing Faculty member in the Richard W. Riley College of Education and Leadership.

Allison H. Blosser (allison.blosser@gmail.com) holds a PhD in Cultural and Educational Policy Studies from Loyola University Chicago. She is currently a part-time faculty member in the School of Education at High Point University in North Carolina. She also serves as Co-chair of the Teaching Comparative Education Special Interest Group for the Comparative and International Educational Society. Her research examines the teaching of comparative education, multicultural education, diversity in private schools, and the global spread of market-based educational reforms.

Mark Bray (mbray@hku.hk) is UNESCO Chair Professor in Comparative Education at the University of Hong Kong. At the time of writing he was President-Elect of the Comparative & International Education Society and responsible in 2016 for the 60th anniversary conference in Vancouver, Canada. Mark Bray has been based at the University of Hong Kong since 1986, prior to which he taught in secondary schools in Kenya and Nigeria and at the Universities of Edinburgh, Papua New Guinea and London. Between 2006 and 2010 he worked on secondment in Paris as Director of UNESCO's International Institute for Educational Planning. He is a past-president of the Comparative Education Society of Hong Kong and of the World Council of Comparative Education Societies.

José Cossa (mozambicanscholar@gmail.com) is a Visiting Associate Professor at the American University in Cairo and serves as a methodologist at Walden University. He is the author of the book *Power, Politics, and Higher Education: International Regimes, Local Governments, and Educational Autonomy*, and is the recipient of the 2012 Joyce Cain Award for Distinguished Research on People of African Descent, awarded by the Comparative and International Education Society. Cossa's research focuses on power dynamics in negotiation over educational policy; higher education policy and administration; system transfer; international development; and global and social justice.

Kenneth Cushner (kcushner@kent.edu) is Professor Emeritus, Kent State University, and directs the new student teaching initiative for the ECIS global network of international schools. He is author/editor of several books and articles including: *Human Diversity in Education: An Intercultural Approach* (8th ed., 2015) and *Intercultural Student Teaching: A Bridge to Global Competence* (2007). He has taught in schools in Switzerland, Australia and the United States, and has traveled with young people and teachers on all seven continents. Dr. Cushner is a Founding Fellow and Past-President of the International Academy for Intercultural Research; was a Fulbright Scholar to Sweden; and twice coordinated Semester at Sea's Teachers at Sea program.

Erwin H. Epstein (eepstein@luc.edu) is Professor Emeritus at Loyola University Chicago. He is a former President of the Comparative and International Education Society and of the World Council of Comparative Education Societies. He has served as Editor of the *Comparative Education Review* and Historian of the CIES. Before his retirement, he was founder and Director of the Center for Comparative Education at Loyola, and prior to his appointment at that university he was Director of the University Center for International Studies at the Ohio State University. His research has focused on epistemology in comparative education and on the impact of education on national identity in socio-culturally marginal communities.

Mariusz Galczynski (mariusz.galczynski@mail.mcgill.ca) is a lecturer at McGill University and administrator of the Québec Ministry of Education's English Exam for Teacher Certification. A former secondary school teacher in Texas and Illinois, his research interests include multicultural education, comparative education, teacher policy and professionalization, and assessment literacy. He was very active in the organization of the 2011 Annual Conference of CIES in Montreal and served as the student representative on the CIES Board from 2012-2015. He was also Co-chair of the New Scholars Committee from 2011-2012.

Ratna Ghosh (ratna.ghosh@mcgill.ca) is James McGill Professor and William C. Macdonald Professor of Education at McGill University where she was Dean of Education. A member of the Orders of Canada and Quebec, a Fellow of the Royal Society of Canada, she is the recipient of several awards from national and international organizations. She was President of the Shastri Indo-Canadian Institute, on the Board of the Canadian Human Rights Foundation and active in several other organizations. As President-Elect of the Comparative and International Education Society she organized the 2011 Annual Conference in Montreal and was President of CIES in 2011-12. Her research has focused on education and diversity, gender and development, and recently in education's role in combating religious extremism.

Sahtiya Hosoda Hammell (Sahtiya@virginia.edu) has over a decade of experience in the education sector as a K-12 educator, university instructor, and director of out-of-school time programs. A doctoral candidate in education at the University of Virginia, her undergraduate degree in English from Princeton focused on issues of normativity and post-colonialism in literary curricula in the US and New Zealand. Sahtiya's current research builds upon her earlier work to examine the construction of national identity in textbooks, and includes interests in citizenship education and social justice pedagogies. Sahtiya is Co-Chair for the Comparative and International Education Society's New Scholars Committee.

Halla B. Holmarsdottir (Halla-Bjork.Holmarsdottir@hioa.no) is a Professor in Multicultural and International Education at Oslo and Akershus University College. Professor Holmarsdottir has more than 25 years of teaching and research experience in formal and non-formal education. Her work covers a wide range of topics such as gender and education, bilingual education, adult education, and teacher training and training of trainers. Other areas of expertise include the education of youth, development cooperation, capacity development in the university and public sector, post-conflict reconstruction and development, qualitative research methods, indigenous peoples and human rights, and education for marginalized groups.

Maria Ishaq Khan (mikhan@albany.edu) is a Pakistani doctoral student at the Department of Educational Administration and Policy Studies (EAPS) at the State University of New York at Albany. Maria earned a BS in Mathematics and a MS in Accounting and Finance from Kinnaird College for Women, Lahore, Pakistan before beginning her Master's degree on a Fulbright scholarship at EAPS. Her focus on comparative and international education as soon she began her academic journey in the US, helped her frame educational challenges that her country faces in an international context. Maria's research interests include educational development and aid, state of education and educational policies in developing countries, the role of governments and inherent politics, as well as the intercultural, economic and social factors that affect access to education in many parts of the Muslim world.

Patricia K. Kubow (pkubow@indiana.edu) is Professor in Educational Leadership and Policy Studies and Curriculum and Instruction at Indiana University. She is also Director of the Center for International Education, Development and Research (CIEDR) in the Indiana University School of Education. Her research interests focus on the comparative study of constructions of democracy and citizenship education in Sub-Saharan Africa and the Middle East. Kubow is Co-Chair of the Teaching Comparative Education Special Interest Group of the Comparative and International Education Society and a member of the CIES Publications Committee.

Hilary Landorf (landorfh@fiu.edu) is the Director of Florida International University's (FIU) Office of Global Learning Initiatives where she oversees FIU's successful university-wide curriculum internationalization initiative, *Global Learning for Global Citizenship*. She is also an Associate Professor of International and Intercultural Education in FIU's College of Education. Landorf has published over 35 articles and book chapters on international education, has been an internationalization consultant to several colleges and universities, and has given over a hundred presentations and workshops on internationalization in K-20 settings. Among her recent publications is a case study on global learning at FIU in the NAFSA publication *Improving and Assessing Global Learning*.

Caroline (Carly) Manion (<u>carlymanion@gmail.com</u>) is a Lecturer in the Comparative, International and Development Education (CIDE) collaborative program at the Ontario Institute for Studies in Education (OISE), University of Toronto. With over 15 years of research and teaching experience in the broad area of gender and education, Caroline has examined the construction of gender equality in education knowledge, the scope and nature of gender-based inequalities in education, their connections with social, economic and political processes, and a variety of policy responses in North American and African school systems.

Maria Manzon (<u>maria.manzon@nie.edu.sg</u>) is Research Scientist at the Centre for Research in Pedagogy and Practice, National Institute of Education (NIE), Singapore. She is Research Convenor of NIE's International and Comparative Studies Task Force. She is Editor of *CIEclopedia* and Chair of the Admissions and New Societies Standing Committee of the World Council of Comparative Education Societies (WCCES). She is author/editor of several volumes on the institutional and intellectual histories of comparative education worldwide. Her research currently focuses on Asian pedagogies and parent involvement in education.

Vandra L. Masemann (<u>vandra.masemann@utoronto.ca</u>) is Adjunct Associate Professor at the Ontario Institute for Studies in Education at the University of Toronto. She is a former president of the Comparative and International Education Society of Canada, of the Comparative and International Education Society, and of the World Council of Comparative Education Societies. She has also served as Secretary General and Historian of the WCCES. She has taught at the University of Wisconsin-Madison, the Faculty of Education at the University of Toronto, State University of New York at Buffalo, the State University of Florida, and the University of Pittsburgh. Her research interests have been in the anthropology of education, multicultural and cross-cultural education, and theory and methods in comparative education.

Cheryl Matherly (<u>cheryl-matherly@utulsa.edu</u>) is Vice Provost for Global Education at The University of Tulsa. In addition to providing strategic leadership for the university's international education initiatives, she teaches in the graduate program in Educational Studies. Dr. Matherly's research has focused on the impact of education abroad on the development of students' global competencies. She has received three National Science Foundation grants to examine the impact of international experiences on learning outcomes for students in STEM fields. She is the recipient of two Fulbright grants for international education administrators (Germany and Japan). She has an EdD in Education Leadership and Culture Studies from the University of Houston.

Martha C. Merrill (mmerril@kent.edu) is an Associate Professor of Higher Education at Kent State University. She is the Coordinator of the Higher Education program's International Education certificate and teaches most of its comparative and international education courses. Her research focuses on university reform in Central Asia, particularly Kyrgyzstan, where she lived for five years. She currently is studying Kyrgyzstan's shift from state attestation to independent accreditation and the impact of international accreditation on higher education systems in Central Asia.

Karen Mundy (karen.mundy@utoronto.ca) is a Professor of International and Comparative Education at the University of Toronto (on leave) and the Chief Technical Officer and Director of Strategy, Policy and Performance for the Global Partnership for Education (2014-2017), a multi-stakeholder partnership whose mission is to ensure good quality education to children in the developing world. Her research has focused on the global politics of "Education for All" programs and policies; educational policy and reform in Sub-Saharan Africa; and the role of civil society organizations in educational change. She has published four books and more than 50 articles and chapters.

Bjorn H. Nordtveit (bjorn@educ.umass.edu) is Associate Professor at the University of Massachusetts-Amherst, and editor of the *Comparative Education Review*. Prior to his current appointment, he served on the faculty of the University of Hong Kong. He has worked as a technical expert for UNESCO, including five years in the Lao People's Democratic Republic; and for six years with the World Bank, working on non-formal education in francophone Africa. His research focuses on child protection, child labor, and aid effectiveness, and he is currently working on girls' education with the International Rescue Committee in the Democratic Republic of the Congo.

Oren Pizmony-Levy (pizmony-levy@tc.columbia.edu) is an Assistant Professor of International and Comparative Education at Teachers College, Columbia University. He is broadly interested in education, globalization, and transnational movements. In one line of research he examined the socio-historical roots of international large-scale assessments and factors affecting country participation in these assessments. In another line of research, he is exploring the expansion of environmental education worldwide and the ways in which students in 17 countries engage with environmental education. Between 2013 and 2016, he served on the CIES Ad Hoc Committee on SIGs. Dr. Pizmony-Levy earned his PhD in Sociology and comparative and international education from Indiana University, Bloomington.

Robyn Read (robyn.read@utoronto.ca) is a PhD candidate and Canada Graduate Scholar studying comparative, international development education at the Ontario Institute for Studies in Education, University of Toronto. Her research interests include knowledge mobilization and education policy in the developing world, with a specific focus on how research influences policy in educational development.

Linda F. Robertson (lfrobert@kent.edu) is the Director of the Gerald H. Read Center for International and Intercultural Education at Kent State University. She is a former Ohio Principal of the Year, and public school administrator, at Aurora High School, which gained National Blue Ribbon School recognition under her leadership. The Read Center, under her direction, has been awarded the U.S. Department of State's the International Leaders in Education Program all nine years of the program's existence. Other funded projects have been awarded by UNESCO, USAID, U.S. Department of State, American Councils, Martha Holden Jennings Foundation, Toyota Foundation, and Harmony Foundation. She administers special contracts with International Baccalaureate World Schools and Avropa Foundation Schools in Istanbul.

Iveta Silova (isilova@gmail.com) is a Professor and Program Director of Comparative and International Education at the College of Education, Lehigh University. Her research focuses on the study of globalization and post-socialist transformations in education, including privatization in public education, the role of non-governmental organizations in education change, the politics of policy borrowing, and childhood studies. She is the co-editor (with Noah W. Sobe) of the journal *European Education: Issues and Studies*.

L. Bahia Simons-Lane (lsimonsl@fiu.edu) is currently earning her PhD in Curriculum and Instruction, with a concentration in Language, Literacy, and Culture, at Florida International University. She is also a graduate assistant at FIU's Office of Global Learning Initiatives where she writes and conducts research related to FIU's university-wide curriculum and co-curriculum internationalization initiative Global Learning for Global Citizenship. Previously, she taught English in Japan as part of the Japan Exchange and Teaching (JET) Program. She is currently the president of the Florida chapter of the JET Alumni Association.

Gita Steiner-Khamsi (gs174@columbia.edu) is Professor of Comparative and International Education at Teachers College, Columbia University, New York. She assumed the position in 1995. Prior to her emigration to the United States, she worked for 10 years for the Ministry of Education of the Canton of Zurich (Switzerland) as director and policy analyst in the area of multicultural education. A past president of CIES, and editor of the *World Yearbook of Education* series (Routledge), she has published eight books and numerous journal articles on comparative policy studies, policy borrowing and globalization, and case study methodology. Her geographic focus is on Europe, Caucasus, Central Asia, and Mongolia.

Kathleen M. Stone (kstonegift@aol.com) received her PhD from Loyola University Chicago. Her professional focus is Educational Psychology and Comparative and International Education. She provided leadership in the original development of the CIECAP project, and continues as a CIECAP resource. Her research concentration includes Comparative and International Education, Gifted and Talented Education, and policy issues related to international testing. She facilitates international research through her consulting practice, INSTEAD International (International Network Supporting Transnational Education and Diplomacy). Her website (www.insteadinternational.com) supports transnational research and global education diplomacy.

Nelly P. Stromquist (stromqui@umd.edu) is Professor at the University of Maryland. She is a former president of the Comparative and International Education Society. She has served in the past as associate editor of the Comparative Education Review. She is the current director of the International Education Policy Program at UMD. Her research covers a wide range of issues: gender and education; popular and nonformal education; social movements in education; global and national equity policies; and the impact of globalization on education, particularly on professorial identity. She is the author of seven books and co-editor of 13 books; in addition, she has written numerous book chapters and articles. She examines educational phenomena from a sociological perspective that builds upon critical theory.

Elizabeth Sherman Swing (eswing1@verizon.net) is Professor Emerita of St. Joseph's University in Philadelphia where she taught for most of her academic career. She was the first CIES Historian from 1999-2008. She was also a Board Member of the journal, *European Education*. In 1990 she was named Knight in the Order of the Crown (*Ridder in de Kroonorde*) for her research on the Belgian language controversy. Her research interests have been focused on the teaching of languages, official bilingual policy, and bilingualism, particularly in Belgium and in Europe generally. She has also written on multiculturalism and multicultural policy.

Maria Trakas (mtrakas@gmail.com) is an immigration attorney in Chicago. Prior to earning a Juris Doctorate from DePaul University College of Law with a Certificate in International and Comparative Law, she studied at Loyola University Chicago, earning a Master's degree in Cultural and Educational Policy Studies with a concentration in Comparative Education.

Alexander W. Wiseman (aww207@lehigh.edu) is Associate Professor of Comparative and International Education in the College of Education at Lehigh University. Dr. Wiseman conducts internationally comparative educational research related to large-scale data, information and communication technology, teacher quality, and evidence-based decision making. He serves as Series Editor for the International Perspectives on Education and Society volume series (Emerald Publishing), Editor of the *Annual Review of Comparative and International Education*, and Senior Editor of *FIRE: Forum for International Research in Education*.

Index

CERC Studies in Comparative Education (ctd)

14. W.O. Lee, David L. Grossman, Kerry J. Kennedy & Gregory P. Fairbrother (eds.) (2004): *Citizenship Education in Asia and the Pacific: Concepts and Issues*. ISBN 978-962-8093-59-5. 313pp. HK$200/US$32.

13. Mok Ka-Ho (ed.) (2003): *Centralization and Decentralization: Educational Reforms and Changing Governance in Chinese Societies*. ISBN 978-962-8093-58-8. 230pp. HK$200/US$32.

12. Robert A. LeVine (2003, reprinted 2010): *Childhood Socialization: Comparative Studies of Parenting, Learning and Educational Change*. ISBN 978-962-8093-61-8. 299pp. HK$200/US$32.

11. Ruth Hayhoe & Julia Pan (eds.) (2001): *Knowledge Across Cultures: A Contribution to Dialogue Among Civilizations*. ISBN 978-962-8093-73-1. 391pp. HK$250/US$38. [Out of print]

10. William K. Cummings, Maria Teresa Tatto & John Hawkins (eds.) (2001): *Values Education for Dynamic Societies: Individualism or Collectivism*. ISBN 978-962-8093-71-7. 312pp. HK$200/US$32.

9. Gu Mingyuan (2001): *Education in China and Abroad: Perspectives from a Lifetime in Comparative Education*. ISBN 978-962-8093-70-0. 260pp. HK$200/US$32.

8. Thomas Clayton (2000): *Education and the Politics of Language: Hegemony and Pragmatism in Cambodia, 1979-1989*. ISBN 978-962-8093-83-0. 243pp. HK$200/US$32.

7. Mark Bray & Ramsey Koo (eds.) (2004): *Education and Society in Hong Kong and Macao: Comparative Perspectives on Continuity and Change*. Second edition. ISBN 978-962-8093-34-2. 323pp. HK$200/US$32.

6. T. Neville Postlethwaite (1999): *International Studies of Educational Achievement: Methodological Issues*. ISBN 978-962-8093-86-1. 86pp. HK$100/US$20.

5. Harold Noah & Max A. Eckstein (1998): *Doing Comparative Education: Three Decades of Collaboration*. ISBN 978-962-8093-87-8. 356pp. HK$250/US$38.

4. Zhang Weiyuan (1998): *Young People and Careers: A Comparative Study of Careers Guidance in Hong Kong, Shanghai and Edinburgh*. ISBN 978-962-8093-89-2. 160pp. HK$180/US$30.

3. Philip G. Altbach (1998): *Comparative Higher Education: Knowledge, the University, and Development*. ISBN 978-962-8093-88-5. 312pp. HK$180/US$30.

2. Mark Bray & W.O. Lee (eds.) (1997): *Education and Political Transition: Implications of Hong Kong's Change of Sovereignty*. ISBN 978-962-8093-90-8. 169pp. [Out of print]

1. Mark Bray & W.O. Lee (eds.) (2001): *Education and Political Transition: Themes and Experiences in East Asia*. Second edition. ISBN 978-962-8093-84-7. 228pp. HK$200/US$32.

CERC Monograph Series in Comparative and International Education and Development

12. Raymond E. Wanner (2015): *UNESCO's Origins, Achievements, Problems and Promises: An Inside/Outside Perspectives from the US*. ISBN 978-988-14241-2-9. 84pp. HK$100/US$16.

11. Maria Manzon (ed.) (2015): *Changing Times, Changing Territories: Reflections on CERC and the Field of Comparative Education*. ISBN 978-988-17852-0-6. 105pp. HK$100/US$16.

10. Mark Bray & Ora Kwo (2014): *Regulating Private Tutoring for Public Good: Policy Options for Supplementary Education in Asia*. ISBN 978-988-17852-9-9. 93pp. HK$100/US$16. [Also available in Chinese and Korean]

9. Mark Bray & Chad Lykins (2012): *Shadow Education: Private Supplementary Tutoring and Its Implications for Policy Makers in Asia*. ISBN 978-92-9092-658-0. (Print). ISBN 978-92-9092-659-7. (PDF). 100pp. HK$100/US$16. [Also available in Chinese, Russian and Vietnamese]

8. Nirmala Rao & Jin Sun (2010): *Early Childhood Care and Education in the Asia Pacific Region: Moving Towards Goal 1*. ISBN 978-988-17852-5-1. 97pp. HK$100/US$16.

7. Nina Ye. Borevskaya, V.P. Borisenkov & Xiaoman Zhu (eds.) (2010): *Educational Reforms in Russia and China at the Turn of the 21st Century: A Comparative Analysis*. ISBN 978-988-17852-4-4. 115pp. HK$100/US$16.

6. Eduardo Andere (2008): *The Lending Power of PISA: League Tables and Best Practice in International Education*. ISBN 978-988-17852-1-3. 138pp. HK$100/US$16.

5. Linda Chisholm, Graeme Bloch & Brahm Fleisch (eds.) (2008): *Education, Growth, Aid and Development: Towards Education for All*. ISBN 978-962-8093-99-1. 116pp. HK$100/US$16.

4. Mark Bray & Seng Bunly (2005): *Balancing the Books: Household Financing of Basic Education in Cambodia*. ISBN 978-962-8093-39-7. 113pp. HK$100/US$16. [Also available in Khmer]

3. Maria Manzon (2004): *Building Alliances: Schools, Parents and Communities in Hong Kong and Singapore*. ISBN 978-962-8093-36-6. 117pp. HK$100/US$16.

2. Mark Bray, Ding Xiaohao & Huang Ping (2004): *Reducing the Burden on the Poor: Household Costs of Basic Education in Gansu, China*. ISBN 978-962-8093-32-8. 67pp. HK$50/US$10. [Also available in Chinese]

1. Yoko Yamato (2003): *Education in the Market Place: Hong Kong's International Schools and their Mode of Operation*. ISBN 978-962-8093-57-1. 117pp. HK$100/US$16.

Order through bookstores or from:

Comparative Education Research Centre
Faculty of Education,
The University of Hong Kong
Pokfulam Road. Hong Kong, China.

Fax: (852) 3917 4737
E-mail: cerc@hku.hk
Website: http://cerc.edu.hku.hk

The list prices above are applicable for order from CERC, and include sea mail postage. For air mail postage, please add US$10 for 1 copy, US$18 for 2-3 copies, US$40 for 4-8 copies. For more than 8 copies, please contact us direct. For titles of CERC/Springer Series No.24 and 30, air mail postage is US$15 per copy.

CERC Studies in Comparative Education 21

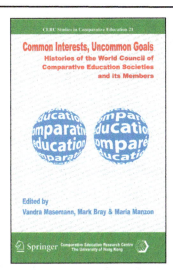

Common Interests, Uncommon Goals: Histories of the World Council of Comparative Education Societies and its Members

Edited by
Vandra Masemann, Mark Bray &
Maria Manzon

Publishers: Comparative Education
Research Centre and Springer
ISBN 978-962-8093-10-6
2007; 453 pages
HKD250/USD38

The World Council of Comparative Education Societies (WCCES) was established in 1970 as an umbrella body which brought together five national and regional comparative education societies. Over the decades it greatly expanded, and now embraces three dozen societies.

This book presents histories of the WCCES and its member societies. It shows ways in which the field has changed over the decades, and the forces which have shaped it in different parts of the world. The book demonstrates that while comparative education can be seen as a single global field, it has different characteristics in different countries and cultures. In this sense, the book presents a comparison of comparisons.

Vandra Masemann is a past WCCES President and Secretary General. She has also been President of the US-Based Comparative and International Education Society (CIES), and of the Comparative and International Education Society of Canada (CIESC).

Mark Bray is also a past WCCES President and Secretary General. He has also been President of the Comparative Education Society of Hong Kong (CESHK).

Maria Manzon is a member of the CESHK and has been an Assistant Secretary General of the WCCES. Her research on the field has been undertaken at the Comparative Education Research Centre of the University of Hong Kong.

More details:
http://cerc.edu.hku.hk/product/common-interests-uncommon-goals-histories-of-the-world-council-of-comparative-education-societies-and-its-members/

CERC Studies in Comparative Education 19

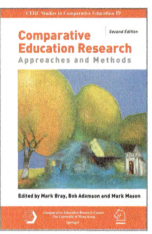

Comparative
second edition
Education Research
Approaches and Methods

Edited by
Mark Bray, Bob Adamson and
Mark Mason

Publishers:
Comparative Education Research Centre and
Springer
ISBN 978-988-17852-8-2
2014; 453 pages
HKD250/USD38

Approaches and methods in comparative education are of obvious importance, but do not always receive adequate attention. This second edition of a well-received book, containing thoroughly updated and additional material, contributes new insights within the long-standing traditions of the field.

A particular feature is the focus on different units of analysis. Individual chapters compare places, systems, times, cultures, values, policies, curricula and other units. These chapters are contextualised within broader analytical frameworks which identify the purposes and strengths of the field. The book includes a focus on intra-national as well as cross-national comparisons, and highlights the value of approaching themes from different angles. As already demonstrated by the first edition of the book, the work will be of great value not only to producers of comparative education research but also to users who wish to understand more thoroughly the parameters and value of the field.

The editors: Mark Bray is UNESCO Chair Professor of Comparative Education at the University of Hong Kong. Bob Adamson is UNESCO Chair Professor in TVET and Lifelong Learning at the Hong Kong Institute of Education; and Mark Mason is Professor and Head of the Department of International Education and Lifelong Learning at the Hong Kong Institute of Education.

This book is also available in Chinese, Farsi, French, Italian,
Japanese, Portuguese, Russian and Spanish.
Website: http://cerc.edu.hku.hk//product/comparative-education-
research-approaches-and-methods/

CERC Studies in Comparative Education 24

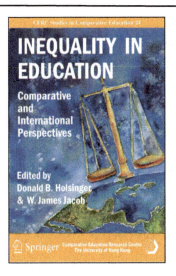

Inequality in Education: Comparative and International Perspectives

Edited by
Donald B. Holsinger &
W. James Jacob

Publishers: Comparative Education Research Centre and Springer
ISBN 978-962-8093-14-4
2008
HKD300/USD45

The book is a compilation of conceptual chapters and national case studies that includes a series of methods for measuring education inequalities. It provides up-to-date scholarly research on global trends in the distribution of formal schooling in national populations. It also offers a strategic comparative and international education policy statement on recent shifts in education inequality, and new approaches to explore, develop and improve comparative education and policy research globally. Contributing authors examine how education as a process interacts with government finance policy to form patterns of access to education services. In addition to case perspectives from 18 countries across six geographic regions, the volume includes six conceptual chapters on topics that influence education inequality, such as gender, disability, language and economics, and a summary chapter that presents new evidence on the pernicious consequences of inequality in the distribution of education. The book offers (1) a better and more holistic understanding of ways to measure education inequalities; and (2) strategies for facing the challenge of inequality in education in the processes of policy formation, planning and implementation at the local, regional, national and global levels.

Donald B. Holsinger is Professor Emeritus in Education and Development Studies at Brigham Young University, and has held academic appointments at the University of Chicago, the University of Arizona, and the State University of New York (Albany). He is a former President of the Comparative and International Education Society and Senior Education Specialist at the World Bank.

W. James Jacob is Acting Director of the Institute for International Studies in Education at the University of Pittsburgh's School of Education, and is the former Assistant Director of the Center for International and Development Education at the University of California (Los Angeles).

More details:
http://cerc.edu.hku.hk/product/inequality-in-education-comparative-and-international-perspectives/

CERC Studies in Comparative Education 29

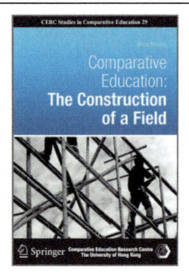

Comparative Education: The Construction of a Field

Maria Manzon

Publishers: Comparative Education Research Centre and Springer

ISBN 978-988-17852-6-8
2011; 295 pages
Price: HK$200 / US$32

This book is a remarkable feat of scholarship — so remarkable in fact that I put it in the same league as the great classics of the field that had so much to do with setting the direction of Comparative Education. Indeed, this volume goes further than earlier classics to reveal, through textual analysis and interviews with key figures, how the epistemological foundations of the field and crucial professional developments combined to, as the title indicates, construct Comparative Education.

Manzon's work is indispensable — a word I do not use lightly — for scholars who seek a genuine grasp of the field: how it was formed and by whom, its major theoreticians, its professional foundations, and so on. Clearly too, this book marks the rise of a young star, Maria Manzon, who shows promise of joining the ranks of our field's most illustrious thinkers.

Erwin H. Epstein
Director, Center for Comparative Education
Loyola University, Chicago, USA

Maria Manzon is a Research Associate of the Comparative Education Research Centre (CERC) at the University of Hong Kong. She was Editor of CIEclopedia in 2009 and 2010, and Assistant Secretary General of the World Council of Comparative Education Societies (WCCES) in 2005.

More details:
http://cerc.edu.hku.hk/product/comparative-education-the-construction-of-a-field/

CERC Studies in Comparative Education 17

Portraits of Influential Chinese Educators

Ruth Hayhoe

Publishers: Comparative Education
Research Centre and Springer
ISBN 978-962-8093-40-3
2006
HKD250/USD38

China's economic rise has surprised the world, and most governments and large corporations feel the need for a China-strategy to shape their relations with this emerging super-power. What do they know, however, about the educational ideas and achievements that have contributed to this economic success? Names of political figures such as Mao Zedong, Deng Xiaoping and Jiang Zemin are household words, yet how many people have heard of Li Bingde, Gu Mingyuan, Lu Jie or Ye Lan?

Substantial research has been done on Chinese educational development by Sinologists and Comparative Educationists, making a wealth of data and analysis available to the specialist reader. Most of these studies have been framed within Western social science parameters, integrating an objectivist assessment of Chinese education into the international research literature.

This book conveys an understanding of China's educational development from within, through portraits of eleven influential educators whose ideas have shaped the educational reforms initiated by Deng Xiaoping in 1978. They are portrayed in the context of their cultural heritage, families, communities and schools, offering their own deeply reflective interpretations of Chinese education. The book is written for the general reader, to provide glimpses into the educational context of China's recent move onto the world stage.

Ruth Hayhoe is Professor at the Ontario Institute for Studies in Education of the University of Toronto, President Emerita of the Hong Kong Institute of Education, Past President of the Comparative and International Education Society, and an Associate Member of the Comparative Education Research Centre at the University of Hong Kong. She has written extensively on higher education in China and on educational relations between China and the West. She is an Honorary Fellow of the University of London Institute of Education, and was awarded the Silver Bauhinia Star by the Hong Kong SAR Government and the title of Commandeur dans l'ordre des Palmes Académiques by the Government of France in 2002. In the same year she was also awarded an honorary Doctorate of Education by the Hong Kong Institute of Education.

More details:
http://cerc.edu.hku.hk/product/portraits-of-influential-chinese-educators/

CERC Studies in Comparative Education 30

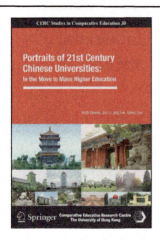

Portraits of 21st Century Chinese Universities: In the Move to Mass Higher Education

Ruth Hayhoe, Jun Li, Jing Lin, Qiang Zha

2011; 483 pages
ISBN 978-988-1785-23-7
HK$300 (local), US$45

This book received the 2nd place in the 3rd Annual Comparative and International Education Society (CIES) Higher Education Special Interest Group (HE-SIG) Best in Books for the academic year 2011-2012!

This book examines the ways in which China's universities have changed in the dramatic move to a mass stage which has unfolded since the late 1990s. Twelve universities in different regions of the country are portrayed through the eyes of their students, faculty and leaders.

The book begins with the national level policy process around the move to mass higher education. This is followed by an analysis of the views of 2,300 students on the 12 campuses about how the changes have affected their learning experiences and civil society involvement. The 12 portraits in the next section are of three comprehensive universities, three education-related universities, three science and technology universities, and three newly emerging private universities. The final chapter sketches the contours of an emerging Chinese model of the university, and explores its connections to China's longstanding scholarly traditions.

Ruth Hayhoe is a professor at the Ontario Institute for Studies in Education of the University of Toronto. **Jun Li** is an associate professor in the Faculty of Education at the University of Hong Kong. **Jing Lin** is a professor of international education policy at University of Maryland, College Park. **Qiang Zha** is an assistant professor at York University.

More details:
http://cerc.edu.hku.hk/product/portraits-of-21st-century-chinese-universities-in-the-move-to-mass-higher-education/

CERC Studies in Comparative Education 32

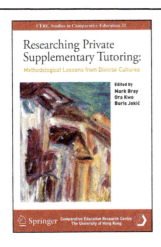

Researching Private Supplementary Tutoring:
Methodological Lessons from Diverse Cultures

Edited by Mark Bray, Ora Kwo & Boris Jokić

October 2015; 292 pages
Published by Comparative Education Research Centre (CERC) and Springer
ISBN 978-988-14241-3-6
HK$250 (local), US$38 (overseas)

Private supplementary tutoring, widely known as shadow education because of the way that it mimics mainstream schooling, has greatly expanded worldwide. It consumes considerable family resources, provides employment for tutors, occupies the time of students, and has a backwash on regular schools.

Although such tutoring has become a major industry and a daily activity for students, tutors and families, the research literature has been slow to catch up with the phenomenon. The topic is in some respects difficult to research, precisely because it is shadowy. Contours are indistinct, and the actors may hesitate to share their experiences and perspectives.

Presenting methodological lessons from diverse cultures, the book contains chapters from both high-income and low-income settings in Asia, Caribbean, Europe and the Middle East. Separately and together, the chapters present valuable insights into the design and conduct of research. The book will assist both consumers and producers of research. Consumers will become better judges of the strengths, weaknesses and orientations of literature on the theme; and producers will gain insights for design of instruments, collection of data, and interpretation of findings.

The editors:

Mark Bray is UNESCO Chair Professor in Comparative Education at the University of Hong Kong.

Ora Kwo is an Associate Professor in the Comparative Education Research Centre at the University of Hong Kong.

Boris Jokić is a Scientific Associate in the Centre for Educational Research and Development at the Institute for Social Research in Zagreb, Croatia.

More details:
http://cerc.edu.hku.hk/product/researching-private-supplementary-tutoring-methodological-lessons-from-diverse-cultures/

CERC Monograph Series in Comparative and International Education and Development 11

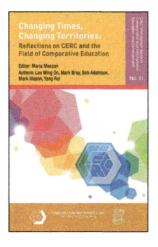

Changing Times, Changing Territories:
Reflections on CERC and the Field of Comparative Education

Edited by Maria Manzon
Authors: Lee Wing On, Mark Bray, Bob Adamson, Mark Mason, Yang Rui
February 2015; 105 pages
Published by Comparative Education
Research Centre (CERC)
ISBN 978-988-17852-0-6
HK$100, US$16

This CERC monograph differs from others in the series in that it is not a research report but a commentary on a research institution: the Comparative Education Research Centre (CERC) at the University of Hong Kong (HKU) which was established in 1994. The monograph documents the trajectory of CERC as narrated by its five Directors and with a commentary by the editor.

Historically, the value of the monograph lies in encapsulating the collective efforts of its founders and their successors. It reflects on why CERC was formed and how the Centre's "tribes and territories" and their work have evolved over time. Sociologically, CERC as a unit for analysis provides an example of the institutionalisation of the field of comparative education. Viewed from a sociology-of-knowledge perspective, CERC exemplifies the dynamic interplay of international and domestic politics, episteme, personal biography, and the internal sociology of universities.

Maria Manzon is a Research Scientist at the National Institute of Education, Singapore. She is also an Associate Member of the Comparative Education Research Centre at the University of Hong Kong. She was co-editor of a volume of histories of comparative education societies (2007), and of another volume about comparative education in universities worldwide (2008). Her 2011 book entitled *Comparative Education: The Construction of a Field* has been acclaimed for its comprehensive approach and path-breaking conceptualisation.

More details:
http://cerc.edu.hku.hk/product/changing-times-changing-territories-
reflections-on-cerc-and-the-field-of-comparative-education/

—

CPSIA information can be obtained
at www.ICGtesting.com
Printed in the USA
BVOW10*0216090816

458406BV00001B/6/P